NORThUMBRIA

NORThUMBRIA
THE LOST KINGDOM

PAUL GETHING AND EDOARDO ALBERT

The History Press

Front cover: Bamburgh Castle. *Darren Turner/iStockphoto*
Back cover: Hadrian's Wall. *Simon Fraser, Northumberland National Park
    Authority*

Quotations from J.R.R. Tolkien's works © Fourth Age Limited 1954,
    1955, 1966.

First published 2012

The History Press
The Mill, Brimscombe Port
Stroud, Gloucestershire, GL5 2QG
www.thehistorypress.co.uk

© Paul Gething & Edoardo Albert, 2012

The right of Paul Gething & Edoardo Albert
to be identified as the Authors of this
work has been asserted in accordance with
the Copyrights, Designs and Patents Act 1988.

British Library Cataloguing in Publication Data.
A catalogue record for this book is available from the British Library.

ISBN 978 0 7524 5970 7

Typesetting and origination by The History Press
Printed and bound by TJ International Ltd, Padstow, Cornwall

CONTENTS

Introduction 7

1 Northumbria: A Brief History 9
2 Laying Down The Land 23
3 The First Northumbrians 33
4 Religion 51
5 War 71
6 Society 87
7 Culture 104
8 Food 118
9 Technology 126
10 Trade and Travel 147
11 Burial at Bamburgh 158
12 Decline and Fall 170

Notes 179
Bibliography 184
Kings of Northumbria 186
Acknowledgements 188
Index 189

INTRODUCTION

Remember when you were young, you shone like the sun.

('Shine on you Crazy Diamond', Pink Floyd)

If Northumbria is a lost kingdom, where would you find it? It's not on the map. Sure, there's Northumberland, but while that is certainly composed of land north of the Humber, it's separated from the river by the whole of Yorkshire. It's a curious name for a county; transplanting the nomenclature to countries, it's like calling Canada North Mexico. But the distance of the modern county from its name source gives us a clue: once upon a time, Northumbria was bigger. Much bigger. For a couple of hundred years, between the withdrawal of the Roman legions and the arrival of the Vikings, the kingdom of Northumbria was the pre-eminent realm in the land, its dominion stretching from the Humber in the south to Edinburgh in the north. Before Northumbria's kings, the rulers of the other kingdoms of Britain bent their knee and offered their homage. To put it bluntly: Geordies ruled us all.[1]

Not only did they rule us, they renewed us. The kingdom of Northumbria was the fount and inspiration for a cultural and political renaissance that first transformed Britain and then the rest of northern Europe. It produced the brightest scholars, the holiest saints, the greatest kings, the fiercest warriors, the most beautiful art and the most innovative technology of its time.

But then it was forgotten. Most people today will have heard of Bede, but apart from labelling him 'venerable' – which relegates the monk to a dim past rather than suggesting him worthy of regard – that will be about the limit of their knowledge. Oswald, Wilfrid, Alcuin, Edwin? Names that have fallen out of fashion, rather than four of the key figures in British and (in Alcuin's case) European history. There are many reasons for the forgetting, but they can be summed up as fate and fortune, or geography and war. Northumbria's position at the edge of the world, which once served it well, isolated it in the end. But unfortunately its isolation was not sufficient to protect it from the whirlwind that came out of the north: the Vikings. In the desperate struggle against the northmen, the kingdom of Wessex, insulated by geography from raiders who regarded the North Sea as their private pond, took first place, and history accorded its king, Alfred, the deserved title of 'the

Bamburgh Castle.

Great'. But two centuries before Alfred, Northumbria's King Oswald was Britain's first royal saint – and martyr.

In this book, we hope to bring the lost to light, and reveal the splendour of the lost kingdom of Northumbria. To do so, we will use the knowledge gained by archaeologists and historians over the last few decades, knowledge that has produced such a lightening of what were once called the Dark Ages that they're now called – admittedly with rather less pzazz but considerably more accuracy – the early medieval period.

Of the authors, Paul Gething is an experimental archaeologist, smelter and bladesmith, and one of the directors of the Bamburgh Research Project, an ongoing series of excavations that has been instrumental in our reassessment of the kingdom of Northumbria. He provides the archaeological and historical weft for the other author, writer Edoardo Albert, to weave into a tapestry of the life, times, culture and people of the lost kingdom of Northumbria.

We hope you enjoy the journey.

1

NORTHUMBRIA:
A BRIEF HISTORY

Quam cito transit gloria mundi. (How quickly the glory of the world passes.)

(Thomas à Kempis, *The Imitation of Christ*)

The Dark Ages[2] are full of obscure kingdoms that briefly rose to power, only to sink slowly – or catastrophically – back into oblivion. What makes Northumbria worth writing about rather than Rheged, Lyndsey or Elmet, or any number of petty kingdoms that have been swallowed up over time?

And yet Northumbria is different. Its kings were no less violent; its battles were as often ignoble and rapacious as glorious and decisive; and its peasants have left as little a trace as peasants have elsewhere. The kingdoms of Britain in the early medieval period were no different from their inhabitants' lives: nasty, brutish and short.

While we grant that Northumbria was a relatively short-lived kingdom, and its wars were certainly nasty, one look at a page of the Lindisfarne Gospels will reveal that it was far from brutish.

On the contrary, perhaps because of the sheer fragility of civilised life, beauty became all the more precious. A monk might spend six weeks working on a single letter, only to have it lost to fire, while a smith might hammer a sword blade 10,000 times and then see it shatter as a result of the quenching process. Beauty was something hard won, and harder still to preserve. But in the brief period of its heyday, in conditions that are as perfect an example of a Hobbesian world as one would not wish to find, Northumbria's inhabitants made a civilisation that stood shoulder to shoulder and eye to eye with Byzantium (the eastern, enduring arm of the Roman Empire) and the new power of the Carolingian Empire under Charlemagne.

It might be hard to imagine that kings who could not read and whose preferred method of dealing with an inconvenient relative was assassination, might be bulwarks of civilisation, yet they were. For a brief time, little more than a couple of centuries, an extraordinary kingdom flourished, creating islands of culture in the land by the sea.

The kingdoms of Britain and Ireland in the seventh century. There may have been others, too short lived to leave any historical trace. *Wikimedia Commons*

TWO BECOME ONE

Northumbria, as it became called, resulted from the forced union of the neighbouring kingdoms of Bernicia, centred on Bamburgh in Northumberland, and Deira, which had its heartland in Yorkshire, centred on York, which was known at the time as Eoforwic. As Northumbria, the kingdom became the most powerful in the land, with at least two of its rulers powerful enough to be known as *Bretwalda*, high king of Britain. But tensions between the old Bernicia and Deira ruling families ensured that there were always plausible alternative claimants to the throne. When you add one of the peculiarities of Anglo-Saxon kingship into the mix – if you weren't constantly bringing new petty kingdoms under your control and scattering the largesse of battles won among your followers, then those followers would slowly drift away to rival courts and kings – and combine this with the lack of an established system of precedence, then you have a recipe for terminal instability. It took an extraordinary personality to hold things together at all and Northumbria had a supply of these for a while. But then, inevitably, factional fighting and the renewed strength of rival kingdoms, Mercia in particular, led to Northumbria's decline. The decline turned into a fairly rapid fall with the arrival of the Vikings, who annexed the Deiran half of the kingdom in AD 867 and turned the Bernician rump of Northumbria into a dependent earldom.

However, the Northumbrians were still sufficiently sure of their ancient rights to self-determination to prove a major irritation to Harold Godwinson's attempts to claim the throne for himself after the death of Edward the Confessor in January 1066.

Unfortunately for Northumbrian independence, Harold lost to William, and after a number of failed attempts to pacify the north, the Conqueror decided to destroy its powerbase. The record of the Domesday Book, compiled some sixteen years later, is a grim testimony to how thoroughly his troops despoiled Northumbria. That pretty well marked the end of the kingdom of the north, although the earls of Northumberland continued to play a major part in British history, most notably when Hotspur rebelled against Henry IV in 1403. The fifteenth-century Wars of the Roses were also principally northern affairs, with both the houses – Lancaster and York – once having been part of the kingdom of Northumbria.

ÐARK BEGINNINGS

Historically speaking, we know next to nothing about what happened in Northumbria after the withdrawal of the legions and the foundation of the kingdom. This is traditionally dated to 547, when Bernicia was founded by a travelling warlord and his band of merry plunderers. Ida, an Anglian adventurer, spotted the potential of a huge isolated craggy rock by the sea – Bamburgh. Generations, stretching back to the Stone Age, had seen its defensive possibilities. The basalt rock, and the succession of strongholds upon it, command the coastal plain. In those days the sea washed right up to the base of the rock, ensuring easy communications up and down the coast and making a siege all but impossible to maintain.

Ida and his men took the stronghold that was already in place, presumably killing or driving out the previous British king of the area.[3] What happened then? The most honest thing would be to say 'we don't know', and move on to other matters. But hey, this is a book on archaeology: we're not going to let a lack of historical sources stop us speculating about what did and didn't happen!

Exactly how many men Ida had with him is impossible to say, but it was enough. Enough to hold and consolidate his new kingdom, to fight off the attempts by the native British to take back their land[4] and enough to be able to pass it on to his heirs. Ida's achievement is all the more impressive given that the British were well organised, had several strongholds, including Edinburgh, and were capable of fielding armies, if the sources are to be believed. Strathclyde was still a large kingdom in its own right. The Angles, on the other hand, would have had to cross the sea to call on reinforcements. In any case, the early kings would have had only family allegiances to draw on, since fealty was normally only given once a king had proved that he was actually worthy of being a king. So Ida and his sons and followers probably carved out their realm with limited resources and little or no back up.

It is not until Æthelfrith, some fifty years and, according to the king list, seven rulers after Ida – which gives a good idea of the short tenure of a king at that time – that we reach firmer historical ground.

It was Æthelfrith who conquered the neighbouring Anglian kingdom of Deira and brought Northumbria into being, turning it into a real player in the power struggles of sixth- and seventh-century Britain.

But what of the other half of Northumbria? What of Deira? Unfortunately, if the origins of the northern half of Northumbria are dark, those of its southern end, Deira, enter the realm of mystery. One of the few sources we have is the *History of the Britons*, ascribed to Nennius,[5] a Welsh monk, and probably written in the ninth century. The problem here of course is that this is so much later than the events we are interested in. To give a rough comparison, it would be like relying on a contemporary book for news of what happened during the French Revolution.

Of course, our most important written source is Bede, the author of the *Ecclesiastical History of the English People*, and one of the most remarkable men of Northumbria's flowering. He wrote the *Ecclesiastical History* in AD 731, which puts him somewhat closer to events, and undoubtedly his accounts of the later history of the kingdom are the best evidence we have.

Gildas, writing from the perspective of the Britons who were being slowly pushed out of the east and into the west of the country, is our earliest source, probably writing his *Ruin of the Britons* in the sixth century. According to him, the Anglo-Saxon invaders first arrived as paid mercenaries, hired to fight by British kings who no longer had the services of the professional armies of Rome to call upon. But the mercenaries stayed and gradually started carving out kingdoms for themselves in what became England as the original Britons were pushed west and became the Welsh. But almost everything Gildas says must be taken with a pinch of salt as his account is loaded with his own agenda.

When Augustine, the missionary sent by Pope Gregory the Great to convert the English, reached Canterbury in 597 there was an English king ruling in Deira. The genealogy of the kings in the *History of the Britons* gives a list of predecessors to the kings of Deira and Bernicia, and both lists terminate with the god Woden. But even assuming the king list is accurate, it still gives us no more than a bald list of names begatting other names for the crucial foundational years of these kingdoms.

So what really happened?

This is the question that has exercised generations of historians and archaeologists. It is in this interregnum between the fall of Rome and the pagan English converting to Christianity that the legends of Arthur originate. But of course, the once and future king was warchief of the Britons in their struggle against the invading Anglo-Saxons – the leader of the (soon to be) Welsh against the English! Ultimately, the Britons lost and the English won, pushing the Celtic peoples into the extremities of the island – Cornwall, Wales and Scotland. But what remains an open question is how much this national transformation was brought about by mass migration and how much by a change in the ruling elite.

HISTORY RESTARTS

From our vantage point, nearly a millennium and a half after the events we're going on to describe, one major problem remains the predilection the Northumbrian ruling families had for beginning their sons' names with a vowel, in particular O and Æ. It can be difficult to separate Oswald from Oswiu from Oswine, or Æthelfrith from Æthelwod and Ælfwine in one's mind. It's hard not to think that these were dynasties in desperate need of an injection of consonants.

There is a complete list of the kings of Northumbria on p. 186, with their dates of reign (as far as these can be attested). But the story of the kingdom is not the same as the story of the kings; some of them can simply remain as names on the list, with nothing more said. But after Ida, the first king we must speak of is Æthelfrith, traditionally the eighth king of Bernicia and the first to rule Deira as well.

Æthelfrith became king of Bernicia around 593. From about 604 he was also king of Deira, thus uniting under him the constituent kingdoms of Northumbria. It is with him that history restarts; an ironic destiny for an illiterate warrior who was one of the key figures in driving the still literate and Christian Britons out of what became England.

In the desperate Darwinian struggles of the sixth century, Æthelfrith proved a master. Bede records him inflicting a devastating defeat on the Scots in 603, ensuring, according to Bede, that no king of the Scots attempted to attack English land again up until Bede's own day, some 130 years later. With Deira annexed the following year – we don't know how it was done, whether by force, persuasion, intimidation or some combination of the three – Æthelfrith turned his attention on the Welsh, winning a crushing victory over them around 615.

At the time, the victory must also have seemed a triumph of the old pagan gods over the new Christian God, for as a prelude to the actual battle, Bede tells us that Æthelfrith ordered his warriors to attack and slaughter the Welsh monks who had come to pray for their side's victory.

This victory established Northumbria as the most powerful kingdom in the land. It would be tempting to think of it as the most extensive too, but that would be carrying modern categories into the past. Nowadays, we tend to think of wars as battles over territories, with armies struggling to take and hold land and cities. The Romans too must have seen things quite similarly, with Hadrian's Wall marking the limits of empire. But in the semi-anarchy of the sixth and seventh centuries, a more apt image would be of a tooled-up gang venturing into its rival's territory, aiming to catch those rivals napping and dispose of them before hightailing it back home with all the booty they could carry. There were virtually no towns, castles or centres of population. A king travelled; his retinue accompanied him, and allegiance was marked by giving gifts and pledging aid rather than parcelling things out on maps that didn't exist. The only form of quasi-taxation came in the responsibility of local landowners to provide accommodation and supplies for the army of the king.

What is clear, even from our distance in time, is that Æthelfrith and his gang were hugely capable warriors who kept their eyes open for the main chance. After all, the Welsh nicknamed Æthelfrith *Flesaur*, which translates as 'the Twister' or 'the Artful Dodger'. Such a man was not likely to be overly troubled by questions of probity, honour or chivalry. This pretty much epitomised the pagan Anglo-Saxon ideal of a warrior chief: a man who won battles by fair means or foul, disposed of rivals with threats, poison or treachery, and doled out the winnings to his followers. In many ways, the comparison with a modern-day mob boss is closer than a comparison with our modern ideas of kingship, influenced as they are by 1,000 years of Christian and philosophical refining.[6]

According to Bede, Æthelfrith:

ravaged the Britons more cruelly than all other English leaders, so that he might well be compared to Saul the King of Israel, except of course that he was ignorant of true religion.

He overran a greater area than any other king or ealdorman, exterminating or enslaving the
inhabitants, making their lands either tributary to the English or ready for English settlement.

(Bede, *Ecclesiastical History*, p. 97)

Although Æthelfrith had taken control of Deira, at least some of its ruling family had
escaped into exile, notably Edwin, the son of the previous king of Deira, and Hereric,
Edwin's nephew. Hereric was disposed of by poison while in exile, with some writers discerning Æthelfrith's fingerprints all over his murder.[7] Edwin proved harder to
dispose of.

Once in exile, Edwin seems to have led a wandering life. He must surely have stayed in
the kingdom of Mercia, or else it would be all but impossible to explain how he came to
have children with a Mercian princess called Cwenburg. The Welsh remembered him too,
but not fondly, calling Edwin one 'of the three chief pests of Anglesey nurtured by itself'.[8]
There was a tradition that Edwin was raised as foster brother to Cadwallon, later to be
king of Gwynedd. If true, there must have been a truly spectacular falling out between
them, as when Edwin became king of Northumbria he attacked Gwynedd and conquered Anglesey, driving Cadwallon into exile, only for the Welsh king to gain revenge in
blood and battle some years later. But more of that anon. First, we must set Edwin upon
his throne: no easy task, as Æthelfrith, having disposed of one Deiran exile in order to
secure his throne, had turned his attention to Edwin.

At the time, Edwin was staying with Raedwald, the king of East Anglia, and thus chief of
another branch of the Angles. According to Bede, Æthelfrith attempted to bribe, threaten
and cajole Raedwald into disposing of his guest and thus removing the last credible claim-
ant to the throne of Northumbria. Raedwald was minded to agree, but his wife persuaded
him that to do so would be wrong. Instead, Raedwald, with Edwin, rode out against
Æthelfrith, and taking him by surprise, defeated his army and killed the first king of the
combined kingdoms of Northumbria. Æthelfrith's sons survived however, and went into
exile. We shall hear more of them later.

By right of battle, and the sufferance of Raedwald, Edwin was now king of Northumbria.
But while Raedwald was alive, the East Angle held overlordship over Edwin and indeed,
much of Britain; Bede records Raedwald as the fourth Bretwalda, or high king of Britain.
While he was prominent in life, he became even more so in death. It is widely accepted
now that Raedwald was the king buried in the Sutton Hoo ship.

But once Raedwald died, Edwin ruled supreme. And he set about making himself
more supreme.

BRITAIN DIVIDED

To understand the situation in Britain at the time, we need to abandon completely any idea
of a country. The land was divided into petty princedoms, many no bigger than a county,
and these were ruled by so-called kings. Loyalty was the fundamental binding agent of this
society, but it was a personal loyalty, owed to a particular person who happened to be king
of, say, Northumbria, rather than there being any obligation to Northumbria itself. You
served the king, and were bound to him through personal honour, bought through the

ancient rite of gift giving. You did not serve your country, for such a thing barely existed – you served a king.

To give an idea of how small the princedoms could be, Bede tells us that a West-Saxon king sent an assassin to kill Edwin. One of Edwin's retainers, exhibiting the loyalty that existed between king and man, put his unarmed body between the king and the assassin's knife, and took the strike himself. In revenge, Edwin set off for distant Wessex and killed no less than five West-Saxon kings. We don't even know if those five kings exhausted Wessex's king list – there may have been more! Such was the bond between king and retainer: each was sworn to protect and avenge the other.

Given the tiny size of so many kingdoms, and the small numbers involved in so many 'armies', it must have been relatively straightforward for Edwin, with the resources of two large kingdoms at his disposal, to assemble a war band that would overcome most of his opponents. Which is exactly what he did. To Deira and Bernicia, he added Elmet, a British kingdom that roughly occupied the West Riding of Yorkshire (think of the region around modern-day Leeds). Most travel in Anglo-Saxon Britain was done by sea, so Edwin put his ships to good use and invaded and conquered the Mevanian Islands, believed to be Anglesey and the Isle of Man.

If that makes Edwin seem nothing but a bloodthirsty warlord, we must remember that it was this king that Bede said brought such peace to the land that a woman could cross the country from sea to sea with a newborn baby in her arms and not be harmed, and who caused bronze drinking cups to be hung by wells at the side of the road so that travellers might be able to drink. And 'no one dared to lay hands on them except for their proper purpose because they feared the king greatly nor did they wish to, because they loved him.'[9] Machiavelli would have approved in part. This was a king that men feared, one that could parade with a standard bearer like the emperors of old and not seem like a popinjay but a ruler of genuinely imperial stature, even if his lordship was over a straightened land in straightened times.

And Edwin eventually became the first Christian king of Northumbria.

The king was baptised on Easter day AD 627. There's much more about this key event in our chapter about religion.

In the end, this Christian king of the English Northumbrians was killed in battle by the Christian king of the Britons, who had allied with the pagan king of Mercia. In an age of small realms and shifting alliances, some strange leagues could form, and none was more unusual than that between Cadwallon of Gwynedd and Penda of Mercia.

Having been defeated and driven into exile by Edwin, Cadwallon had regrouped and, with Penda of Mercia,[10] attacked Edwin. In October 633 Cadwallon and Penda met and defeated Edwin, killing the king. His two older sons by his first wife were with him at the Battle of Hatfield Chase: one died there, the other was taken prisoner by Penda and killed later.

The victorious Cadwallon drove on to Northumbria and, according to Bede, laid the kingdom waste, conducting what was almost a war of ethnic cleansing against the inhabitants. While it's unlikely that Cadwallon really aimed to exterminate every Anglo-Saxon in the country – after all, he was allied with the thoroughly Saxon Mercians – he does seem to have reserved an unusual fury for the defeated Northumbrians. Wars were generally a matter of kings and their war bands; the outcome for the peasants usually meant little more than a change in the man they paid their duties to. But Cadwallon seems to have extended his campaign to the non-fighting sections of the population in Northumbria.

The Return of the King

For a time it may have appeared that the British might succeed in regaining their lost dominion in the north. But when Edwin slew Æthelfrith and took the Northumbrian throne for himself, Æthelfrith's wife and surviving children had taken the normal course of action of a defeated ruling family: flight into exile. But though their actions were expected, the destination they chose was less so – the island of Iona.

This island off the west coast of Scotland had become the key centre of Christianity in the region. Given that Bede tells us that Æthelfrith had killed some 1,200 Christian monks before his successful battle against the Welsh, the decision of his still pagan family to seek refuge among those monks' co-religionists seems noteworthy. We know nothing more of why they made this decision, but the welcome they received suggests that it was the right one.

The four children of Æthelfrith stayed on Iona for some years, growing to adulthood there. It must have been on Iona that Oswald, later to be king of Northumbria and saint and martyr of the Universal Church, received instruction and entered into the faith that his father had fought against: Christianity. And it was from Iona that Oswald returned to the mainland with a small army to attempt to wrest his father's kingdom from Cadwallon.

Before the armies met, at a place called Heavenfield near Hexham in modern-day Northumberland, within sight of Hadrian's Wall, Oswald had a cross erected and knelt, holding it in position as its setting in the earth was filled. This was a time when men expected their gods, or their God, to deliver in this world as much as the next: victory under the sign of the cross would lead to Oswald and his men taking up the cross across Northumbria. Defeat meant death unshriven. It was time for God to put up or push off. He put up.

The present-day Iona Abbey, Scotland. *Wikimedia Commons*

Despite inferior forces, Oswald won, and Cadwallon was killed. Oswald, in the year of Our Lord 634, became king of Northumbria. Cadwallon's Britons were decisively defeated. Never again would the Britons come close to re-establishing control over their former territory. In fact, the Britons were now well on their way to becoming the Welsh.

God having delivered for Oswald, the new king did the same for God. He invited a mission from Iona to come to Northumbria. Aidan[11] arrived in Northumbria in 635 and established a monastery on Lindisfarne, the soon-to-be Holy Island, within sight of the royal stronghold at Bamburgh.

From there, Aidan and his monks set out to evangelise Northumbria, with the king acting as patron, sponsor and, initially at least, translator. When Aidan first arrived he could not speak the language of the locals, whereas Oswald, having lived on Iona, was fluent in both British and English.

Not only was Oswald king of Northumbria, but he seems to have exercised dominion over the other kingdoms of Britain. His reign lasted eight years, and firmly established Christianity in Northumbria in a way that Edwin's conversion had not.

But it was Edwin's old enemy, Penda of Mercia, who brought him down. In 642 Penda defeated Oswald at the Battle of Maserfield. The victorious pagan cut up Oswald's body and stuck his head and arms on poles.

If God rewarded his adherents and punished those who fought against him, this seemed to be a devastating setback for Christianity. The stubbornest pagan in the land had defeated a man whom Bede writes of as being a saint in his life as well as his death. The situation surely could only get worse for the new faith, for Penda was now the most powerful king in the land, installing and removing monarchs at whim. Possibly to ensure the permanent weakening of Northumbria, Penda split the kingdom into its two constituent realms. Oswald's younger brother, Oswiu, ruled Bernicia, but he did so at Penda's pleasure.

Politics is personal, and possibly no more personal than at this time, when people looked to their immediate families and kin for support, aid and refuge. You might kill one king, but a glance at the royal genealogies of the time shows that a nemesis often took the form of a relative of the slain monarch. Penda was no exception. His death eventually came at the hands of Oswald's younger brother, Oswiu.

Oswald. © *2012 Walters Art Museum*

However, Penda's blood stayed in his veins for many years after Oswald's death. Oswiu was king at the sufferance of his brother's killer, but, displaying a sound grasp of the practicalities of the power politics of the time, he apparently bought off the Mercian ruler by paying him huge amounts in tribute.

Quite why Penda eventually decided to take the money in a more direct manner – that is, over dead bodies – is not certain, but in 655 he invaded. As so often, the exact details, or indeed locations, of what happened next are not entirely clear, but the outcome was as stark as it usually was in sixth-century politics: Penda died, Oswiu won.

The death of Penda, who had remained stubbornly, perhaps even magnificently, pagan throughout a time of extraordinary religious change marked the effective end of paganism as a political and religious force in the land. While it no doubt took many, many years before the general population could be effectively evangelised, from now on all the country's rulers, whether they were English, British, Scottish, Pictish or Irish, were Christian. Even Penda's own sons, who went on to rule Mercia, were Christian.

As for Oswiu, he was now the dominant king in the land. And though his domination did not last that long – the Mercians revolted against the client king he'd established and put one of Penda's sons back on their throne – he did achieve something unique among Northumbrian kings up to that time: he died, in his bed, after falling ill. It was 15 February 670 and he was the first Northumbrian king not to die in battle.

His son, Ecgfrith, was not so fortunate. He ruled over a Northumbria at the height of its power, but died during a disastrous sortie against the Picts of Scotland in 685. Bede states that Northumbria's political decline began with his death, although historians argue that power had already started to shift south to Mercia during his reign.

In any case, the most important aspects of Northumbrian history shifted from the political and military to the cultural and religious.

Think on this. In 635, when Aidan arrived in Northumbria, he found a pagan and illiterate people. Within a century, Northumbria had become the key intellectual, religious and scholarly centre of northern Europe. Its priests and monks, men and women such as Bede and Hilda, Wilfrid and Alcuin, studied the Scriptures and works of classical learning, produced exquisite volumes of the Gospels, sent missionaries and representatives to the pagans of Germany and the court of Charlemagne, and assembled the finest libraries to be found

Viking ship detail. *Wikimedia Commons*

A model of the Viking ship burial excavated at Gokstad in Norway. The original would have been more frightening.
Wikimedia Commons

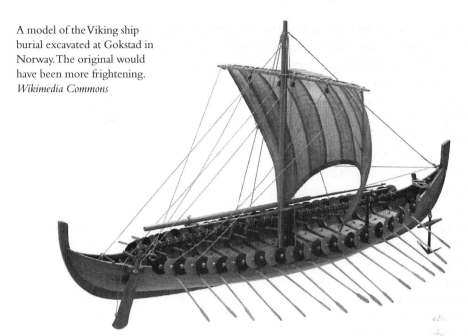

in northern Europe. Men who, in the words of Pope Gregory, had worshipped sticks and stones but a generation ago, spoke in Latin, read Greek, wrote treatises on the tides and established that the world was, against the apparent evidence of the senses, round.

It was, in its own way, a golden age. Indeed, so thoroughly had the new religion penetrated at least the upper echelons of society that Ecgfrith's successor, Aldfrith, was seen as a scholar as well as a king. In fact, Bede records only one battle as taking place during his reign, which suggests a period of quite unparalleled peacefulness.

Thereafter, a number of unremarkable kings ruled, generally for short periods of time, trialling the chronic instability that would eventually so weaken the kingdom. What is notable is that two of them, rather than following the time-honoured tradition of violent death, voluntarily gave up their crowns and entered monasteries: Ceolwulf (reigned 729–737) and Eadberht (ruled 737/8–758). But afterwards, the history of the kings of Northumbria becomes a sad, bitter and, for our purposes at least, slightly pointless tale of usurpation and murder, with names passing in a blur of dates.

And then the Vikings came.

Yes, we know all the historical revisionism, we know the Vikings were great traders and travellers, we understand that history is usually written by the victors, but if the victors are illiterate then the losers get an unexpected chance to paint their enemies in all the gory colours of their defeat; we know all this, and some of it is even true.

But for the kingdom of Northumbria, history ends when the long ships appear. The *Anglo-Saxon Chronicle* records:

> In this year [793] fierce, foreboding omens came over the land of Northumbria. There were excessive whirlwinds, lightning storms, and fiery dragons were seen flying in the sky. These signs were followed by great famine, and on January 8th the ravaging of heathen men destroyed God's church at Lindisfarne.

Interview with Graeme Young

1. Who are you and what is your area of expertise?
My name is Graeme Young and I am a 46-year-old professional field archaeologist. Over my career I have excavated a considerable variety of sites dating from the Mesolithic to the industrial era, but my particular area of expertise is in the medieval period, both early and later. I am also one of the four directors of the Bamburgh Research Project.

2. Describe your specialism simply.
The meticulous excavation and recording of complex and deeply stratified archaeological sites would about sum up what I do best.

3. How have archaeological investigations, such as those at Bamburgh, changed our views of Northumbria?
The story of Northumbria at one time was very much based on the historical evidence of texts such as Bede's *Ecclesiastical History*. Archaeology over the last few decades has transformed our understanding and brought these texts to life, particularly with the excavation of sites like Wearmouth and Jarrow illuminating the pages of Bede by revealing a monastic culture every bit as sophisticated as that he described. With secular sites such as Bamburgh (high status) and Shotton (low status) we have very little descriptive evidence, as monks tended to write more about monasteries, so the archaeology takes on an additional significance as it is often the only way we can get close to the architecture and cultural life of the period.

4. What do you consider the most important change in our views of Northumbria?
I would say that archaeology has painted a more sophisticated cultural picture of Northumbria over recent years than we had deduced from texts. I would also add that cemetery sites have put us closely in touch with the often painful and brutal lives of medieval Northumbrians. Bamburgh in particular is providing evidence that stone architecture was in use in a secular context from a much earlier period than had previously been thought. I would add my voice to those who see archaeology countering the historical label of the early medieval period as the 'Dark Ages'.

5. Who do you consider to be the most important figures in Northumbrian history?
There are obvious answers such as King Oswald, who played such a key role in the Christianisation of the kingdom, bringing it into the European medieval cultural and intellectual mainstream. Given the importance of Northumbria at the time, this has significance for the wider development of England. There is also Bede, who has such a key role in the development of an English intellectual culture and the recording of history. Perhaps

even the creation of an idea of England itself. In fact he is really of such significance that he should be seen as a European figure.

I would add the almost unknown figure of Oswulf, one of the tenth-century Bamburgh earls. He was in no small part involved in ending Eric Bloodaxe's reign as king of York, which led to the final creation of a kingdom of all England. It's quite an important role to have played and should be better remembered.

6. Which areas of Northumbrian history are most likely to change in future with further investigation?
I think there is a great deal that archaeology has to add with regard to reconstructing the past economy. At the moment, we have a rather limited data set with which to map the scale and productivity of early medieval farming, which would have so much to tell us about the lives of early medieval Northumbrians. I think further palaeoenvironmental work, from Bamburgh not least, will add hugely to our understanding of the Northumbrian economy.

7. Why was Northumbria important?
Northumbria played a major role in the introduction of Christianity to England and perhaps the key role in the decision to turn to Roman rather than the Irish Christian tradition for its lead. This led to an alteration in the outlook of England, moving from a more Scandinavian one to a Franco-Italian one. The implications of this are still unfolding today in terms of our relationship with our continental neighbours.

8. Why is Northumbria important?
I think all history starts as local and regional history, so for those of us from Northumbria, its history still has an impact on how we see ourselves. The history of the region has real relevance today, particularly with the rise of the Scottish independence movement. Why, if not due to Northumbria's history, is the border where it is and England and Scotland the places they are? We are still in so many ways the border region that links London and the south to what lies beyond the immediate English orbit.

9. Is there anything else you would like to add?
At a time of such tumult and with economies and so many peoples' lives in jeopardy, archaeology and history can seem a little frivolous. I would argue though that it is at such times of crisis, or potential crisis, that knowing how we got here and what failures and successes past generations have had can help us find our way. Or at the very least give us some comfort that all troubles pass in time.

What is Archaeology?

Archaeology is a science. Many people see archaeology as an art rather than a science, but in fact archaeology is one of the broadest of sciences, its range of constituent disciplines ranging from the hardest of hard sciences – isotopic analysis, say, or neutron activation analysis – to the social sciences such as sociology and psychology. The findings of archaeologists can also illuminate and be illuminated by disciplines such as art history and history itself, which aren't sciences but do have rigorous intellectual foundations. In fact, we're hard put to think of a science that uses a wider range of intellectual and technical tools to interrogate its subject. But then, that is to be expected, since the subject of archaeology is humanity and its interaction with our world and its physical, animal and plant constituents. It's a big subject; quantum mechanics is easy peasy by comparison.

2

LAYING DOWN THE LAND

The green earth, say you? That is a mighty matter of legend, though you tread it under the light of day!

(J.R.R. Tolkien, *The Two Towers*)

Standing on the rock at Bamburgh, walking the Cheviot Hills, marking the old Roman bounds along Hadrian's Wall or pitching out to the Farne Islands on a boat, the visitor to Northumberland is brought face to face with a land where geography dominates. Humanity has always been thin on the ground here, and our presence still feels tenuous. In this chapter, we will look at the long history of Northumbria and try to understand how the forces that formed the land gave birth to, nurtural and constrained the civilisations and peoples that have lived there over the centuries.

CATASTROPHE AND CONTINUITY

Dropping into the personal for a moment, both authors remember the quite literally jaw-dropping impact of first seeing Northumberland's unique combination of landscape, history and architecture brought into stark focus by Bamburgh Castle, squatting on the horizon and dominating land, sea and sky. But how did the landscape assume its current form? To answer that, we have to go back a long, long way.

In the late eighteenth and nineteenth centuries, the abyss of time was slowly being plumbed. Geologists such as James Hutton and Charles Lyell proposed that their nascent science should seek to 'explain the former changes of the Earth's surface by reference to causes now in operation'.[12] Floods, catastrophes and acts divine or unexplained were unnecessary for understanding the nature of the earth. All that was required was time: time for processes such as erosion, deposition and weathering to lay down hills and carve out valleys. The Victorian buzzword was 'uniformitarianism' and uniformitarianism allowed extraordinary advances in our understanding of geology. It also, not entirely coincidentally, allowed the self-confident pioneers of the new science to cut themselves free from what many of them saw as the dead hand of religion. No longer was the earth to be

The topography of Britain: flat in the east, knobbly in the west. *Wikimedia Commons*

dated by arcane researches into the book of Genesis by the Archbishop of Armagh and Primate of All Ireland, James Ussher. The world, it was realised, began a little before Sunday 23 October 4004 BC; new men, new ideas and a new paradigm now held sway.

But revolutionaries, if they are successful, in turn become the establishment, with as much invested in their ideas and prestige as their predecessors. In the last two decades of the twentieth century the realisation began to slowly dawn in geological circles that the drop-by-drop, grain-by-grain accumulation of change was insufficient to explain the history of the planet. Sometimes, not often, but often enough to make a profound difference, things happened suddenly. Earth-shattering things. Indeed, it's now widely held that the Moon itself was the result of a collision between the earth and a body the size of Mars some 4 billion years ago. More recently, the key hypothesis leading to the acceptance of catastrophic events in the planet's history was the discovery of a layer of iridium, deposited over the earth, coinciding with the extinction of the dinosaurs 65 million years ago. Since iridium is an uncommon element on earth but abundant in meteorites, father and son scientists Luis and Walter Alvarez (the father a physicist, the son a geologist) proposed that an asteroid between 6 and 9 miles in diameter had struck the earth with an explosive power 1 billion times that of the atomic bombs dropped on Hiroshima and Nagasaki. The later discovery of a hole 110 miles wide off the Yucatan Peninsula in Mexico provided the smoking crater.

Bamburgh Castle.

Hard core: coring at Bamburgh. *Bamburgh Research Project (BRP)*

The 2004 Indian Ocean tsunami killed over 230,000 people. *Wikimedia Commons*

Earth, it turned out, was not the sleepy old lady she had appeared to be, but one who rather burst from the slumber of millennia into a frenzy of shaping, only to settle back down to unquiet, rumbling sleep. Even the old Biblical myth of the world-swamping flood proved not so mythical after all, with a veritable wave of inundations being proposed over the last couple of decades, starting with the flooding of the Black Sea in 5600 BC and coming right into home waters with the megafloods that separated Britain from the Continent 180,000 years ago and then drowned Doggerland beneath the North Sea in 6100 BC.

Flood, fire and earthquake, wonders in the heavens and chthonic stirrings in the ground have occasionally but devastatingly changed everything, either locally or, sometimes, over the whole globe.

So we are faced now with a history, deep beyond our imagining, where the very ground upon which we walk is shifting in the long slow continental waltz; where mountains rise and fall, seas grow and fail, and solid earth, if we could view it through its ages, would show as many moods as the shifting sea.

Squeezing history from a stone

Some of the most important rock in Northumbria formed 295 million years ago. The Great Whin Sill is a vast layer of rock, stretching from Teesdale in the south, up through the Pennines to Bamburgh and the Farne Islands. Most of it is still underground. To understand how that can be so, we have to go deep. We're all familiar, at least on television, with molten lava spurting from a crater or crawling down the flank of a volcano.

But not all lava gets to the surface: 295 million years ago, when Northumbria was near the equator and covered by a shallow and, in comparison to today's version, pleasantly warm, sea, magma was squeezed up from deep in the earth. However, rather than finding a channel to the surface, this slow-flowing rock, heated to about 1,100°C, diverted into the fault lines between the layers of softer sedimentary rock that formed the bottom of the shallow sea. Imagine squeezing the contents of a tube of toothpaste into a gap where the mortar has fallen out between two bricks; that gives a sense of what happened. Toothpaste, of course, goes hard when it comes out of the tube; lava goes harder. In the case of the Great Whin Sill, the rock is called dolerite, but for our purposes that is not particularly important. What is important is that the rock is hard, and the rock above and below it is much softer. So, a sheet of rock, concealed beneath the earth, and formed in a relatively short space of time, was gradually revealed by classically Lyellian processes: the sea retreated, and the forces of erosion worked on the exposed sedimentary rock, wearing it away until the Great Whin Sill was slowly revealed beneath. The process is continuing today: much of the Whin Sill is still below ground, its presence obvious more by implication than action. But where it has been exposed, this rock has left its mark, on geography and our interaction with it.

Hadrian's engineers employed exposed ridges of the Great Whin Sill to add ready-made height to their already high wall. Elsewhere along its length, sweating soldiers had to dig a ditch on the northern side of the wall, and where the Great Whin Sill cut across the landscape, the legionaries needed only to build the rampart on top of its shelf.

At the coast, the great rock of Bamburgh, squatting by the sea, is also made of dolerite. Across the waves, the Farne Islands, present-day home of hundreds of thousands of breeding seabirds and past home of Cuthbert, Northumbria's greatest saint, are also part of the Great Whin Sill.

Thus geology, in the shape of rocks formed hundreds of millions of years ago, makes history in the form of strongholds both military and spiritual.

We are creatures of our landscape, and this landscape is deep.

The Rhythms of Stone

The long, slow dance of the continents has waltzed across the surface of the earth ever since there was a planet to move over. In that time, the land that today is England, Wales and Scotland has migrated over much of the globe. No doubt Scottish nationalists will be pleased to know that, for most of the period, Scotland was separate from England and Wales, the lands only joining a mere 420 million years ago. In the succeeding aeons, the country was periodically submerged beneath the oceans, where much of the land we now walk upon was laid down in the sediment of shallow seas, only to re-emerge, blinking, into the light.

The Cheviot Hills are the oldest feature of the Northumbrian landscape, having been formed by a volcano spewing magma over some 600sq km. The granite hills we see today are the much-eroded remnants of that volcano, which exploded 380 million years ago.

The land that slopes down to the sea, forming the coastal plain, is a young stripling by comparison, with the sandstones, mudstones and limestones that form its foundations having been laid down in estuaries and shallow seas around 340 million years ago. Overlying this is a layer of thick-grained sandstone, siltstone and mudstone that was deposited when big river deltas spread silt over a shallow sea 300 million years ago. This coastal environment supported fecund swamp forests that fell back into the water to eventually produce thick layers of coal.

Thus the skeleton of Northumbria formed. The gritty flesh overlying it that we walk on today was mainly the result of the Ice Ages of the last 100,000 years leaving layers of sediment as the glaciers pulsed to and fro.

Beating Out the Bounds

Look at the map of Britain on p. 24. It's a truism that geography defines us, but some places are more defined than others and a glance at the map will show why Northumbria is one of them. To the east, the Cheviot Hills form a brooding backdrop to the royal dramas at Bamburgh, the capital of the northern half of Northumbria, Bernicia. The Pennines continue southwards, forming the offset spine of the country. To the east, the land slopes downwards in rich agricultural rolls to the sea. Rivers cut through the fertile farmlands around York, providing easy access to the capital of the southern half of Northumbria, Deira. And it is the sea that defines the eastern flank of Northumbria, providing food, offering island sanctuaries and allowing travel with a speed and security impossible on land.

Another look at the map will reveal a further consequence of England's geography. It's possible to penetrate deep into the expansive plains of the eastern half of the country by sailing up one of the many rivers that flow across the plains: the Ouse, the Tyne, the Tees, the Tweed and the Wear. The western half of the country is less accessible. The raiders and settlers who became the English predominantly settled in the east, most obviously because it was closer to their original homes, but also because it was so straightforward to sail their boats miles inland.

But the English were latecomers. The first people to see Northumbria arrived on foot. What did they see?

Trees. Lots of trees. But not the Wildwood of legend that supposedly blanketed Britain from coast to coast. Even before humanity arrived, the landscape was much more varied than the Wildwood legend suggests. In fact, people may have arrived before the trees. There is some evidence of human presence even during the last Ice Age, with fire sites found on the caves of the Hebrides, and other indications of human presence in Wales and the south of England.

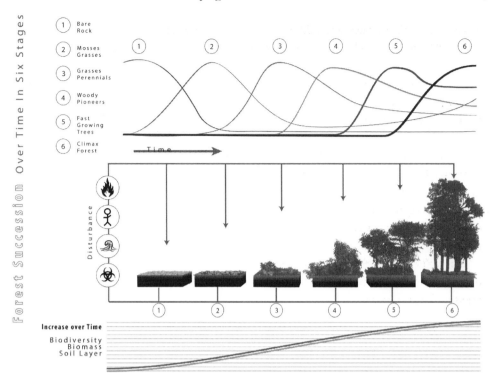

From bare rock to climax forest, nature follows a schedule. *Wikimedia Commons*

But whether people or trees arrived first, the land uncovered by the retreating ice was a blank canvas awaiting a living script. That script is pretty well predetermined, with a well-established succession of plants moving in to take advantage of the exposed ground. First, lichens and mosses, then grasses and other hardy, windblown plants. All of these set about the hard work of creating soil, only for their labour to be taken up and used against them as birch and willow and pine, not quite so hardy but taller and thus able to shade out their predecessors, came in and displace the pioneers.

The pioneer trees were shaded out in their turn by the late-arriving, slower-moving oak, hazel, elm and alder, which formed the forests that eventually covered much of Britain. But even when the Wildwood was established, the effect of local conditions – the variations in soil, exposure and altitude, and the general vicissitudes of weather, fate and the fancy of grazing herds of megafauna – would have ensured a landscape that was more mosaic than monoculture.

Those first human visitors would have had further to walk to find the sea. The Farne Islands were, like the rock upon which Bamburgh Castle sits, outcrops on the Northumbrian plain, while the shores of the gradually expanding North Sea were still far to the east. What better vantage point could those prehistoric gatherers and hunters have asked for than the eminence of Bamburgh rock, commanding the level plain for as far as the eye could see?

There is evidence of human activity on and around Bamburgh from Palaeolithic times onwards. Although those early men might not have needed strongholds and defences in the way that their successors would – people were so spread out that isolation was more likely to be a problem than aggression – still they recognised what others were to see later. This was the place to be.

TAKING THE LOW GROUND

A look at the topography of the region immediately shows something important. The higher ground is offset to the west, the coastal plains being correspondingly broader in the east than they are in the west. The weather, in particular the rain, generally comes from the west, and falls more on the western plains and the highlands than the eastern plains. But wheat and barley – two typical crops from the Bronze Age to the present – don't grow well when they receive more than 75cm of rain a year. So it's little surprise that the eastern plains were more intensively settled and harder worked than the uplands or western plains. And since they could support a larger population, the chief of the eastern plains had an immediate advantage over his rivals.

This climactic advantage was supplemented by the best soils being concentrated in the east, in particular in East Yorkshire. But archaeology suggests that the Bronze Age settlements in the Cheviots were generally on the higher ground. How can we explain this discrepancy? One possibility is that after the ice retreated, woods re-established themselves across the area. For several thousand years, the long, tangled roots of this wood bound the soil together and acted as a buffer against the effects of heavy rainfall. At this time, the bare ridges of the Pennines and the Cheviots would have had a shaggy appearance to passing hunters, clothed as they were in ragged trees and forests.

So where did the trees go? They were cut down by men, first wielding stone and then bronze axes. But what those early woodcutters did not realise was that once the stabilising mat of tree roots was lost, then the topsoil could be washed away by the region's heavy rainfall. Thus, the accumulated fertility of thousands of years of leaf mould was unlocked for a few years' crops, before it followed the rain down the hillsides, staining the streams and rivers brown. The rich soil of the hilltops was washed off them, and in its place, peat formed and bogs grew.

By the Bronze Age, 100 generations of farmers had been swinging axes and setting fires. The archaeology reveals a landscape that had become degraded. So began the slow retreat from the hills. Bronze Age settlements gradually abandoned the high ground and moved downhill, with the later settlements to be found below 300m.

Interview with Ian Boomer

1. Who are you and what is your area of expertise?
My name is Ian Boomer. I'm an earth scientist, a geologist. I reconstruct past environments, whether they're 200 million years old or 5,000 years old. That brings my work into archaeology, where I'd probably be called a geoarchaeologist.

2. Describe your specialism simply.
My main expertise is in using microfossils to reconstruct past environments. These are usually less than 1mm long, so I spend a lot of time using microscopes! One of my main areas of research has been the ways we can use these microfossils, together with details of the sediments that they came from, to tell us how coastlines have changed in recent millennia. So coastal change has always been an interest of mine, particularly how it responds to natural changes in sea level.

3. Can you describe the geomorphology of Northumbria in layman's terms?
A series of hills or uplands to the west (such as the Cheviots), grading down into a rich coastal plain that is bounded to the east by a combination of rocky and sandy beaches with many rivers, large and small, cutting west to east through that landscape.

4. How was the geomorphology of Northumbria determined?
It began with the underlying geology, with many millions of years of deposition, intrusions, uplift and erosion. This provided the canvas, giving us the uplands, lowlands, and the coastline. More recent events have painted this canvas: the ice sheets of the last 2 million years eroded and smoothed the landscape, leaving behind a collection of sands, gravels and tills that covered much of the land. This was then sculpted by the rivers and coastal processes that we see today.

5. What techniques do you use?
We learn a lot just from observing and describing, but that's only on the surface. To understand what's happening underneath the ground, we have to dig. Digging large holes in the ground is useful but expensive. I tend to use cores. These aren't quite the boreholes that engineering and mining companies use, but are drilled with smaller, lighter equipment. A couple of people can easily reach 10–12m down in the right type of sediments.

Sediments are like a tape recorder: as they accumulate, they record sediments, plants and animals that tell us about the past environment. That's where my interest lies. We can also take this to a further level and look at the chemistry of the sediments and fossils through time.

6. How has the land changed since the Ice Age?

The first thing we would have seen at the end of the Ice Age would have been a lot of water. All that ice had to go somewhere and it generally went back into the sea via rivers, so the rivers would have been carrying much more water in the immediate 'post-glacial' period than they do now. That may help to explain why some Northumbrian rivers are small but are set within very deep cut gorges.

There was no soil and no plants to begin with. The first soils would have been mineral rich till with relatively little humus material. It would have been a grey and brown world 20,000–16,000 years ago. The vegetation established slowly. First a few cold-type grasses and sedges, then gradually some low-lying, cold-adapted herbs, followed by more herbs and high-latitude trees such as conifers before we get broad-leaved trees sometime after about 10,000 years ago. By about 8,000 years ago, trees and shrubs covered much of the landscape – and they still would if it wasn't for man's intervention.

7. If we watched a speeded-up film of the changing geology/geomorphology of Northumbria, what would we see?

It depends when you start the film. Geology works on very long timescales. It takes millions of years for sediments to be deposited, lithified (turned into rocks) and then uplifted to form mountains/hills. Geomorphology is what happens to geology at the earth's surface, it's the combination of weathering, erosion and biological impacts on the upper few metres of geology.

The geomorphology is basically the result of the Ice Age(s). Geologically, go back about 370 million years and the first part of the modern landscape comes with the intrusion of magma deep below ground (that would eventually become granite) and the outpouring of volcanic lavas onto what was then the land surface to form what we know today as the Cheviot Hills. Come forward to about 340 million years ago (mid-carboniferous) and Northumbria was under subtropical waters with sands, muds and limestones being deposited in warm shallow waters during a series of cycles, as global sea levels rose and fell (sometimes, the sea level fell enough for coals to form at the tops of these Yoredale Cycles). The whole sequence was then uplifted as Britain sat on the northern margin of a closing ocean and associated with that was lots of volcanic activity. The result of this was the creation of large dykes and sills deep below ground towards the end of the carboniferous. The remains of one of the large sills has now been brought to the surface through erosion – the Whin Sill.

3

THE FIRST NORTHUMBRIANS

Remember me when I am gone away,
Gone far away into the silent land.

(Christina Rossetti, 'Remember')

The history of human habitation in Britain stretches back to a time before humans – *Homo sapiens sapiens* – actually existed. Successive waves of our ancestors – *Homo heidelbergensis* and *Homo neanderthalensis* – travelled up into the far north-west of the world, only to retreat before the advancing glaciers of a series of ice ages. For most of our ancestors, a little global warming might have seemed very welcome indeed. The earliest evidence of human activity in Britain is, in fact, hominid rather than human, but moving on to anatomically modern humans, archaeologists have found tantalising traces of them in these islands from before the last Ice Age. Considering the way advancing glaciers scour the land back to bedrock and the minuscule populations that must have existed then, the fact that there are any remains at all is almost miraculous.

On the other hand, it's worth bearing in mind that archaeologists are now reinterpreting how the series of ice ages over the last 100,000 years affected human activity in Britain. The conventional image of implacable sheets of ice advancing south as far as Sheffield and turning the rest of the country into a sub-Arctic wasteland of howling winds and frozen tundra is being questioned, most notably by acknowledging that there's no reason to expect all the ice ages to have come the same distance south. Think of waves on a beach. Some waves reach far higher up the strand than others and though glaciers appear solid, they are in fact governed by laws of flow dynamics that allow them to move, in fact to flow, rather like an advancing wave. So it's likely that the succeeding glaciations covered more or less of the British Isles. Furthermore, the evidence of steady occupation at places like Cresswell Crags in Derbyshire suggests that even when the ice came south, people did not abandon the land but rather adapted to the changed conditions and stayed.

Mesolithic art

During the Mesolithic, people started engraving what today
we call cup and ring marks on rocks. There is usually a central depression (the cup) and concentric grooved circles
surrounding it. Northumbria has more of this rock art than
anywhere else in Britain, with particularly good examples
to be found at Roughting Linn, Dod Law, Lordenshaw and
Weetwood Moor. It's worth bearing in mind that while all
we have today are stone examples, it's perfectly possible that
people carved similar patterns into trees or other organic
substances that have long since decayed. As to their meaning,
well, they are something of a Rorschach test for archaeologists, as their
mute witness brings forth as many explanations as there are surviving examples. Some
people say they're maps of the stars, others that they're property markers or contracts
literally set in stone, or maybe they're the visual representations or way markers for a
Mesolithic shaman's hallucinogenically inspired spirit journey.[13]

Flood alert

Once, where the North Sea and English Channel are today, there was a low-lying plain
of lakes and rich hunting – Doggerland. The assumption was that Doggerland gradually
receded beneath the waves, but recent evidence, uncovered by Professor David Smith,
indicates that the end might not have been so gentle. He found a thick layer of sand in
the Montrose Basin in Scotland, but this was sand where it shouldn't be: far above the
high-water level. What seems to have happened is that part of what Norwegians today call
the Storegga (the Great Edge), the wall of rock that rises out of the abyss to form the first
buttress of the Eurasian continent, collapsed into the deep. When it fell, water flooded into
the suddenly empty space, then just as suddenly exploded outwards, unleashing a 30ft-high
tidal wave down along the eastern side of Britain that reached as far as 50 miles inland and
finally, and catastrophically, broke the link between Britain and the continent. There were
no doubt many settlements and groups of gatherer-hunters in the low land along the coast
and camped in Doggerland. They wouldn't have stood a chance. We can imagine them,
staring in bewilderment as the sea drew back and back and back from the land.

  Then the wave came, as pitiless as death and just as implacable. It was in 6100 BC that
Britain became an island, and further folk memories of the flood were cemented into our
collective psyche.

The Good Life

The first evidence of human activity in what was the kingdom of Northumbria was excavated at Seamer Carr in North Yorkshire. The hunter-gatherers who left their flint hand axes and chopping tools at Seamer Carr were there at the latest in 10,000 BC and possibly tens of thousands of years before. These early hunter-gatherers were following the movements of animals and the seasonal fruiting and ripening of plants. In fact, the order should probably be reversed: these people were gatherer-hunters more than hunter-gatherers and so the prevalence of nuts, fruits, berries and edible grasses most likely had the biggest influence on their travels. Plants are also usually more reliable than animals: after all, even today if you find a particularly fecund blackberry bush you know it's worth going back at the same time next year to harvest the fruit. These gatherers were not simply subsisting though – far from it. They had a good quality of life, picking highly nutritious plant products and hunting small game, while seasonally harvesting the migrating herds that they followed when seasons allowed. They had plenty of leisure time and a rich culture, creating clothing, tools and art.

The life of gatherer-hunters does not change much through the centuries. This Pomo woman photographed in the early twentieth century would have slipped seamlessly into Neolithic Northumbria. *Edward S. Curtis Collection/Wikimedia Commons*

… as would this Klamath canoeist. *Edward S. Curtis Collection/Wikimedia Commons*

One of the key constraints on gatherer-hunters is what, and how much, they can carry. This, in turn, is dependent on their luggage technology. Unfortunately, bags, baskets and slings, since they were made of organic materials, seldom leave archaeological remains. Women of childbearing age would have had to carry a baby; the men, older women and children had to porter the rest. Although the traces are slight, the transition from carrying things in arms to carrying things in bags seems to have occurred at the changeover from the Palaeolithic age to the Mesolithic age, roughly 10000 BC.[14]

The remains at Seamer Carr are the only traces of Palaeolithic activity in Northumbria to be discovered so far, but things pick up considerably during the Mesolithic. The climate at that time, around about 11,000 years ago, was increasingly wet and mild, producing a country of woods and glades, lakes and rivers that was the matrix of the haunted, hunted Wildwood of the British imagination.

Just across the water from Seamer Carr is Starr Carr, one of the most famous Mesolithic sites in the world. At the time, what is now the Vale of Pickering was a large lake, reed fringed and wooded around its banks with alder, willow and birch. Such a place was rich in game and forage, and it attracted centuries of hunters. No doubt there were many other such habitual hunting and gathering grounds around Britain, but this one is special: this one left remains of much more than stone. Because the lake laid a thick layer of sediment down on its shores, organic material lost or deposited in the water was preserved because the lack of oxygen in the mud prevented the normal processes of decay from happening.

Archaeologists have found remains of the oldest permanent house in Britain here and a wooden platform or pier that extended out over the surface of the lake some 20ft. Apart from Mesolithic carpentry – skilfully carried out with stone tools – excavators have found harpoon points made from antler and bone, wooden tools, and amber and animal-tooth jewellery. But most famously, and intriguingly, of all, archaeologists found 21 headdresses, made of the hollowed-out upper skull and antlers of a red deer. Looking at the artefact, it's impossible not to imagine a cord inserted through the holes and tied under the chin to hold the top-heavy headdress in place.

Spectacular though the finds at Starr Carr are, the earliest evidence of Mesolithic habitation in Northumbria was found on a clifftop in Howick, not far south of the village of Craster, well known for its smoked kippers. At Howick, archaeologists discovered a hut that had been inhabited for at least a century, having been constructed around 7800 BC. Apart from the hut, which was constructed around a framework of wooden poles sunk into the ground and then thatched over, the site has produced huge amounts of flint, indicating that the people who lived in the hut ran a thriving workshop, producing flint tools and weapons, such as arrowheads, knives and scrapers, from the flint that was harvested from the cliff and shore below.

These finds, together with other discoveries in the British Isles, have been vital in allowing archaeologists to peer behind the flint screen that had previously obscured the Mesolithic. Very often all that survived of our Mesolithic ancestors was flint, but these finds seem to us to herald something of a reinterpretation of the period, away from one based on rather simplistic parallels with American Indian and other extant hunter-gatherer societies, to a view of Mesolithic society as more complex, ingenious and differentiated than previously thought. For instance, it seems highly unlikely to us that Mesolithic man limited his use of stone to flint and only his Neolithic descendants had the wit to use other types of stone for monuments and henges. The mastery of flint revealed at Howick, and the wide variety of natural materials excavated at Starr Carr and other places, suggest a culture ingenious and confident enough to make use of every material to hand.

Life in a Day

Is it possible to write an account of an ordinary day in the life of a Mesolithic man or woman? Many archaeologists have done so, but in truth their reconstructions probably tell the reader as much about the writer as they do about the subject. There are almost as many different models of the Mesolithic as there are Mesolithic sites, and all of these models depend upon a particular philosophical or theoretical framework. So there are Marxist interpretations that view the Mesolithic as a time of social equality, Hobbesian analyses that see it as a time of vigorous competition between tribes with gender-based divisions of labour that started off seeing women as out gathering nuts and berries while big hairy men hunted deer and wild cattle and then, with the rise of feminism, saw Mesolithic men getting in touch with their inner botanist and harvesting fruit while women fished and set traps.

Whether this wealth of interpretations will ever be thinned out remains to be seen, but there are a lot of reputations riding on the lack of definitive evidence. If firmer conclusions are eventually possible, it's likely that there will be embarrassments similar to the chagrin that greeted the carbon dating of Stonehenge to a time after the pyramids in Egypt, when many scholars had confidently dated it to before the Pyramid of Djoser (built 2700 BC). In archaeology, many a reputation has evaporated in a single moment of scientific breakthrough or been gradually washed away by the slow accumulation of evidence. There is too often a lack of rigorous testing, which has led to an overabundance of theorising, with whole models resting on insubstantial foundations.

With all these caveats in place, and bearing in mind that we are not party to any privileged information, so take our theorising with as much salt as anybody else's, here's our take on the Mesolithic.

Within the broad church of the Mesolithic there were small family units, consisting of probably fewer than 30 people, with two or three core families living together. These families may have split up during parts of the season, or aggregated with other groups at different times. The central dynamic of Mesolithic culture was movement, but movements that returned to specific areas at specific times to harvest seasonal crops or hunt migrating animals. Some activities were very much helped by people collecting in larger groups, like fish-

An aerial view of the BRP excavations at Bradford Kaims. *Horizon AP*

ing for salmon during their annual run or hunting larger animals such as caribou and auroch, the wild and distinctly dangerous ancestors of today's cattle. Other activities, such as fruit or fungus gathering, benefited from people being more spread out. An ethnographic parallel would be American Indian tribes that hunted white-tailed deer for one season, rabbit for another and harvested wild growing corn at a different time. The regular travels probably resolved into a rough circuit, but over generations that circuit expanded and spiralled outwards as people sought out new hunting and gathering grounds.

It's hard to imagine nowadays, when people would rather buy blackberries from a supermarket than pick them from a bramble, but people then had an extraordinary connection with nature. In fact, the Mesolithic may have represented a high-water mark in our communion with nature, since mankind had sufficient technological resources to allow people to thrive, but that thriving depended on and was fed, literally and spiritually, by being part of nature's weave rather than standing apart from it. Even warfare, mankind's perennial pastime, was probably not waged – there wasn't the population and any conflict over resources could be solved more easily by moving on rather than by fighting it out.

Lest we seem to be painting a rosy picture of an Edenic Mesolithic world where all the people were 'living life in peace' then the flip side was that Mesolithic life was hard, short and often painful. In times of plenty, people feasted and put on as much fat as they could, because in times of shortage they knew they would starve. However, numerous studies of present-day hunter-gatherer societies suggest that in the normal course of events they only needed to work for about 10 per cent of the day to gather their food requirements; the rest of the time was devoted to some heavy-duty dossing. The people of the Mesolithic were practical botanists par excellence and while life on a cold winter's day in Northumbria must have been hard (it can be pretty unpleasant even today!), lolling at day's end by a trout-filled lake at the end of August must have been really rather pleasant.

Stone Age clothing

Did Palaeolithic man wear any clothes? We're talking about people who lived between 40,000 and 10,000 years ago during a period that's called the Upper Palaeolithic. The short answer is that we don't know. The evidence is scantier than the outfits at the Rio de Janeiro carnival, so archaeologists have been reduced to inferring an answer from climactic evidence. Some archaeologists claim that it would have been simply impossible for people to survive during this period – which included the last glacial period – without warm clothing. Of the two authors of this text, the effete southern one has considerable sympathy with this argument. Other archaeologists, citing the lack of evidence of clothing and the fact that the Aboriginal inhabitants of Tasmania made do without clothing, say they didn't. The northern author, being made of considerably sterner stuff, finds this credible in principle.

BRAVE NEOLITHIC WORLD

Starting from any point during the Mesolithic, the changes that finally tipped society into the Neolithic must have seemed small individually. But the changes slowly accumulated and gathered into an extraordinary wave of cultural transformation. Through the thousands of years of human existence up to and including the Mesolithic, the basic elements of human existence had remained unaltered: birth, death, speech, movement. By the end of the Neolithic, while there was still birth and death, the other fundamentals of existence were changing fast: people settled down, stopped moving and started growing, and speech was on the verge of being set down and stored for generations in writing, as vital a resource as grain kept in a jar but far less predictable.

The change from Mesolithic to Neolithic cultures is one of the most investigated areas of archaeology, and one of the most perplexing. The evidence, ranging from the domestication of animals and plants to permanent settlements and changing diets, is wide-ranging, but the range of possible interpretations is just as wide and perhaps the most honest account is to say we simply don't know exactly how the transformation occurred. Take the domestication of wild plants into the cereal crops that allowed people to grow enough food to become static. Was this a case of people taming and mastering nature – the prevalent view for many years – or was it rather that plants like the wild grasses that became wheat and rice entered into a symbiotic relationship with people, exchanging the loss of seed in the harvest for the planting and protection of next year's crop. If nothing else, for the plants concerned the relationship ensured a huge multiplication in the number of their descendants, thus maximising their place in the gene pool.

We suspect, although we certainly can't prove, that one of the crucial turning points was when people had filled in enough of the land that there came borders and defined

The axeman cometh. A selection of Neolithic axes. *Wikimedia Commons*

territories that allowed for the formation of trading networks. Because once you know that at this time next year, when the salmon are running, there will be a great gathering of people on the River Tweed, or when you've found out that the cliffs at Howick produce enough flint to support a semi-permanent settlement of tool makers, then it becomes possible to trade, because you know there'll be someone at these places at these times to trade with. Once trading begins in earnest, then a level of ownership of what you're trading becomes necessary; after all, you don't want someone else sneaking in and getting all the best flint before you. Thus the concept of ownership really gets going. Supposing your family knows a stretch of coast is very rich in shellfish. The population has grown sufficiently for you to know that if word gets out then that stretch of coast will soon be exhausted, so you either keep the location secret or warn intruders away from what is now your territory.

One of the reasons for this growth of population was the reduction in mobility. Once a group had settled in one spot – or even if they moved once or twice a year – it became possible for women to give birth more frequently; children could toddle around through their infancy and didn't require someone on hand to carry them all the time.

Once people had settled down, they could start growing things. There are, of course, many debates and almost as many disputes as to what exactly happened when people started farming – far too many to go into here. Our opinion, for what it's worth – and we do encourage you to read further on this subject – is that agriculture was mixed in with the other concomitant changes in Mesolithic society. So people that had moved frequently became more and more aware that certain plants flourished at certain times of year and started influencing that by not eating everything, for by leaving some plants to set seed, more would be produced the next year. What's more, by transporting, eating and then excreting seeds, the travelling groups started spreading their harvest plants around their normal travelling route. This does seem to be one of those chicken-and-egg paradoxes though, where the birth of agriculture requires people to adopt a sedentary lifestyle, but there's no way to support a static but growing population without agriculture: each requires the other, so it seems impossible to state which came first.

With a larger, more settled population, it became possible to start building on a far grander scale and, sure enough, the Neolithic saw the construction of henges all over the country. The most famous is, of course, Stonehenge in Wiltshire, but the basic design doesn't actually require great big stone monoliths. What all henges share is a roughly

A reconstruction of the henge at Maelmin.
Courtesy of geograph.org.uk, 420781

circular shape, defined by a ditch and bank, with a level plateau in the centre. There would often be stone or wooden uprights, but the earthworks appear to be the structural fundamentals of a henge.

Now, what was a henge for? It's a good question. Unfortunately, the answers aren't quite as good. Henges seem to be ritual structures. Despite the earthworks, they don't serve any defensive purposes, since the earthworks are the wrong way round: the bank has the ditch on the inside, which would be like putting the moat of a medieval castle inside the walls. We believe the idea that they were used to process through in ritual parades is correct. This hypothesis comes from excavating postholes in henges. Where now there is a hole, there must once have been a vertical pole, and if the space in-between the poles is wattled, a complicated, almost maze-like series of passages are created, with certain areas cut off from external view. We think that henges may have been used by people, men and women, of a priestly caste processing through their temple of mysteries. There are interesting parallels between the structure of henges and the cup and ring marks cut into rocks.

One of your two writers has had unusual experience of a henge: Paul helped build one. With twelve other volunteers in April 2000 (the wettest April since records began!) he dug, mounded, sculpted and shivered through the reconstruction of a previously excavated henge at Milfield North. The new henge is at Maelmin in Northumberland and it's still there. As far as was possible, Paul and the other builders limited themselves to building techniques, clothing and food that would have been available to the original henge builders in the Neolithic. One notable effect of this was the way time passed differently without a watch or any other mechanical timepiece: everything was regulated by the sun. As far as the rain of the wettest April was concerned, the builders adopted the Neolithic approach: they got wet. The conditions being so poor, the henge builders had to first construct a shelter, and the fire burning continuously within it ensured that there was always somewhere to dry off. The labour was hard, physical work, but an unexpected consequence of the conditions was that someone was required to constantly watch and maintain the fire and perform running repairs on the roof of the shelter to keep the rain out.

The technological and cultural innovations that produced the Neolithic created a more differentiated society. For thousands of years, people had been generalists, jacks or jills of all trades, able to do or produce pretty much anything that anyone else could. But with increasing technological developments and the creation of specific castes of people, the

One of the largest surviving Neolithic cairns: Barpa Langass on the island of North Uist. It's still possible to enter. *Wikimedia Commons*

era of the specialist had begun. By the end of the Neolithic, coppersmiths and smelters were making their first assays at what must have seemed magical transformations of the properties of things and there are the first signs of a warrior class in the increasingly brutal weapons being created, with arrowheads designed as man killers (judging from skeletal remains complete with embedded arrowheads, they were all too efficient), maces and, at the transition into the Bronze Age, swords and daggers whose only function was fighting.

One of the first markers of the transition to the Bronze Age is seen with the construction of large cairns in prominent positions in the landscape. These seem to have served as burial chambers, but also they signified that the builders of the cairn had sufficient manpower to build such an impressive structure – so if you've got any ideas about settling here, think again – and that this land had belonged to the cairn builders for generations. Ownership of land, intimately tied to ancestors and family, had well and truly begun.

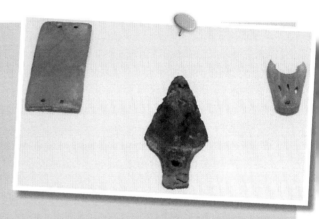

It's a fair cop

The earliest copper knives were replicas of their flint precursors. Which is odd, since copper knives aren't as good as flint knives: copper is soft and malleable, doesn't hold an edge and is rubbish for cutting things. So why make knives out of copper at all? After all, flint was readily available, it could be knocked into a knife in half an hour and it did the job. Copper, on the other hand, had to be mined, smelted and forged in the first place, a job carrying with it significant danger from arsenic poisoning,[15] and even once you'd got a copper knife, it wasn't nearly as good at its job. So why bother? Well, we don't really know, but if there's one thing we can say, it's that copper was the shiny new technological kid on the block, and owning a copper knife would immediately set you apart from other people. Maybe the copper knife owners of the early Bronze Age were the ancestors of today's early adopters, the people who pride themselves on having the newest gadgets and the coolest accessories.

More seriously, a copper implement manifests an awareness of one of the key new powers that people of this age were appropriating: the power to transform and transubstantiate materials. They took a stone, extracted copper from it by fire – itself surely one of the key symbols of transformation – and made something entirely new that had a unique appearance and properties. Could there be a more high-status item to own? Of course, status and differentiation are not necessarily incompatible reasons for acquiring a copper knife.

BRONZE AGE BEGINNINGS

Bronze is made by mixing copper with a little bit of tin and arsenic. There are no sources of copper and tin in Northumbria, so to acquire these items people had to trade, either for already-forged weapons and jewellery, or for the raw materials to make them. But how did this newfangled technology arrive in Britain in general and Northumbria in particular? Unusually for archaeology, there are only two contending explanations: invasion and adoption. The evidence is pretty much the same, it's the interpretations that are different. Either a people, whom we call the Beaker folk, arrived in Britain as invaders and displacers. They brought with them, well, beakers, along with beer, and bronze weaponry with the necessary technology to mine, smelt and smith bronze. According to this interpretation, the Beaker folk arrived around 2300 BC and they took over and started to run the British Isles.

The competing explanation, which is also based on the beakers, beer and bronze found in the archaeological record, is that the native inhabitants of Britain simply imported and adopted foreign customs and technologies. This argument resonates in modern Britain, with our Japanese televisions and German cars, since it seems clear that it's possible to import ideas and goods on their own, without accompanying invasion fleets.

Before coming to a conclusion one way or another, we have to bear in mind that this was a time when there were folk movements, with the exact nature, scale and numbers involved very hard to determine. Archaeology, being as subject to fashions as any other discipline, has reacted strongly against an earlier tendency to view everything through a prism of marauding Vikings, and for a while all change was viewed as benign and mutually beneficial trade exchanges between peoples who valued each other's cultural differences and celebrated diversity: a bit like *Balamory*. Now, hopefully, there's some acknowledgement of the necessity to bear trade and terror in mind when interpreting the past.

Three Bronze Age axes. *Wikimedia Commons*

Of course, it's worth bearing in mind how few men, relatively speaking, it can take to subjugate an area. The German army of occupation that held France during the Second World War was some 300,000 strong – a large number, but small compared to the population of the country at the time, which was around 40 million. So a third possibility would be small incursions of warrior bands, presumably encouraged by beakers full of beer, killing or driving out the top tiers of native British Bronze Age society and replacing them. For the labourers in the fields, it probably made little difference who was in charge: they still worked and the guys with the swords creamed their share off the top.

The hard stuff: the Iron Age

Bronze was hard but iron was harder still. It made sharper swords, better daggers and firmer ploughs. An iron sword could go right through a bronze shield like, well, probably not butter but maybe a firm cheddar. And around 700 BC–600 BC the Iron Age arrived in Britain. Things were starting to change much faster than before.

Many of the most impressive prehistoric structures in Northumbria date from this era, when people began to build the hillforts that dot the country. The most impressive of these is at Yeavering Bell, but there are many more examples in Northumbria. Today, climbing

The hill where the hill fort of Yeavering Bell
perches. The stone ramparts enclose the summit.
Northumberland National Park Authority

Yeavering Bell takes you up an almost perfectly conical hill that rounds out to a fairly smooth twin-peaked plateau at the summit. The summit is encircled by the still impressive remains of what must once have been quite awe-inspiring ramparts some 8ft high. The area within the walls contains traces of around 130 dwellings, made of the local andesite rock. It might be hard to imagine now, but when the houses were first built, they would have been bright pink, since freshly quarried andesite comes out of the ground looking like freshly cooked salmon before weathering to a dull grey. A climb to the top of Yeavering Bell or any other hillfort impresses on the climber an understanding of the difficulty of attacking or taking by surprise the inhabitants of the fort, and a conviction that our Iron Age ancestors must have had thighs like tree trunks.

But apart from defence, the positioning of hillforts is also a statement of power and an implied threat to any intruders: a single glance from afar would be enough to tell any marauders that it took a lot of men to build that hillfort and therefore the local area might not be the best place to look for plunder.

Living on the hilltops, the hillfort dwellers took advantage of a slightly more benign climate than we have today, to drive agriculture up to higher levels than before, finishing the work of clearing the Cheviot Hills of their trees that earlier generations had begun.

Since people had returned to the British Isles following the Ice Age, there had been huge changes: ways of life had changed completely, with the scattered bands of Mesolithic hunter-gatherers giving way to the highly structured and militarily minded societies of the Iron Age. But there was one common characteristic of all these societies: they were all, historically, dumb. They left physical traces, but of their words and thus their hearts and souls we have no direct testimony. But all this was about to change, for in AD 43 the Romans came.

Tools for the journey

Which tools and implements did hunter-gatherers carry around with them from one site to another? After all, they didn't have pockets or beasts of burden, so there was a limit to what they could carry. The answer is, not very many. Most of their tools were straightforward to fabricate from readily available natural materials, so the natural response was to jettison everything bar the essentials and make new ones when they got to a fresh site. It was a throwaway society too!

By their tools you will know them

In the Palaeolithic, people used big, stone hand axes and hammers. Tools and weapons didn't have hafts but were simply held in the hand. This would have reduced leverage, but even so, a blow from a Palaeolithic hand axe would have been pretty devastating.

By the Mesolithic, people started to have proper tool kits and this period saw the first appearance of tools that were designed specifically to make other tools. The key components of the Mesolithic tool kit were, on the face of it, not very impressive. Microliths – literally, 'little stones' – are nothing like as eye catching as the big hand axes of the Palaeolithic, but by sticking them onto shafts and hafts, Mesolithic tool makers could create a far greater variety of tools and start to employ leverage to multiply human strength. Flint tools became even more complex, including barbed and tanged arrowheads and broadhead arrowheads, where the head was fixed to the haft via the apex of the triangle and the flat base of the triangle was the cutting edge, designed to cut tendons and arteries and therefore to kill or immobilise quickly.

A WALL RUNS THROUGH IT

Famously, the Romans fixed the northern boundary of their empire along a line that ran right through the middle of the later kingdom of Northumbria. Hadrian's Wall, following the Roman genius for practical engineering solutions, cuts across Britain at one of its narrowest points. The Emperor Hadrian, on his tour around the far-flung provinces of the Empire, visited Britain in AD 122. Where before the Romans had been set on a path of everlasting expansion, Hadrian seems to have established the idea that it was time for consolidation. The empire had reached its limits. It need go no further.

Although the wall marked the usual limit of empire (there were periods when the Romans expanded into Scotland and a second wall, the Antonine, was built in AD 142 between the Firth of Forth and the Firth of Clyde but it was only garrisoned for short periods of time) there was of course still considerable contact between the peoples north and south of the wall – not least the Votadini tribe whose land the wall bisected. Trade was frequent and many Roman artefacts have been found in Scotland, but the area north of the wall remained largely unromanised. Given the lack of urban centres, and the identification of Roman life with towns, this may have been inevitable. Where there were towns, such as York, daily life was thoroughly Roman, to such an extent that York was twice the administrative centre of the whole Empire: from AD 208 to AD 211, when Emperor Septimius Severus lived in the city and then from AD 305 to AD 306, when Constantine was proclaimed Emperor in York and set out to conquer and consolidate the Empire.[16]

Hadrian's Wall. *Simon Fraser, Northumberland National Park Authority*

The Romans liked accessible fertile valleys with easy access to resources that they could drive good straight roads through. York and the fertile, generally flat land around it, was ideal, and also provided prime sites for the other typical Roman habitation: the country villa. This was essentially an agricultural business and rural retreat: Latin literature is replete with pastoral poetry extolling the simplicity of country life against the corruption and decadence of the city. Surviving British villas range from palatial complexes complete with baths and mosaics covering every floor to simple establishments that could only stretch to a single mosaic on the floor of the main public room.

While Latin was the *lingua franca* that allowed the functionaries of empire and the officers of the Roman Army to communicate with each other, most other people would have spoken local languages and dialects, with a higher or lower ratio of Latin to native tongue depending on the amount of interaction with the representatives of empire.

The year 410 is the usual date for the end of direct Roman rule in Britain. That was when the Emperor Honorius replied to a request for aid from Britain with the answer that they were on their own: a refusal known as the Rescript of Honorius. In 409, Roman magistrates had been expelled from Britain as Rome again fell prey to civil war and the garrisons that had previously protected the country against Saxon incursions crossed the Channel to support their candidate for emperor. The legions never returned. And while Roman ways of life carried on for a number of generations, the empire slowly receded into memory and legend. Britain retreated into prehistory and began upon the long, gradual process of becoming England, Wales, Scotland and Ireland.

Interview with Clive Waddington

1. Who are you and what is your background?
My name is Clive Waddington. I'm a land-
scape archaeologist with a speciality in
prehistory, in particular the Mesolithic and
Neolithic. But with respect to Northumbria,
I've worked on almost its whole history,
from the Palaeolithic through to the early
medieval. I was the director of the Milfield
Geoarchaeology Project, the Till-Tweed
Project and Howick Project.

2. What are your areas of expertise?
I'm particularly interested in the interaction between humans and landscapes, how people
have adapted to landscapes in different ways through time and how the landscape itself has
been adapted as a consequence of human activity. So that's from the post-glacial through
to the heavily farmed landscapes of the early medieval period.

3. Can you outline the history of Northumbria as revealed by your research?
We begin at the end of the last glacial, where we have evidence for hunter-gatherers
operating inland. From flint finds we can trace these people following herds of reindeer
and so on. But by 8000 BC, we see a secondary colonisation by hunter-gatherers who I
believe were people displaced from the flooded plains of Doggerland. They brought with
them a new, narrow-blade microlith technology. Since all the evidence for the early stages
of narrow-blade microlith technology is found along the north-east coast of Britain I
think that's further support for these people being refugees from the lands that the North
Sea had recently swamped. They followed a very different way of life to the first hunter-
gatherers: they were living on the coastline, and their whole economy and tool kit were
adapted to a maritime way of life, unlike the first hunter-gatherers, who were forest dwellers and herd followers. There's oblique evidence for their use of skin boats, in that we
found seal paws, tools for softening skin and ochre. Ethnographic parallels suggest that the
skins of seals were sewn together, stretched over a wooden frame and then the ochre was
mixed with pine resin to waterproof the joins.

Moving on to the Neolithic, we have recently found some new evidence in
Northumberland of post-built timber structures. There's at least seven of them at the
Lanton Quarry site. Carbon dating puts these buildings in the fourth millennium BC.
This is in line with new thinking about the Neolithic, which sees it as produced by a
wave of incomers, up and down the eastern seaboard: a third identifiable phase of colonisation in Northumbria. All the early Neolithic sites in Northumberland are coastal or
riverine, which marries up with the idea that people arrived by boat and sailed up the
rivers and settled on the gravel terraces next to their banks. This is a pattern that recurs
throughout Britain.

4. Does Northumbria have a distinct prehistory or does its history simply recapitulate the wider story of Britain?

I think Northumbria does have a prehistory different from central and southern England. There was the early phase of narrow-blade microlith Mesolithic culture I mentioned above, there were local burial traditions in the Neolithic and distinctive hill forts in the Iron Age. Northumbria is a crossroads, because it occupies the narrowest isthmus east-west across England and this position means that it controls communication between north and south as well as east and west. This is reflected in the unique mixture of archaeological remains that can be found there.

5. When does the prehistory of Northumbria start and when does it end?

It currently starts at the end of the last glacial, but when it ends is an interesting question. I would argue it continues until the arrival of the Anglo-Saxons, since the Roman occupation in the north is a military occupation. There are few villa sites, people continue to live in round houses and of course north of Hadrian's Wall it's completely unromanised. So it seems reasonable to assume that people went on living according to prehistoric values. It's only with the Christianisation of Anglo-Saxon Northumbria, the use of Latin and the flowering of learning that we get the creation of a historical record separate from the occasional Roman text or inscription. So prehistory in Northumbria starts about 10000 BC and continues to the sixth or seventh century AD.

6. What techniques do you use to study this long period?

I use a wide variety of techniques, particularly field walking to look at the early Stone Age, aerial surveys, crop-mark formation, and in the uplands there are a lot of standing-stone monuments. Air surveys are also good for the later Stone Ages, and the Iron Age. We also use coring to reconstruct the environment and the extent to which people managed the landscape by obtaining information from pollen and plant remains. Large-scale strip, map and sample excavation has also had a transformative effect on our knowledge of Northumbria. This has opened up huge swathes of landscape to archaeological view. It has brought to light smaller features never before found, for instance the Neolithic structures observed at Lanton Quarry.

7. How has our understanding of Northumbria changed recently?

Ten years ago we had one carbon date for the Mesolithic in Northumbria. Now we have forty just for the Mesolithic! We've even got human footprints from that time preserved in peat – and the feet were wearing boots or sandals! As for the Neolithic, all we used to have were the henges and occasional burial monuments. Now, we've got several settlement sites, a carbon-14 chronology, we know quite a lot about what they ate, and we have good evidence for early cereal grains, in particular wheat and barley. In the Bronze Age, we have good evidence for mixed farms in lowland and upland situations, and evidence for expansion into the uplands. There's not been so much work done on the Iron Age, but strip, map and sample work has revealed late Roman sites at East Brunton, West Brunton, and Pegswood, where we have multiphase sites, with round houses and small enclosures, suggesting intensive use over many generations. It looks like the lowlands were quite densely settled in the late Iron Age.

There have also been occasional Iron Age burials found in recent years, which have helped our understanding of the burial practices of the time.

One thing that's interesting is that I believe we can see a precursor for the kingdom of Bernicia in the area controlled by the Votadini, where we have their tradition of burying people in cist graves.[17] There's quite a few examples of these graves in the Borders region and East Lothian, but we've recently found these sort of graves in the Milfield plain and Beadnell. So if these burials do represent the burial practice of the Votadini, we can use them to map out the area of their kingdom and see if it coincides with the successor kingdoms of Bernicia and Manau Gododdin.

8. How did the landscape define Northumbria?

The thing that characterises Northumbria for me is its incredible diversity. It's a very fragmented landscape: hills, valleys, lowland plains, indented coastline. This has given rise to valley-based communities, and for me this is what defines northern Britain and Northumbria. The allegiances of people are defined by valley catchments. These catchments develop at different rates due to the self-sufficiency demanded by this geography. Then there's the great productivity of the coastal plains contrasted with the poor uplands where today it's sheep farming at best. This variation is reflected in the people. Through much of prehistory, I think people in the uplands lived fairly insular lives, since while valley-based communities encourage self-sufficiency they also produce parochialism. This has always, I think, been a characteristic of upland Northumbria and its people. But coupled with that, and in distinction to it, there's the Northumbrian relationship to the sea and the way rivers and sea allowed for wide-ranging communication and travel throughout prehistory and in Anglo-Saxon times. In the Neolithic, Northumbria was part of a sea-based culture, defined by cup-and-ring artwork, that included Scotland, Portugal, Ireland and western France but, interestingly, not central and southern Britain.

4

RELIGION

Behold, all things are become new.

(2 Corinthians, 5:17)

At the start of the twenty-first century, we stand at a peculiar juncture of history: in the lands that now stand on Northumbria the gods are forgotten, while God himself was pronounced dead in the nineteenth century and the twentieth provided His funeral rites. The default assumption seems to be that this process will continue.[18]

But this belief leaves us ill-equipped to enter into times and places where religion was central to people's lives and God was so tangible a part of human experience as to be almost viscerally present. What do we make of an age when mouldering bones commanded more money and veneration than a Premiership footballer, and learned men could come to blows over a date in the calendar? In the end, we have to use the tools at our disposal to understand Northumbria in our own light *and* its own.

BEÐE WORK

If poetry is emotion recalled in tranquillity, then history is the imagination disciplined by facts. In Northumbria during the seventh and eighth centuries, religion took on an entirely new cast and moved from open groves and idols into buildings made of wood and stone.[19] Exercising that imagination, think about approaching a group of stone-built buildings. Their windows are narrow and few, but some of them are glazed, and there is a bustle of activity around the complex that is not found in many places in Anglo-Saxon Britain. Coming closer, the sound of voices chanting in unison floats over the river beside which the monastery stands. The singing is beautiful, but the words are different from those being shouted at the busy jetty nearby. The monks are singing in Latin, while the boatmen are calling out to each other in early English. This is Bede's monastery in Jarrow, standing by the River Don, which provides easy access to the River Tyne and the sea routes that bind Britain together, and the monks are at work.

This monastic labour consisted of following the monks' rule of life and singing the 'Divine Office', a practice that goes back to the earliest days of the Church and has its ultimate roots in Judaism. To this day, monks and the other religious of the Catholic, Orthodox and Anglican churches recite basically the same words. So, in some respects, the religious life of Northumbria was similar to what we might encounter in a monastery or cathedral today. But there were other aspects of the religious life of the time that would have looked very strange to twenty-first-century eyes. At the most visible level, the monks and the other religious were tonsured: in Bede's monastery, that meant their heads were shaved at the crown, with a ring of hair left that was meant to recollect Christ's crown of thorns. But elsewhere, we might see men with the front half of their heads shaven, and then as now, such distinctive cuts indicated different allegiances.

While Bede and his fellow monks lived in a monastery, organised under an abbot and living a rule, there were other, wilder, freelance religious, wandering the countryside in solitary peregrinations or withdrawing to places remote, unpopulated and invariably windswept. These were the hermits, or anchorites. This new religion was open to interpretation, and different people chose different ways to view the word and will of God.

GETTING AWAY FROM IT ALL

St Benedict of Nursia (AD 480–AD 547), whose rule became the foundation of most of Western monasticism, recognised a division in the monastic calling between the active life of those living and working together in communities – the cenobites[20] – and the solitary hermits. Monasticism first developed in the Egyptian desert. Men and women withdrew into the wilderness to escape the temptations and trials of civilised life. In this escape they were following scriptural patterns: Jesus himself frequently went into the desert to pray, most notably for forty days after his baptism in the River Jordan, and John the Baptist and other prophets also withdrew into the desert. However, there was a problem for would-be Irish, British and English anchorites – deserts were in short supply. But there was no shortage of cold, wet and windy islets, off the coast, bisecting rivers or lost among marshlands, and this 'green' martyrdom (as distinct from 'red' martyrdom, which involved large amounts of blood and a painful death, and 'white' martyrdom, which meant sailing off into the unknown, following the Spirit and spreading the Gospel) became widespread, and crucial in the spread of Christianity, particularly in Northumbria. It may have looked different to the deserts of the Bible, but it was no less challenging and just as inhospitable.

Monasteries were the first centres of Christianity in Northumbria and the new religion's key organisational centre for its first centuries. An archbishopric had been instituted in York, and there was a bishop in Hexham, but the parish-based organisation of the Church had hardly begun. Minster was the English word for a monastery, so even York with its archbishop was ministered to by priests from its minster.

To get a sense of how important these concentrations of religious men were, compare the two bishoprics in York and Hexham to the number of monasteries in Northumbria: Lindisfarne, Coldingham, Abercorn, Melrose, Carlisle, Hexham, Monkwearmouth/Jarrow, Tynemouth, South Shields, Gateshead, Dacre, Hartlepool, Gilling, Lastingham, Catterick, Whitby, Hackness, Stamford, Leeds, Tadcaster, Whalley and Ripon are all named by Bede, and, despite its length, this is not an exhaustive list of Northumbria's minsters. Historical and archaeological evidence adds a score or more monasteries to that list.

Any Northumbrian evincing an interest in the new religion would have found organised and impressive activity, a community of men (and sometimes women too – there were some mixed monasteries) working together, carrying out their opus Dei but also constructing impressive buildings and bringing the land into fruitful use. The Anglo-Saxon nobility in general, and the extended Northumbrian royal families in particular, were generous in endowing land on monasteries, but this land was usually wild, isolated and unworked. Monastic communities were often the first to bring land that had fallen into disuse after the Roman withdrawal back into production. When you add the monks' success in producing a surplus of food to their obligation, as stated by Bede, to help their neighbours by giving food to the hungry and drink to the thirsty, then you have the recipe for an extraordinarily powerful impact on the local population.

The Anglo-Saxon world was one in which there were few concentrations of people. The old Roman towns of Northumbria were largely depopulated. The kings, and there were many, had their bands of retainers, but royalty was mobile, moving from one centre to another. The new monasteries were the first organised, permanent settlements to house more than a few score people for two centuries. The Church, as an institution, brought with it literacy, Latin and reconnection to Romanitas: through these monks England was brought back within the fold of civilisation. What's more, the Anglo-Saxons were often as keen as the initial immigrant churchmen to reconnect with the classical world and lay claim to its dignity and legitimacy.

The everyday experience of Christianity would, in some ways, have been very different to today. Without organised local parishes, in order to minister to its flock, the Church dispatched travelling monks, priests and bishops from the monasteries to far-flung communities. However, their visits would inevitably have been rare, maybe once or twice a year. (Parallels exist today in the less-developed parts of the world, where isolated villages may only see a priest once or twice a year.) But there were two other avenues by which ordinary people could encounter the Christian religion: hermits and wandering preachers. We surmise, and this is an extremely tentative conclusion based on reading around the literature and sources, that among the English there were more people out proselytising than praying in monasteries in the early years

The South Face of Ruthwell Cross.
Wikimedia Commons

of Christianity. Working in the church of the open air, the peripatetic religious, the hedge priests, would have ministered and preached at significant sites in Northumbria: standing crosses, river fords, boundary stones.

However, farmers were not tied to their fields all year round, and it's likely that families travelled to a local monastery occasionally. There, they would have seen and heard and been taught wonders, as well as trading and selling to the monastery or obtaining alms. For anyone trading, a monastery and its environs were obvious focal points too.

The old gods fight back

From the vantage point of the twenty-first century, the replacement of Anglo-Saxon paganism by Christianity might seem inevitable. As a religion, Christianity boasted a vigorous intellectual life, honed in disputes with the representatives of the schools of classical philosophy, an organised structure that could call on support from many sources, and an imperative from its founder to spread. On the face of it, paganism had no such advantages. But how then to explain the apparent total extirpation of Christianity from much of the country between the fifth and seventh centuries, particularly when it had had four centuries to establish itself securely? The answer is straightforward enough – war.

To put it shortly, and to blithely ignore all sorts of nuances and caveats, the pagan Anglo-Saxons won and the Christian Britons lost. The Britons retreated into the west of the island, or fled to Brittany, and the Anglo-Saxons carved out new kingdoms for themselves. Christianity, which in the Roman Empire had been very much an urban phenomenon, seems to have died out with the gradual depopulation of the towns and cities.

The question of whether the native Britons really were displaced en masse by invading hordes of Anglo-Saxons accompanied by brawling, puling broods of children, wives and concubines remains an open one. Some archaeologists argue for mass migrations, others for roving war bands that exterminated or assimilated the native gentry and then put the local peasants to work for their new bosses. In this case, the majority of the population remains unchanged. Of course, some combination of the two is also possible.[21]

Whatever proves to be true about populations, what does appear to be incontrovertible is that the native Romano-British culture was pretty well extirpated from the areas of Anglo-Saxon settlement. Towns emptied, elegant country villas were abandoned and all traces of Christianity disappeared. Religion became a matter of blood. Britons were Christians, the Angles, Saxons and Jutes were pagans. Generations of warfare then cemented that division. But if the Britons were chary of preaching the Gospel to the people who had invaded their land,[22] the Irish and the Italians[23] knew no such misgivings. In an evangelising pincer movement, missionaries were sent from Iona around Scotland to Northumbria, and from Rome through Gaul to Kent.

The first Christians in Northumbria

Although Northumbria is known for Holy Island and its connections with the Christianity of Iona and Ireland, the first Christians in the realm came from Kent. Æthelburga,

Augustine of Canterbury sculpture on the outside of Canterbury Cathedral. *Wikimedia Commons*

the second wife of King Edwin of Northumbria, was the king of Kent's daughter and, more importantly, a Christian. Her marriage to the pagan Edwin was contracted on the basis that she and her retinue could continue to practise Christianity. So when Æthelburga travelled north, she brought with her as personal chaplain Paulinus, a Roman who had first come to Britain as part of the mission sent by Pope Gregory to convert the Angles.[24] This mission, under the leadership of Augustine of Canterbury, had landed on the Isle of Thanet in 597.

Æthelburga, who through her mother was connected to the Merovingian kings of the Franks, and Paulinus, a son of the Mediterranean and bishop of the Universal Church, brought a sophistication and breadth to Edwin that must have been unknown before. Soon, the question of conversion came to occupy the king and all his retainers to such an extent that Edwin called his counsellors to debate.

> You are sitting feasting with your ealdorman and thegns in winter time; the fire is burning on the hearth in the middle of the hall and all inside is warm, while outside the wintry storms of rain and snow are raging; and a sparrow flies swiftly through the hall. It enters in at one door and quickly flies out through the other. For a few moments it is inside, the storm and wintry tempest cannot touch it, but after the briefest moment of calm, it flits from your sight, out of the wintry storm and into it again. So this life of man appears but for a moment, what follows or indeed what went before, we know not at all. If this new doctrine brings us more certain information it seems right that we should accept it.[25]

Thus, according to Bede, spoke one of Edwin's men at the debate.

Not even the devotees of the old gods spoke up for them. Bede tells us that Coifi, Edwin's pagan high priest, told the assembly that no one present had served the gods more devotedly than he, and yet he had received no advancement or reward for his devotion. Therefore, Coifi said, let us embrace this new doctrine and, to prove his conversion, he later rode from the assembly (pagan priests were not allowed to ride) and desecrated the nearest shrine by hurling spears into the idols (nor were they allowed to carry arms).

The impact of this must have been like the Pope suddenly declaring Richard Dawkins to be correct. How can we explain such a conversion (leaving aside the intervention of divine grace as being outside the purview of historians)? This was an age when the gods were meant to deliver: any divine being worth its salt had to bring victory in battle, deliverance from disease, children to succeed you. Oh, and gold. Lots of gold. One can imagine Coifi looking around at the magnificent assemblage – and it would have been magnificent, for the Northumbrians wore their wealth on their bodies, in the shape of bracelets, armbands and all manner of shiny, glittery things – and, seeing their golden sheen and comparing their lustre to his own lack of bling, concluding that being a priest of Thor was a mug's game. (Alternatively, think of him as a wily political operative, smelling a change in the wind and getting his denials in first. And, following its establishment under Constantine, opulence had arrived big time in the Church of Rome, so membership could bring great rewards.)

Given the arguments, what else could the council decide?

So Northumbria joined Kent and East Anglia as an officially Christian English kingdom.

Why did the Anglo-Saxons convert to Christianity?

The first converts to Christianity among the Anglo-Saxons were from the nobility. This was different to the early Christians in the Roman Empire, many of whom came from the lowest echelons of society. So what did the Anglo-Saxon nobility see in Christ and Christianity? Were there aspects to their society that predisposed them to accept the Christian message? After all, any message falls on soil that has been culturally prepared in some way or other – there's no such thing as a blank surface in human history. For

the Anglo-Saxons, there were some obvious parallels between Christ's crucifixion and their own tale of Woden sacrificing himself upon the tree of woe for three days to obtain knowledge. Woden had his warriors around him, as Jesus had his disciples, Woden was betrayed by some of his followers as Jesus was sold by Judas and denied by Peter. In a society that placed an absolute value on loyalty, the drama of the Last Supper and Judas's betrayal would have resonated strongly.

Grave goods

Burials are among the richest sources of archaeological remains there are, but they must always be viewed with one key caveat in mind: the person buried is not the one who does the burying. We see burials through the eyes of the people who put the body in the ground, not the person in the ground. The idea that pagans were buried with a rich trove of goods for the afterlife, while Christians were sent forth with just the clothes on their back, is commonplace but does not seem to hold up in Northumbria, at least for the first century or so after the conversion of the kings. However, we can broadly trace the advent of Christianity by the spread of graves aligned roughly east-west and there is a gradual tailing off in the amount of goods that people were buried with.

WOMEN'S WORK

Although Bede places the credit for Edwin's conversion with the Holy Spirit and Paulinus, it's worth noting the profound effect that women had on the religious direction and climate of the English kingdoms of the time. The very first English king to be converted, Æthelbert of Kent, married into the wealthy and powerful Merovingian family that ruled Frankish Gaul. The links between the Kentish and Frankish kingdoms were strong, and it was a natural alliance. But Bertha, Æthelbert's intended, was Christian, as were most of the Franks. Thus the stage was set for Augustine's mission to England. Edwin's marriage to Æthelburga likewise provided an opportunity for a Christian princess to be accompanied by a bishop on a mission and though little is recorded of Æthelburga and the other, later, princesses who went to their pagan husbands with trepidation, as often as not the end result was the conversion of husbands and kingdoms. Though these conversions were also undoubtedly due to the playing out of the power politics of the time, the quiet influence of these women should not be underestimated.

But if Northumbria became Christian, it didn't stay that way. Conversion was by no means a one-way process. Kings and rivals calling on other gods could and did win in battle too, for God or the gods are fickle in their favours and none knows when the blow will fall. Edwin fell at the hands of Penda, the pagan king of Mercia, and Cadwallon, the Christian king of the British (Welsh) kingdom of Gwynedd – politics was a messy business then as now, and forged the most unlikely of alliances.

With Edwin dead, Northumbria – or at least its ruling caste – reverted to paganism. Æthelburga and her children, the first candidates for pruning from the tree of succession, fled back to Kent and Paulinus went with them. Elsewhere, East Anglia also reverted to paganism. The initial mission to Britain, after its first promise, was faltering badly. The smart money of the time would no doubt have been on the Anglo-Saxon kingdoms remaining pagan, and gradually exporting that paganism into the declining, and physically diminishing, realms of the Britons. But there is a clue to what would happen next in the flight of Æthelburga and her children. Exile was common for Anglo-Saxon nobility. Oswald and Oswiu, the sons of Edwin's predecessor as king of Northumbria, had fled when their father was killed, for prudence suggested the wiser course was getting out fast, before Edwin had the chance to tidy up the royal bloodlines with some vigorous pruning. The brothers, although Anglians, went to the kingdom of Dalriada, which covered what is now County Antrim in Northern Ireland and Argyll and Bute in Scotland.

hοw The IRISh SAVeδ cIVILISATION

The conversion of the Irish to Christianity is one of the crucial events in the first millennium. It marked a definitive step for the new religion beyond the boundaries of the old Roman Empire and an encounter with a culture that was, in distinction to the urban classical world, almost entirely rural and tribal. Lacking urban centres of population, the Church in Ireland organised itself around monasteries. Therefore it comes as no surprise that monasteries came to play a key role in the daughter churches that Irish missionaries planted elsewhere. Foremost among these at the time was the monastery on the island of Iona, founded by St Columba in 563, part of the kingdom of Dalriada. It was to here that Oswald and Oswiu fled, and it was here that they converted to Christianity.

Oswald took his faith back to Northumbria when he returned with a small party of men to reclaim his kingdom from Cadwallon. It was time for his new god to show his mettle. And he did. Oswald won the war, took the crown and, installed in Bamburgh, sent to Iona for missionaries to come and convert his people.

Aidan was the man Iona sent.[26] Oswald gave him Lindisfarne, Holy Island, as his base. Even today, a trip to Northumberland will reveal the importance of that decision. Standing on the battlements of Bamburgh Castle, which stands on the site of Oswald's stronghold, Lindisfarne is clear and, by the standards of the time, near. In an age when travelling by boat was quicker, easier and safer than travelling on land, the coastal locations of the temporal and spiritual fortresses of Northumbria made communication between them straightforward: jump on a boat and an hour or two later you'd have arrived. What's more, seaborne travel rendered irrelevant Lindisfarne's twice-daily retreats from the mainland, when the causeway is flooded and Holy Island really is an island.

The missionary bishop swiftly set about converting the pagan Northumbrians. One suspects that eloquence was added to his early teaching by having the king himself do the translating.

> And while the bishop, who was not fluent in the English language, preached the Gospel, it was most delightful to see the king himself interpreting the word of God to his ealdorman and thegns; for he himself had obtained perfect command of the Irish tongue during his long exile.
>
> (Bede, *Ecclesiastical History*, p. 147)

But Bede also highlights the personal examples set by bishop and king. Bede presents Aidan as personally humble and holy, eschewing riding a horse for the connection with people that travelling on foot brought. As for Oswald, Bede paints a picture of a king whose life and rule was holy, most famously in the incident where, when told of beggars at his gate, Oswald ordered not just the food from his silver plate but the plate itself to be broken up and given as alms to those outside his door.

The eight years of Oswald's reign were long enough to firmly establish Christianity in Northumbria. So even when Oswald was killed in battle against the pagan king of Mercia, which might have seemed to indicate the declining ability of the Christian God to win battles and bring favours on his worshippers, there seems to have been no apostasy in the kingdom. This retention of Christianity was no doubt helped by the fact that Penda, while a pagan, did not 'forbid the preaching of the Faith to any even of his own Mercians who wished to listen' (Bede, *Ecclesiastical History*, p. 177) so he seems to have been no zealot.[27]

With the gradual conversion of the ruling families of the remaining Anglo-Saxon kingdoms to Christianity in the latter half of the seventh century, the battle for the beliefs of the people of the British Isles was all but won. All that now remained for the Church was to inculcate its doctrines and practices into the general population. Thus began what was, in many ways, a golden age for Christianity in Northumbria.

Who calls the shots

During the Roman Empire, people's allegiance, at least theoretically, stretched far beyond their immediate loyalty to centurion, landlord, master or employer, reaching as far as the emperor himself. When the Romans left, allegiance was rendered to local chieftains, with no greater or larger authority to call upon. In fact, given the chaotic and fractured nature of the petty chiefdoms that sprouted up all over Britain in the fifth and sixth centuries, in many places it was probably difficult to tell to whom allegiance was actually due. This was important: if you didn't know who your king was, or you were subject to competing claims on your loyalty, to whom could you turn for aid and protection, and to whom should you pay the meagre surplus of your crops in tax?

One of the key things Christianity does is to reorder and broaden allegiances and loyalties. The early bishops ruled vast territories, particularly in the north, and their episcopates covered many different kings and rulers. But the bishops owed their primary allegiance not to any local king but to the Pope in Rome. The establishment of Christianity in Britain meant that for the first time since the Roman withdrawal there was an aggregation of power that drew its legitimacy and ultimate direction from an outside source.

The Flowering of Faith

Cuthbert, Bede, Wilfrid, Aidan, Hilda, Benedict Biscop, Alcuin, Chad, Caedmon, Willibrord. These are just some of the names of the extraordinary efflorescence of Christianity that took place in Northumbria in the seventh and eighth centuries. As to what they were, mystic, historian, scholar, founder, traveller, poet, counsellor and missionary are just some of the roles that they undertook.

But how were they to be Christians? What models should the Northumbrians follow, and where were they to look for inspiration? They looked both ways, to the Irish who had sent Aidan, and to Rome, whence Augustine had been dispatched. Being part of a

Reconstructed Anglo-Saxon buildings at Bede's World in Jarrow. © *Andrew Curtis*

A reconstructed Anglo–Saxon building. *Bede's World*

church with claims to universality and a presence through much of the world opened up the imagination of the Northumbrians. Some travelled to Iona and on to Ireland to study in the monasteries there, others crossed the English Channel, learning from the practices of the Church in Gaul, before eventually reaching Rome. Bede mentions many of these travellers in search of food for their faith by name, and alludes to many more. Most notable of them all, at least so far as Bede was concerned, was Benedict Biscop, the founder of the twin monasteries of Monkwearmouth and Jarrow where Bede himself lived. Benedict Biscop was an indefatigable traveller, with five journeys to Rome and many other ventures overseas to his name. He's also a fascinating example of an increasingly common theme of Anglo-Saxon life at this time: the fighting man who renounces arms and turns to God.

Bede records that Benedict Biscop was one of King Oswiu's thegns. At the age of 25, the absolute prime for a fighting man of that era, the king settled on him the land due to his rank, but rather than accruing honour, glory and an arm covered with gold bands, Benedict Biscop forsook his place at the king's side and set off on pilgrimage to Rome. He spent the next 20 years of his life going back and forth to Rome, although he did not return to Northumbria in that time. Almost as important as his time in Rome were the two years that Benedict Biscop spent at the monastery of Lérins, set on a small island in the Bay of Cannes in southern France. It was here that Benedict Biscop became a monk and, since

A fortress of the soul. The church and monastery of Lérins Abbey. *Wikimedia Commons*

Lérins produced men who were steeped in classical learning and Christian teaching, it was likely the place that cemented Benedict Biscop's own scholarly inclinations. For when he finally returned to Northumbria, and founded the monasteries at Monkwearmouth and Jarrow, he sent to the continent for the craftsmen and builders to make something completely new in Anglo-Saxon England: a church made of stone.

> When the building was nearing completion he sent his agents across to France to bring over glaziers – craftsmen as yet unknown in Britain – to glaze the windows in the body of the church and in the chapel and clerestory. The glaziers … helped the English to understand and to learn for themselves the art of glass-making.
>
> (Bede, 'Lives of the Abbots of Wearmouth and Jarrow' p. 191, *The Age of Bede*)

Once the stone bones of his establishment were in place, Benedict Biscop set off to Rome again, returning this time with books, relics of the saints, paintings to adorn his church and even the chief cantor of the church of St Peter in Rome. This displaced choirmaster, John by name, taught the monks of Monkwearmouth and Jarrow how to sing and chant according to the Roman fashion. Thus a place that must have seemed, at least to the transplanted Roman choirmaster, to lie at the very ends of the earth, moved firmly within the intellectual currents of Europe. In fact, in some ways, despite its remote location, Northumbria lay at the intellectual crossroads of Europe. For the establishment of the links with Rome and continental Christianity via Northumbria also brought the insular but scholarly Christianity of Ireland back into the mainstream of European culture.

Anglo-Saxon paganism

What do we know about Anglo-Saxon paganism? The short answer is not very much. It was an oral tradition and the monks of the new religion had little interest in recording the tales, beliefs and practices of the old faith.

It was a polytheistic religion, with a pantheon that resembled that of the Norsemen. The gods were responsible for particular areas of human and natural activity – most obviously Thor provided the thunder – and there were myths of the creation of the world and its final destruction in a day of wrath that would consume the gods too. Aside from that, our few remaining texts, such as *Beowulf*, pretty well take the religion and the gods for granted, in the sense that they were the basis of society and thus didn't require explicit mention.

CHASUBLE AND STRIFE

But of course, when two currents meet, the water is likely to get choppy. In Northumbria, with its twin inheritances from Ireland and Rome, that was indeed the case. The Church in Ireland, and its daughter churches, had developed a different method for calculating the date of Easter, its monks' tonsures were different,[28] the Irish Church practised private confessions[29] and its religious were wont to go wandering, *in peregrinatio pro Christo* (exile for Christ). But the founder of their religion had enjoined unity upon his followers (John 17:20) and this was something the religious of the time took seriously. Apart from the religious imperative to unity, there were strong practical, cultural and philosophical reasons for the practices of the different branches of Christianity in Northumbria to be unified. The shadow of the lost empire lay long over Europe, and much of European history has revolved around attempts to regain the lost unity of Rome, starting with the coronation of Charlemagne as Holy Roman Emperor on Christmas Day AD 800 right up to the European Union of today.

From our perspective, the differences between the Romans and the Irish, particularly over the date of Easter, seem pettifogging. Bede devotes several slightly tedious chapters to explaining exactly why the Roman method of calculating Easter was correct. But think of it this way. It's Lent in the household of King Oswiu. This is the season of penance and fasting – and these Christians were serious about their fasting and their penance. Then there comes a Sunday when the king breaks his fast, and finishes mortifying his flesh. It's Easter, and Christ is risen, and it's time to celebrate. The problem was, his wife, Eanflæd, had been brought up in Kent, and followed the Roman method of calculating Easter, and she and her household were still busy mortifying their flesh.[30] There can hardly have been a more visible sign of disunity than to have one group of Christians celebrating Easter when the others were still in sackcloth and abstinence.

Unity was imperative, and as Constantine had discovered three centuries earlier, when faced with a group of bickering clerics, the best way to achieve unity was to bring them together and bang some heads. So Oswiu convened the Synod of Whitby in 664. In the end, it came down to King Oswiu asking if it was true that St Peter really was God's gatekeeper (Matthew 16:18–19). When the assembled clerics agreed, the decision was made

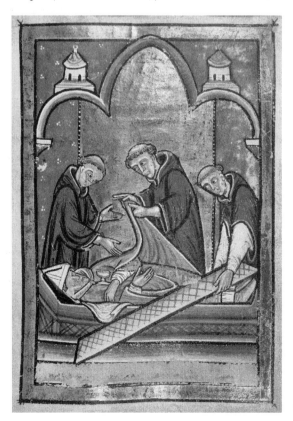

and the Church in Northumbria fell into line with Roman practices. Any clerics – and there were a few, including the incumbent abbot of Lindisfarne – who wanted to retain their old Irish customs had to withdraw to Iona.[31] The Synod was a triumph for another Northumbrian churchman, Wilfrid. He was the prime spokesman for the Romanists and duly reaped the benefits of victory: when Colman, bishop of Lindisfarne, returned to Ireland after the synod, the bishopric was moved to York and Wilfrid assumed the office. At least for a while. Looking at their respective lives, it would seem that Wilfrid far more than Thomas Beckett deserved the sobriquet 'turbulent priest'.

St Cuthbert discovered undecayed.
Wikimedia Commons

During his career, Wilfrid was also imprisoned, exiled, deposed. He travelled to and fro between Rome – usually seeking the Pope's aid in his reinstatement as bishop – he converted the people of West Sussex, founded monasteries and churches, and travelled everywhere in great style. In fact, Wilfrid acted like a Renaissance Prince of the Church some 800 years before there were Renaissance Princes of the Church (although there is no hint that he was personally unchaste, any man who could throw a three-day banquet was one familiar with the finer things in life).

Bede's respectful but slightly distant appreciation of Wilfrid's career is symptomatic of a fault line that has existed in the church from its early days, between the withdrawn and abstemious monk and the urbane and engaged clergyman. But a closer look will reveal unexpected incongruities to this neat pattern. Take, for instance, the archetypal holy hermit of Northumbria – Cuthbert. Here was a man who attracted miracles like other men attract midges, and who repeatedly withdrew from contact with the society of the day to more and more remote refuges – cave, islet, island – although that of course only made people more determined to come and see him. Yet his final place of refuge from the world – one of the Inner Farne Islands – is 2 miles out to sea and in plain sight of the Northumbrian capital, Bamburgh. In fact, the islands are the single most striking sight in the whole magnificent panorama visible from the rock upon which the castle sits. The holy hermit hid in plain sight, his withdrawal a living witness and, possibly, a signal reproof to the king. For hermits, by their radical refusal of the world, have ever been a fascination and a temptation to the worldly.

As an indication that this fascination exerted a strengthening pull over the Northumbria of the eighth century, two successive kings, Ceolwulf and Eadberht, who between them ruled for 29 years, both abdicated the throne to become monks. Their example can be matched in some of the other newly Christian Anglo-Saxon kingdoms. Something really had changed in the culture of the country.

The Venerable Bede

The man upon whom we rely for much of the history of this period – and the content of this chapter! – is perhaps the best example of the cultural revolution that occurred in Northumbria. Bede (672/673–735) was almost certainly of a noble family. If he had lived a century earlier, the only real option for him would have been to strengthen his arm and perfect his sword skills, although he might possibly have become a bard. But in a Christian Northumbria, the young Bede was placed in the monastery at Wearmouth. He was 7, and the abbot there was Benedict Biscop. It was common practice for children to be fostered with other noble families, and since Benedict Biscop was certainly a nobleman, Bede's arrival at the monastery was quite normal. Soon afterwards, Bede was placed under the care of Ceolfrith, abbot of the newly constructed Jarrow monastery, and moved there.

> But in the monastery which Ceolfrith ruled, all those who could read or preach or were able to sing the antiphons and responsories were carried off by the plague except the abbot himself and one small boy.
>
> ('The Anonymous History of Abbot Ceolfrith', *The Age of Bede*, p. 218)

The boy is believed to be Bede. Together, the abbot and the boy rebuilt the monastery, maintaining its work of singing the Divine Office between the two of them until help could be summoned or trained. Many years later, when Ceolfrith was an old man in his seventies, he called together the monks he had ruled for decades to tell them that he was resigning his office and leaving on a final pilgrimage to Rome the very next day. Bede was so upset at the news of his old friend's departure that he was unable to continue with his work for a long time.

Blessed with access to the books brought to the monasteries by Benedict Biscop (the sources tell us that Ceolfrith doubled the collection in his time as abbot) Bede was symptomatic of something entirely new in the Anglo-Saxon world: scholarship. Fluent in Latin, able to read Greek, and blessed with a library containing over 200 books, Bede had access to as extensive a pool of knowledge as existed in Europe at the time, and he dived in deep. In some ways, he can seem disconcertingly modern to a contemporary reader: he demonstrated, for instance, that the world was round – so much for the current trope that people of the time thought they'd sail off the edge if they went far enough. But in other areas he manifests a worldview utterly different from our own, as when he recounts miracles, visions and incorruptible bodies as testament to the sanctity of various religious lives.

But if he is known as a scholar in our day – as indeed he was in his own – it's worth noting that Bede himself placed his learned activities second, behind the performance of his duties as a monk, namely singing the Office and carrying out the acts of corporal and spiritual mercy that formed the heart of his monastic vocation. For the key to Bede, and indeed all the great flowering of Northumbrian culture in the seventh and eighth centuries, is that it took place within the context of the sudden opening of possibilities and broadening of horizons that conversion to Christianity brought. That expansion brought with it the impulse to bring their newly embraced faith to their pagan cousins in the Anglo-Saxon heartlands. Willibrord, a Northumbrian trained in Wilfrid's monastery at Ripon, set out to convert the Frisians, who lived in what is today the coastal regions of the Netherlands and Germany, and the two Hewalds made for the German heartlands and the remaining Saxons. Alcuin was headhunted by Charlemagne himself to become the pre-

Beda venerabilis

Venerable Bede, from the Nuremberg Chronicle. *Wikimedia Commons*

Modern-day Benedictines still sing the Divine Office that Bede recited over a millennium ago.
Wikimedia Commons

siding genius over the Carolingian renaissance in France. Boniface, the greatest of the Anglo-Saxon missionaries, was actually from Wessex. He too concentrated his efforts on his Germanic cousins, and is today commemorated as the patron saint of Germany.

So, in the end, the descendants of the pagan Anglo-Saxons who had extirpated Christianity from the parts of Britain where they had settled, returned to the countries whence they had come and were crucial in the conversion of their cousins, now much removed by time but still united by closely related languages and cultures. History, when viewed through the glass of the centuries, is a strange and often ironic business.

CHRISTIANITY TAKES ROOT

The history of Christian evangelisation among the Anglo-Saxon kingdoms is mainly one of the conversion of kings. But the king's word was by no means absolute – a king ruled in a delicate symbiosis with his warband and nobles, attracting followers by means of his largesse, luck and readiness to go to war – and Edwin, for example, certainly thought it wise to get his counsellors on board before publically committing to the new religion. Within the space of two generations, the rulers of the Anglo-Saxon kingdoms were all Christian, at least in name. However, the renunciation of throne and privilege by a number of kings in the seventh and eighth centuries certainly suggests that the conversion ran very deep in some cases. While there may not have been too much to differentiate between the life of an Anglo-Saxon nobleman and the life of an Anglo-Saxon churchman in the Wilfrid stripe, there were others who abandoned the trappings of wealth and power.

But if we can say with some degree of certainty that Christianity had supplanted paganism among most if not all of the nobility by the eighth century, what of the rest of the population, the people who grew the food and tended the land and provided the surplus that kept their lords and masters in their estates? That is much harder to tell.

Churches were still few and far between in this period, and even if a peasant visited a monastic centre to see the new wonders on show, what could he or she have made of the liturgy, and the readings from a strange book, all chanted in an unfamiliar tongue? How did the Northumbrian clergy set about evangelising the mass of the people?

Bede, as ever, provides us with most of the clues. One way for the religious to evangelise an illiterate population was with their actions. Bede wrote as a historian and a teacher. As a pedagogue, he wrote to instruct the clergy of his day how they should behave, and he did this by providing illustrations of the sort of behaviour he believed they should emulate in the conduct of the saints of the past. Thus, he highlights Aidan's preference for walking over riding, and his readiness to engage with everybody he met. He writes of King Oswald breaking up his own silver dish and distributing it to the poor. Most explicitly, in one of his homilies (*The Age of Bede*, p. 203) Bede recalls his listeners, all fellow religious, to the twin aims of their lives: to remain untarnished by the world and to render aid to the neighbour, by feeding the hungry, giving drink to those who were thirsty and clothing to the cold (an injunction that particularly resonates with a soft Southerner huddled up against a *nor'easter*), by aiding the weak against the powerful, caring for the sick and burying the dead. In a time when there was precious little in the way of safety nets for anyone, this must have resonated with the populace.

However, it was one thing to provide an example of Christian living, but quite another to inculcate knowledge of Christian doctrines in an illiterate, non-Latin-speaking population. We need to be careful here, however. While pre-Christian Anglo-Saxon culture was largely illiterate, that does not mean it did not appreciate words. Storytelling, poetry, songs, riddles and eloquent boasting were all staples of the lord's hall. We have scant evidence for the culture of the peasants but we have no reason to suspect that it was devoid of songs and stories. Indeed, Bede, in telling the story of the most important poet of Northumbria, indicates quite the opposite.

Caedmon, the poet in question, was tending the cows one night. He was outside

because he'd been at a gathering and, seeing the harp coming his way, had escaped before it could reach him. Think of someone tone deaf at a karaoke bar, seeing his turn coming around. But to really appreciate Caedmon's plight, add in the fact that he would have had to accompany himself on the harp and that he was supposed to extemporise a song on the spot. No wonder he escaped to the cows. But when Caedmon fell asleep, he saw a man who called on him by name and asked him to sing a song. Caedmon, in the dream, explained that he couldn't sing and that was why he was out there with the cows, but the man

The memorial to Caedmon. © *Rich Tea*

insisted, telling Caedmon that he was to sing about the creation of all things. And in his dream, Caedmon sang. However, unlike Coleridge, Caedmon successfully remembered the poem when he woke up, and added to it. The new poet was taken before Hilda, the abbess of the monastery where he probably worked. Caedmon recited the poem, and told of the dream that had precipitated it. Hilda, no mean figure herself in the history of Northumbria, must have at once seen the possibilities offered by this unexpected gift of tongues, for she asked Caedmon to enter the monastery as a monk. Once there, he was taught the key stories of the Bible (it appears he never learned to read, so the information must have been memorised), and from these he produced a wide range of verse, in the native language and using the rhythmic structures familiar to the people of the time. It may be hard to imagine the impact of such a thing now, for we have become an overwhelmingly visual culture, saturated in images. But the Anglo-Saxons were aural: knowledge, information, beauty and most of their culture were transmitted to the ear. In such a culture, the beauty of language has a transformative power that we are almost entirely unaware of today.

Sadly, almost all of this poetry is utterly lost. The clanging, declarative 'Hwaet!' ('Listen!') at the start of *Beowulf* and *The Dream of the Rood* is, for us, as much a statement of loss as it would at the time have been a call to attention. However, the fragments that are left reveal a poetry of extraordinary vigour, depth and richness.

Now, we may be in a position to answer the question posed at the start of this chapter: how Christianity came to supplant paganism in the Anglo-Saxon kingdoms of Britain. First, and probably most importantly, the Church, as an institution and as individuals, kept trying. Secondly, and only just less importantly, the Christian Anglo-Saxon kings won more battles, and ascribed their victories to their God, as did the Church. To these, we must add the influence of Christian princesses marrying pagan kings, and the fact that conversion to Christianity brought with it entry into *Romanitas*, the civilised world. First-generation barbarians will burn down cities and put people to the sword, but come the third generation they almost invariably find themselves being lectured on the etiquette of dining implements by the supercilious descendants of their previous victims. Shame of ignorance may be one of the most unsung civilising forces in history. Finally, there is the explosion of possibilities that Christianity brought to the Anglo-Saxons. A culture that already had a rich hoard of words and an honoured place for storytellers and singers could suddenly add the scholar, the monk, the priest and the lord bishop to its store of roles. Women could lead monasteries, men could devote their lives to thought and study, exploiting their rich linguistic heritage and putting it to the service of entirely new ends. It's instructive here to think of a similar warlike, largely illiterate but inveterately poetic society that accepted a new religion: the Arabs. In both cases, the acceptance of a holy book transformed cultures, unleashing an explosion of energy and possibility.

The Northumbrian Golden Age was cut short by the political difficulties the kingdom endured in the eighth century, and brought to an end by the Viking incursions of the ninth century, but in its flowering it produced some of the most extraordinary men and women these islands have ever seen. If it was a Dark Age, would we had more darkness today.

Bishops bearing gifts

Anglo-Saxon culture revolved around gift giving: horses, swords, torcs, princesses. Marriage between royal families was a key way of cementing ties and alliances, and if the royal betrothed was a Christian princess then, naturally, she would include a bishop in the wedding party that brought her to her new home. (The cleric was normally a bishop because, with an eye to the future, a bishop could consecrate more priests in the kingdom and hence prepare solid foundations for its evangelisation. An ordinary priest could baptise pagans, but he could not ordain more priests.)

But there was another aspect to the bishop's presence. Gift giving was taken seriously in Anglo-Saxon culture; in our efforts to understand it today we too often view it through a cynical lens purely as a means to the end of influence and power. But generosity was one of the fundamental virtues and what could be more generous than for a king to dispatch with his daughter a man who brought eternal life and the written word? Eternal life was a promise that depended on faith, but the written word was visible to everyone. Anglo-Saxon culture was based on recital and the spoken word. The first word of *Beowulf* is '*Hwaet!*' 'Listen!'. Everybody listen. Everybody did listen. Everything stopped, people sat around and the scop (an Anglo-Saxon poet) began his story of who and what and why they were. The bards commanded as much attention and prestige as kings.

But words are fragile things, no sooner uttered than lost, and the tales and genealogies and histories that formed the basis of Anglo-Saxon culture were fundamentally dependent on the trained memories of the scops. Although the scops were undoubtedly capable of prodigious feats of recall, all that accumulated knowledge could be lost in a moment's carelessness when crossing a river in spate or risking a shortcut through a winter storm. Memory is mortal. In an age when lives were short, Anglo-Saxons must have been painfully aware of the fragile foundations of their culture. So when men came from abroad with stories of eternal life and the power to make words live forever, it may well have been the immortality granted to words that seemed the greater magic.

This power to fix the past was particularly important to kings, as much of their legitimacy rested upon their genealogies, the proof that they were king by right of blood, and that that blood ultimately flowed from Woden or another of the gods. The royal houses of Bernicia and Deira independently traced their lines back to Woden – who, if royal Anglo-Saxon genealogies are to be believed, seems to have been as active a sirer of mortal children as his Greek counterpart, Zeus. Putting that genealogy down in writing established that claim immutably for their own time and, even more remarkably for the Anglo-Saxons, for the future. It's almost impossible for us today, steeped as we are in centuries of the written word, to realise the impact that writing had on an oral culture but perhaps the phrase 'set in stone' conveys a taste of it. Memory is mortal, but now words could live forever. What greater gift could a king give than immortality?

5

WAR

Who can separate a man and his sword? One is worthless without the other.

(*Klevipoeg*, Estonian epic poem)

Imagine your body pressed against another man, his breath hot on your face, his body pushing back, while to either side your comrades squeeze in against you as the whole line sways and surges in constant dynamic motion. This is about as intimate a physical contact with another human being as is possible outside the marriage bed, but the man you are pushing against is trying to kill you, and you are trying to kill him.

War, in the early medieval period, was waged up-close and personal. Not for Northumbrian warriors the remote dealing of death via bowshot or gun sight, where the target exists as little more than a distant shape. To kill a man at this time was to see him die, to hear the air rattle out of his lungs and the life fade from his eyes. This was the opposite of a sanitised society.

It was in this context and with men schooled in this hardest of schools that the kings of Northumbria – Æthelfrith, Edwin, Oswald and Oswiu paramount among them – ascended to power and exercised authority over the other kings of Britain.

Power politics, Anglo-Saxon style. A sixth-century sword. *Wikimedia Commons*

Stormbringer swords

Within the tale-telling, honour-obsessed world of Northumbrian warriors, the best swords were the ones with a history to them: 'With this blade my grandfather slew Guthlaf and my father felled the thegn of the king of Lindsey.' So close was the connection between a warrior and his sword that one might almost say his soul was as much in his weapon as his body: an idea familiar to all fans of Michael Moorcock's *Elric* novels. Acquiring a sword also meant taking the renown, honour, even the anima, of the man who had wielded it before.

The legend of Wayland the Smith

The Franks Casket, a whalebone chest from the seventh century, is on display in the British Museum. Incised into it are many scenes – pagan, Christian and classical – including a key section from the legend of Wayland the Smith, the forgemaster of the gods in Norse mythology.

When news of Wayland's skill as a smith became known, King Nidud of Sweden sent soldiers to capture him. They found the smith asleep and brought him, and his brother Egil, to the king. To ensure Wayland's service, the king had the smith hamstrung and imprisoned on an island, where he was forced to forge weapons and fancies for Nidud and his family. Wayland had his brother catch birds and from their feathers he made a pair of wings. But he did not put them on and fly away. Oh no. In a long-plotted revenge, Wayland lured the king's sons to his island and killed them. He made the boys' skulls into drinking cups that he sent to the king. When the princes failed to return, Nidud's daughter made the mistake of visiting the smith with a broken ring for repairs. Wayland repaired the ring, drugged the girl and raped her, making her pregnant, before strapping on his wings and flying away. Thus his revenge was complete: Nidud had lost his sons, and his only heir was carrying Wayland's child. Proof positive that it does not pay to mess with the gods. It's curious that Wayland, like Vulcan and Hephaestus, was lame. For ancient peoples, metalworking and smithing carried a price.

MEN AT ARMS

There were a number of things necessary to create an early medieval superpower.

Warriors. Without warriors it was impossible to carve out a kingdom in the first place, or to keep it for long afterwards.

Wealth. To pay the warriors, arm them, feed them, horse them and to generally provide for a standing force that was predominantly idle required great riches. In an age before currency was widespread – although Northumbria was something of an exception in minting widely accepted coins – wealth meant bullion: gold, silver, jewels, and these were woven into ornaments or battlefield tools which were worn and used.

Faith. The certain knowledge that what you were doing was necessary, right and would succeed by God's will and your right hand. If that meant dying, then you were prepared to die, knowing that you had a guaranteed place in Heaven and that tales would be told about your heroics long after your flesh had faded away.

Technology. The better the technology that you had access to and the better the materials you could provide your weapon makers with, then the better the weapons you could supply to your warriors.

All four of these criteria fed and reinforced each other in a self-feeding cycle of success. The key drawback was, like a spiral tightening and tightening as it draws closer to its centre, the successful king had to keep running faster and faster to maintain his position. Success in battle drew more and better warriors to his retinue, but that meant he had to attack further afield to find fresh plunder to provide for them, which meant more enemies and a greater chance of an unexpected and disastrous defeat when caught far from home in unfamiliar territory. Little wonder that few kings of this period died in their beds.

In common with the other early medieval kingdoms, the kings of Northumbria needed warriors, wealth, faith and technology. The basis of the success of Northumbria as an early medieval superpower was its military might and the basis of that might lay in the kingdom's elite warriors and their high-quality weapons. The early medieval kings each kept a small (by modern standards) standing army of household warriors as companions, bodyguards and as the backbone of any larger force that might be needed to attack an enemy or to defend against attack. While this was the face the king's men presented to outsiders and intruders, to the peasants who laboured and sweated to feed them, they acted as much as Mafia enforcers as defenders. There is a case for saying that another possible analogy for these early medieval kings is *The Godfather*, with the king as Don Corleone and his men putting the frighteners on the locals to ensure they paid up and kept the protection racket of kingship running.

Whichever analogy is closer, an Anglo-Saxon army was small, typically numbering a few hundred men. But these warriors were the elite fighters of their time. They trained from an early age, probably starting as children, and they trained hard, every day, to enhance their martial prowess. When they weren't training in a traditional manner they would be enjoying pursuits that enhanced their ability as fighters. Hunting dangerous wild animals was a favourite. Wrestling, weapon practice, horse riding, hand-to-hand fighting and archery would all have been commonplace activities. In the evenings, the playing of strategy games would have helped fill the night-time hours, while the mead hall played a pivotal role in shaping the psychology of the warrior. Sagas and tales were regularly recited or sung. Some of the stories would revolve around the exploits of people actually present in the hall, or their ancestors, while other tales would be apocryphal or aspirational. This was the context in which *Beowulf* would have been sung, to rows of drink-fuddled but attentive warriors each exquisitely attuned to the gradations of praise and honour due to a warrior, his own place in the king's company and how his renown compared to legendary fighters such as Beowulf.

Early medieval warriors lived together, ate together, drank together, fought together (often as a result of the drinking together) and, finally, died together. They shared a deep lifelong bond that fed into all aspects of their lives. It informed them as men and created a camaraderie that was as precious as life itself. The men ate well, drank good-quality alcohol and dined spiritually on a staple diet of sagas, tales and boasts, all centred around the nobility and necessity of fighting, battle and strife, and the quality of that fighting. Think on the most impassioned and opinionated post-match analysis and then multiply it; for these men, what they talked, sang and boasted about really was a matter of life and death. And they loved it!

Kings usually maintained priests or bishops so a warband was often accompanied by a high-ranking holy man, catering for its spiritual wellbeing and assuring the warriors of their place in the afterlife should they serve the king well but fall in battle.

These elite warriors were also paid a tremendous amount when they were successful although pecuniary interest rarely seems to have been the catalyst. The vast scale of the wealth on offer is demonstrated by the Staffordshire hoard,[32] which is either the treasure taken from the dead after a battle, or a tribute paid to avoid war. The huge numbers of sword fittings, mixed with occasional helmet pieces and a crumpled cross, point to the results of battle. Rarely would so many swords be available to strip except after a battle and the helmet pieces, very rare anyway, give strength to this argument.

A BREED APART

Much like our modern standing armies these men did not mix freely with everyday society. They were very much apart. They lived apart, travelled apart, fought apart, died apart and were often buried apart.

The culture was very masculine and thoroughly insular. Honour, loyalty and bravery were highly prized. These were seen as the virtues by which to live one's life, rather than as optional extras. When a warrior pledged himself to his king, it was a pact for life. Many warriors literally gave their lives in service of their king rather than living on with dishonour. The vow could only be dissolved if both king and warrior agreed, and the penalty for breaking the oath of fealty was lifelong dishonour (the stigma of which passed on to the next generation), banishment or death. To illustrate the importance attached to martial valour in general and keeping one's word in particular, the dying Beowulf spent his last moments telling one of his followers of his achievements; and one of the most important of them was that he had never sworn a false oath.

However, it would be naïve to imagine that Northumbrian warriors and noblemen were paragons of round-table-style virtue. They were certainly not above lying, exaggeration and downright dishonesty. Poisoning an enemy was often seen as a valid stratagem, as was ambush. In fact, to take advantage of an opponent through cunning was seen as a mark of being a skilled warrior or king.

The Bamburgh Sword

When Dr Brian Hope-Taylor, the first excavator of Bamburgh Castle, died, one of his former students was telephoned by one of Hope-Taylor's neighbours. The neighbour rang to say that Hope-Taylor's extensive archive and collection were being thrown  into a skip by workmen who had no idea what the dusty, mouldering papers and boxes were. The student, who knew just how important an archaeologist Hope-Taylor had been, went along to the flat to see if there was anything that she could save. It was just as well she did. The workmen had thrown a variety of objects into the skip, but she managed to save the majority of the remains, despite the rough treatment and the fact that they had lain in Hope-Taylor's damp spare room and leaking garage for years.

One of the artefacts saved was a broken sword that Hope-Taylor had excavated from Bamburgh Castle in the 1960s, but had never got round to analysing. When the blade was sent to the Bamburgh Research Project office, Paul Gething had a gut feeling that there was something special about it. He sent the corroded sword to the Royal Armouries for testing.

Paul's instinct was right. An excited metallurgist rang a few days later with the news that the Bamburgh Sword (as it would henceforth be known) was the most extraordinary weapon found in Anglo-Saxon England. Not only was it pattern welded, but it was made of six strands of iron welded together. The next-best sword only had four. This was a blade that had required hundreds of hours to make, and repeated heating and hammering and welding. Thus fused together, the six strands of iron produced a sword that was uniquely flexible and sharp. There can have only been one or two swordsmiths capable of forging such a weapon, and probably just as few men able to pay for it.

We don't know for certain who had the Bamburgh Sword made or who swung it in battle but it was, literally, priceless. It could, quite possibly, have been the king's own sword. Seeing it unsheathed, the naked metal seething with refractive patterns, the most rational response would have been to run away. A blade like this could cut through pretty well everything and never break. (Well, until it did! But it had lasted 300 years by then, so its wielders couldn't really have complained.)

The Bamburgh blade was a single-handed weapon some 30in long when forged. It was consigned to the earth in the tenth or eleventh century, having been forged in the seventh, so for 300–400 years it was handed down, from father to son, as the most prized possession of a royal or noble family. As such, it would have been a physical incarnation of that family's battle prowess, the tale of its battles handed down with the blade from father to son. When it came to the blood feud, the sword was almost a totem of vengeance, for though you might kill a man, the sword he wielded would return through the generations to seek vengeance on you and your kin. These were swords with a personality, almost with a soul, and the Bamburgh Sword was a Stormbringer among them.

The Bamburgh Sword was forged for a king by a master craftsman at a time when Northumbria was one of the pre-eminent powers in the known world. It combined the height of technology with prestige and fashion. It was not only technically perfect, but physically beautiful too. But, after 300 years' use, finally, under circumstances we will never know, it broke. After three centuries of hard use, much like the kingdom it had protected, it returned to the darkness of the earth.

TOOLS OF THE TRADE

The vast majority of Northumbrian weapons were made from a small number of materials. These were principally iron, steel, wood and leather.

Iron was smelted from bog ore, which Northumbria is rich in. The process is skilled but not particularly difficult and a lot of iron can be made relatively quickly using quite simple techniques. Steel is harder to make, but anyone who can make iron can make steel, as the technology is very similar and steel sometimes occurs as a byproduct of iron smelting. Steel is essentially iron with added carbon; the exact percentage was anything between 0.5 per cent and 1.2 per cent in Anglo-Saxon Northumbria. When it comes to making weapons, iron is often a better material than steel, as it is less prone to snapping and can be pushed back into shape relatively easily.

Wood came from the forests of Northumbria, which were carefully managed to provide long, straight shafts for spears and arrows, as well bows and axes. Pollarding or coppicing was the usual method. This involved cutting the tree to a low height and then harvesting the long, straight boughs that grew from the stump as the tree regenerated. The boughs could be harvested on an annual or biennial cycle depending on what size of shaft was needed. More exotic timber was managed in a similar manner, but some would have been traded from much further afield: places such as the Mediterranean and North Africa.

Leather was provided by cattle, sheep, goats, horses or deer. In fact, any animal that had a hide up to the task. Leather was particularly versatile and was used as a covering, as very strong cord and could even be used to make armour when treated appropriately.

GOING HAMMER AND TONGS

Pattern welding was the most technologically advanced system for making weapons that existed during the early medieval period. Pattern welding is a technology that makes steel and iron weapons that are strong, sharp and flexible: essential characteristics of the best weapons.

So how did pattern welding provide these qualities? Basically, by combining varying types of iron through repeated working – beating and heating – so as to spread out the inevitable impurities within the metal and thus prevent weak points occurring around fault lines of impurities.

Strips of iron were gradually forged together to create the composite parts of the weapons, principally swords. Each weld took great skill, but the real skill came in maintaining

The characteristic markings of a pattern-welded sword. *Paul Gething*

the high level of competency needed to make a pattern-welded blade over the entire process. This could take hundreds of hours, depending on the complexity of the sword. The way that the different metal types were combined created an intricate pattern on the surface of the sword, somewhere between the sand ridges on a beach and the whorls of a tree. The marks resulted from the high and low carbon elements within the metal producing darker and lighter shades depending on the relative carbon content. The pattern was then highlighted and accented, usually by twisting, with the pattern being brought into sharp relief by etching with an acid, often urine.

Once the iron core of the weapon was created, a steel edge was added. The iron core was softer but therefore more flexible and more shock absorbent. The steel edge was more brittle but steel can take and retain a much sharper edge than iron. By combining the two materials, Northumbrian swordsmiths were able to forge weapons that were light and flexible, yet could be sharpened to a razor's edge.

The process of pattern welding was not only time consuming, it was (and is) an extraordinarily difficult and skilful process to master. In the early medieval period, any person who knew its secrets would have been highly valued and safely guarded. Translating the technology into modern terms, the ability to forge a pattern-welded sword was akin to the technology that allows certain countries to produce nuclear weapons. Nuclear technology is jealously guarded in the modern era and in the early medieval period the skills and techniques that allowed the forging of what were to all intents and purposes magical weapons, would have been similarly protected. In fact, from the very beginning smiths have been associated with magic and the gods; it's likely that such a reputation would have served only to enhance the standing of the king's own smith and increase his worth. Smiths were very valuable assets and a king who had a master smith in his service would go to great lengths to keep him.

SWORDPLAY

The most prestigious tool of the Northumbrian warrior was the sword. The majority of elite professional warriors carried a sword and, in many respects, that sword was a symbol of rank, status, profession and affiliation.

The sword was not simply a tool or a weapon. It was bound up in the codes, ethics and beliefs of the warrior system. It symbolised a warrior's rights and responsibilities. It told of his ancestry, and his desires and obligations. It marked out its bearer as a warrior and a man to be respected and feared. Carrying a sword indicated that a man was prepared to use it and thus was ready to back his words with deeds. It's clear that swords were not carried lightly, for bearing the weapon meant that the warrior had to be ready to test himself against anyone and everyone who faced him. In the complicated ethical code of the time, bound up as it was in saga, myth and honour-laden stories, death was, quite literally, preferable to dishonour. In fact, a warrior without honour might as well have been dead.

A sword could also be a direct link with the past. In a time when technology was changing slowly, a sword remained current for centuries, for as long as it had integrity and could hold an edge. Given that a warrior would maintain his sword at all costs, swords lasted many lifetimes. So a sword was often passed from father to son, or from sovereign to warrior. Even when it was given to a new wielder, the sword retained some of the personality of its previous owner and its own history. If a sword had been present at a momentous event or important battle then some of that glory remained locked into the blade and the current owner possessed some of that intrinsic power.

Swords, in Anglo-Saxon times as well as our own, fall into many different categories. Swords could be pattern-welded, plain iron, double-edged, lang-seax, richly jewelled or plain. They could be works of the finest art or simple everyday tools. Visit any of the major museums today and you will see a confusion of different blades.

The sword could have either a single edge, a broad trailing edge, or it could be double-edged and more like our traditional interpretation of a sword. As to weight, there was a great range, from extremely light swords of less than 2lbs (0.9kg) that were very quick in the hand, to more than double this, which made for a heavy and unwieldy weapon, but one capable of delivering a very heavy blow.

The majority of Northumbrian swords were plain iron with a steel edge. The edge was either welded onto the iron or the blade was steeled in the fire by the smith. These were the sorts of swords used by workaday warriors who could not obtain or afford a superior weapon.

Anglo-Saxon pattern-welded swords in Paris.
Paul Gething

Making a sword

Swords are made for fighting, so they need specific properties. They must be light enough to move freely but heavy enough to cause damage. They must be strong enough to parry another blade or withstand hitting a shield, or a bone. They must be sharp enough to cut easily but still be relatively straightforward to sharpen. They must be flexible so that they do not shatter on impact, but not so flexible that they stay bent. They should have a point that does not get blunt and a shaft that does not bend too easily.

This is why the best swords are made from an iron core with a steel edge. The central core of iron is very soft, which makes it flexible. The flex means it will bend, rather than shatter, on impact with something hard, such as a shield boss or another sword or a skull. A sword that shattered in a battle was a catastrophe and would very quickly lead to death or serious injury. In Norse tales and sagas there are references to a warrior standing on his sword to straighten it after it had bent during battle, and Northumbrian warriors would have done the same thing. A bent sword was a lot more use than a broken sword as it could be straightened and its wielder could fight on.

Traditionally the best iron for a sword came from bog ore. This was dug from the base of a peat layer or collected from the banks of streams in iron-rich areas. The raw ore was roasted on a bonfire to remove impurities and was then crushed into smaller lumps. A furnace or kiln was built from clay around a wickerwork frame. The kiln was normally less than 3ft (1m) wide and 5ft (1.5m) tall, narrowing near the top to form a flue. The kiln was thoroughly heated using charcoal. When the kiln was very hot, small lumps of ore were gradually added along with the charcoal to maintain an intense heat. Oxygen was introduced using a bellows to promote and maintain the heat necessary to melt the ore. As the bellows increased the heat, more ore and more charcoal was added over many hours until the smelt was complete.

The intense heat produced by the bellows-enhanced charcoal fire melted the ore, allowing pure iron (fe) to separate from the detritus contained within. The end product of the smelt was a bloom of raw iron. However, the bloom still contained a lot of impurities, so it needed to be heavily worked to drive these out and leave a good-quality, working billet. If too many impurities were left in the iron it would tend to be brittle, thus producing a dangerously fragile sword.

The blooms were heated and worked on an anvil or stump, combining the iron until it was in a workable form. The hot working had a dual purpose: it aggregated the iron and drove out the remaining impurities.

The raw material that was left was iron. If it had enough carbon, it became steel; the more carbon that was added, the harder the steel, but also the brittler.

Even after this, the iron would still have had lots of impurities in it: tiny particles of raw carbon, silica and anything else that survived the smelting process. If these impurities grouped together then there was a potential for stress that, under tension, could result in a fracture. But the more the iron was worked, the more disaggregated the impurities became and the stronger the sword.

The iron was extracted from the ore as close to the source of the ore as was reasonably practical, since ore is heavy. It was much easier to extract the iron on site and then move the bloom to a production centre or smithy.

TO PROTECT AND SURVIVE

Shields were traditionally wooden with an iron boss at the centre. The favoured wood for the Northumbrian shield seems to have been lime, used because it was light yet strong. It was also soft enough to absorb a blow, yet will not split easily. Other woods with similar properties were also used, alder and rowan among them, since Northumbrians were practical people.

A shield varied in size from a tiny 18in through to a full 4ft (0.46–1.2m), but in the main, Anglo-Saxon shields tended to be around the 3ft mark (0.9m). That made them big enough to cover the torso, with enough room left over to duck behind and protect the head. A general rule of thumb when looking at Anglo-Saxon shields is that the earlier ones are smaller than the later shields.

But an effective shield was much more than a big circle of wood. They were generally of planked construction strengthened where necessary with thin metal bands and usually covered in cowhide. The Laws of Ine[33] specifically forbade shieldmakers from using sheep hide, suggesting that sheep hide was used in practice but was inferior to cowhide. A rawhide or leather edging was often tacked to the edge of the shield. The hide would have been applied to the shield when it was still wet. As the leather dried, it contracted, providing increased integrity and strength to the shield, rather like a reinforced rim to a wheel.

As far as shape was concerned, a Northumbrian shield was usually round and flat, although concave shapes were also sometimes used. The shield had a centrally placed boss, which is a bowl or cone, usually of iron. This provided a rigid central point and created a heavily protected area for the hand holding the shield. The combination of wood and iron produced a shield that was strong enough to deflect most blows but light enough to carry and use effectively. Excavated shields indicate that Northumbrian warriors painted their protection, probably using strong, vivid colours to mark themselves out on the battlefield and in life.

As you'd expect, shields were used defensively first and foremost, being raised to ward off blows from above, held in front to protect the upper torso and head or lowered to protect the lower torso and legs. A right-handed man could cover the entire left side of his body with a suitable shield. The right-hander stood with his left foot forward, shield side facing towards the enemy.

The shield was useful, even imperative in single combat, or mêlées, but the true strength of the Northumbrian shield became apparent when it was interlocked with its neighbours. This created a shield wall that was extremely difficult to breach. The warrior's shield protected himself, but also the man to his left (giving rise to the term right-hand man). In *Beowulf*, when Hrothgar lamented Aeschere he described him as:

> my right hand man when the ranks clashed
> and our boar crests had to take a battering
> in the line of action.

> (*Beowulf*, lines 1325–28, Seamus Heaney)

The lines describe just how important a role this was, and demonstrates how trusted a man had be to share a shield with a fellow warrior. Your life depended on him and his shield.

The boss end. The shield boss could be used for attack as well as defence. *Paul Gething*

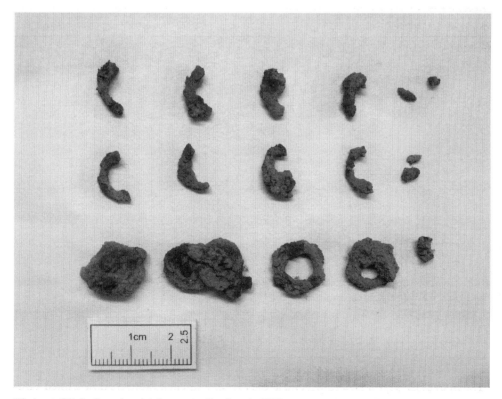

Chain-mail links from the eighth century, Bamburgh. *BRP*

The shield wall was the turning point and trial of strength of most Anglo-Saxon battles. It continued to be a key tactic and mode of attack throughout the early medieval period, and was only completely abandoned when gunpowder made shields obsolete.

But the shield was not only defensive. It was effective to hide behind, it was useful to parry blows, but it could also be used to strike out. The boss was very hard and could be hit into any exposed area of an opponent with immense force, utilising the strength and weight of arm, shoulder and upper body. The general pushing of shield against shield in two opposing shield walls could lead to one side unbalancing, allowing the resultant opening to be exploited by the aggressor. But the shield's rim could also be used to great effect, smashing it into unprotected faces and throats in the battle line. The force of being struck under the chin with a shield rim would break teeth or jaw, incapacitating an enemy or disorientating him enough to make the job of finishing him off relatively easy. A shield wall could not be maintained forever and when it eventually broke up into a general mêlée, where there was more room to wield weapons whether they were pointed or round, the shield could be used horizontally, becoming a formidable weapon and an early entrant for the Captain America shield-throwing contest.

The drawback to using a shield offensively was that it exposed the warrior almost totally. However, it remained a valuable tool in the armoury. What's more, a shield could always be used as a makeshift umbrella, a truly essential accessory in Northumbria.

While shields did provide a great addition to a warrior's power, they were not particularly durable. In accounts of duels from the Norse sagas, two or three shields were often used by the opposing warriors during the course of a single duel, as the wood succumbed to repeated mighty blows.

The Sharp End

Although swords carried the kudos, it was the humble spear that was the principal weapon during Northumbria's heyday. In the early medieval period a spear was a 'must have' object for all free men, akin to a walking stick for the Victorians. It served as a walking aid, a general poking device and a makeshift pole but also as a defence against wild animals and robbers. It is difficult for the modern mind to understand that the spear was such an everyday object as to arouse no attention. Almost everybody carried one: spears lay propped in the corner of most rooms and were carried around when walking. They were as much and as essential a part of everyday life as mobile phones are now.

The ownership of a spear denoted a free man, as slaves were forbidden to carry a spear by Anglo-Saxon law. The spear was the badge of a freeborn man in the same way as a sword marked its bearer out as highborn. However, all warriors of whatever station were intimate with the use of spears and carried at least one.

In battle, spears were used for poking and thrusting and generally keeping the enemy at a distance, although they could also be thrown like a javelin. However, that was a bit of a one-throw shot: miss and you faced the likelihood of having your spear hurled straight back at you.

Excavated spears surviving in archaeological contexts are made up of an iron head, but the shafts rarely survive. Experimental archaeology, ethnographic parallels and the

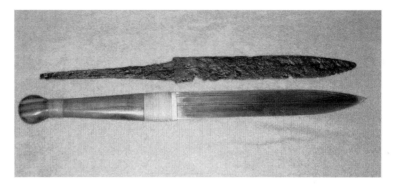

Seax, ancient and modern. *Wikimedia Commons*

dendrochronological samples that survive all show shafts that were made predominantly from ash and hazel. Occasionally, other woods, such as apple, oak and maple were used. The best woods were dense and strong, with a slight flex.

SEAX EDUCATION

The seax was the ubiquitous weapon and tool of the early medieval period. But the word seax covered such a range of items that it started to lose meaning and it is often difficult to know what type of seax was being discussed. Virtually every man, woman and child carried a seax of one type or another. They ranged from small utility blades, 1–2in long and principally for preparing food, through to yard-long single-edged swords used exclusively for fighting. So intrinsic was the tool and weapon to its bearers that the word Saxon itself is said to derive from 'seax'.

Its ubiquity and utility is attested to by the fact that the vast majority of weapons found in graves are seaxes. There are graveyards where virtually every skeleton has a seax on his or her belt.

For one of the king's warriors, the seax was firstly a belt knife, principally used to cut up food, such as bread or meat, at table (the fork only came into use in Britain in the eighteenth century). It was also used for any everyday task needing a knife, and in the last ditch as a weapon. Then, when spears were exhausted, shield was splintered and sword broken or lost, the seax came into its own. When a warrior reached for his seax he was fighting for his life. So, in his final and fatal battle, when Beowulf had fought the dragon to a standstill, he reached for his belt knife. With his dying strength, Beowulf used his seax to kill the dragon.

HARD-HEADED

The problem with helmets is that there are very few surviving from the whole of the early medieval world, let alone Northumbria. Their rarity may be because there weren't many of them in the first place, or possibly helmets weren't put into graves and other places were archaeologists go searching for the past, or maybe a mixture of both. Helmets were (and are) difficult to make and hard to alter, so once a helmet was made it was of little use to anyone without the correct-sized head.

The coppergate helmet. *Wikimedia Commons*

That's not to say helmets didn't exist. The helmet is obviously a very practical solution to humans having heads that are not as hard as swords. If a head was struck with a sword or arrow, or stabbed with a spear, the results tended to be fatal. But if the head in question was shielded by metal, the result was much more in doubt. A blow could be stopped totally or would glance off the helmet, while the trauma from a heavy strike could be alleviated by the padding within. In sum, the helmet was a great leap forward in terms of staying alive during conflict. Added to this, even a light blow to the head when not wearing a helmet could disorientate or stun, leaving the victim pretty helpless before a killing stroke. Disorientation in battle was to be avoided. Helmets helped their wearer keep their heads in all manner of ways.

But a helmet had psychological as well as practical purposes. Putting a helmet on increased the size of the wearer and clearly marked him out as prepared for combat. Since helmets were expensive, anyone wearing one was probably wealthy, well fed and would have had the time and drill necessary to avoid anyone denting his expensive, shiny helmet. The helmet marked the wearer out as 'other'. The man in the helmet was different to you and probably better at the business of war. The implied question was: did you really fancy trying your luck against him?

But putting on a helmet also imbued its wearer with feelings of increased or enhanced power. The feeling may have been an illusion, but it is undeniable that when a helmet is put on the wearer enters a different mental space: the logical conclusion to wearing a helmet is conflict. Wearing a helmet was a tacit acceptance of this combat readiness.

So, the technical superiority of the helmet, coupled with the impact it had on the perception of enemies and the confidence it lent its wearer all conspired towards a helmet being an important part of an elite warrior's equipment.

One of the finest helmets of all comes from Northumbria. The Coppergate helmet is well preserved, still having the obvious form of an actual head shape. It is largely beaten iron, strengthened with iron bands and then decorated with bronze strips and mouldings. The neck part of the helmet has some of the finest mail of all known mail. The links are small and delicate-looking, around 8mm in diameter. It is intricately linked with each individual link threading through four of its neighbours. This metal mesh makes for a flexible protective curtain. The mail also makes a great statement, as mail was costly and time consuming to make. The mail at the back of the helmet would have taken more time to manufacture than the helmet itself.

The overall helmet is extraordinary. It must have belonged to a very high-ranking person, such as a king or a warlord. The manner in which it was deposited in a wood-lined pit in Anglian York indicates that it was hidden quickly, with the mail being folded and placed inside the helmet. It was already old when it was placed in the ground. The fact that it was not recovered suggests that events may have overcome the helmet's last owner.

The elements of an archaeologist

Physically, just about anyone can be an archaeologist. Paul has worked with a man with one arm and a woman who had cerebral palsy. (And both of them outperformed the majority of more able-bodied people!) However, to work at a professional level as a field archaeologist you do need to be physically fit and it does help if you're strong. Just as important is the sort of stoicism that allows somebody to work in poor conditions cheerfully and without complaint. You'll be working in rain, sun, wind; all the extremes of weather the climate can throw at you. At Bamburgh, conditions have varied between -10 and +30°C, with snow, hail and wind strong enough to blow you off your feet. In extreme conditions, the excavation will stop, but the archaeology will carry on: sifting through the results, collating finds, the myriad tasks of a dig.

While the physical demands of archaeology shouldn't rule out many people, its intellectual requirements are more demanding. A reasonable degree of intelligence is necessary. It helps to be well educated, but it's certainly not necessary; some of the best archaeologists have been self taught and, at a practical level, many metal detectorists, who may not have much in the way of formal education, have a great grasp of the historical context of their finds. More than anything else, archaeology requires the capacity to think, combined with a great degree of mental flexibility.

The other great intellectual requirement is imagination. Many archaeologists are hampered by a lack of imagination. For instance, on excavation charts there are unique identifying charts to show colours. This is all very necessary for precision, but UR43 might tell you that something is brown, but not much else. However, describing something as 'the colour of bears' – so long as the numerical description is included as well – provides the spark to set the imagination into burning life.

At a practical and social level, the oil that keeps a site functioning smoothly is good humour. If humour is lacking then, almost certainly, the site will be poor and its findings meagre. Field archaeology involves small groups of people, usually living in basic conditions, doing hard physical work often in difficult conditions. Not surprisingly, the relationships formed during the weeks of a dig tend to be intense. The ability to get on with people under these conditions and, even more importantly, the ability to overlook other people's faults for the month or two of the excavation is important. Things tend to become magnified if you're living in a field with someone for 10 weeks. Foibles that, under normal conditions, would scarcely be noticed, loom large after five or six weeks in such close proximity. It's as intense as the relationships formed between actors on tour, and close to that between soldiers on service.

People love archaeology. Admittedly, they often have only the vaguest idea of the science, usually involving a bullwhip and a fedora, but when people learn that ultimately archaeology is about them, and where they came from, then archaeology becomes contagious.

Archaeology is sharing our rediscovered history and seeing how the light of that knowledge changes other people. Standing on the spoil heap of modern archaeology, we realise that we are standing on the work of everyone who has gone before us. Newton said that he could see further because he stood on the shoulders of giants. Archaeologists, literally, stand upon the accumulated knowledge of their predecessors. We stand on the bones of the past.

Archaeological site.

6

SOCIETY

An armed society is a polite society.

(Robert A. Heinlein, *Beyond This Horizon*)

How people classify and relate to one another is fundamental to the ordering of a society. In the years following the withdrawal of the legions, the Roman civilisation that had organised Britain was completely dissolved (at least in the areas conquered by the Anglo-Saxons) and a new society formed. In most ways, this society was different from what had gone before, from its organisation around the king's retinue of warriors and the central place of kin relationships, to the price placed on each man's life by weregild and the practice of hostage giving. Probably the only area of relative continuity was for the peasants in the countryside. Life was hard under the Roman Empire, it stayed hard under Romano-British petty kings and it didn't improve when a bunch of Anglo-Saxon warlords took over the running of things.

ɷaᴋɪɴɢ ɷoɴaʀᴄʜꜱ

Northumbrian society was hierarchical, with the king at the top and peasants and slaves wearily contending for the bottom of the pile, but it was by no means ossified. Certainly, in the fifth, sixth and seventh centuries, just about anyone could become a king so long as he could take a kingdom and hold it – might made the monarch. By the eighth and ninth centuries, however, ideas of kingship had evolved, and the keeping and holding of a kingdom required legitimacy as well as force of arms – now blood mattered almost as much as blades. But through most of the kingdom's existence – and certainly during Northumbria's ascent to military and political dominance under the successive reigns of Æthelfrith, Edwin, Oswald and Oswiu – there was a considerable element of meritocracy to Northumbrian society. Although kingship required royal blood, given two competing royal houses from the constituent realms of Bernicia and Deira, and an undefined system of royal succession, it was possible for a wide range of claimants to reach for the crown. In the period of Northumbria's decline, the lack of clarity as to who could legitimately be king led to chronic instability and contributed greatly to Northumbria's eclipse, but during the Northumbrian hegemony the brutal competition within and between kingdoms produced a series of exceptional monarchs.

Our idea of kingship has been moulded by centuries of struggle between monarch and parliament, with a leaven of the divine right of kings via Charles I and a dash of monarchical monomania through Louis XIV's '*L'état, c'est moi*'.[34] To get an accurate idea of how the Anglo-Saxons viewed their kings, we have to leave our historical baggage behind. For them, a king's authority was absolute but limited. And yes, it was true, the king was a descendant of Woden and thus had a divine right to rule, but then half the fighting men of the kingdom claimed similar lineage. On the most important decisions, the king took counsel from the chief men of the kingdom, both to gauge their opinions but also to get them on board before the decision was made. As an example, Edwin, when faced with the choice of accepting Christianity, called his advisors together and asked their advice. A king, particularly in the earlier era, could probably decree pretty much what he wanted, and since his will was backed by the only substantial group of fighting men in the kingdom, his word tended to be the law. But the king, despite this primacy of might, was still bound by precedent. Law, in pre-Christian, pre-literate days, was remembrance – it was the way things had always been done. To some extent, this precedent-based system of law came through the person and office of the king, but he was advised by councillors, wise and, not to put too fine a point on it, older men, whose memories reached further into the collective roots of the people. However, we shouldn't be misled into thinking men who had come to rule by the sword and kept their kingdoms and their heads by the same means were constitutional monarchs; if the king really wanted something or someone, he could take it. But it would be equally wrong to see the Anglo-Saxon kings as barbarian exemplars of the triumph of the will: the nets of memory were the foundations, both entangling and constructive, of a non-literate society.

After the conversion to Christianity and the adoption of writing, a body of laws started to be written down and codified. The key change that written laws allowed was that other people could implement the law on the king's behalf: the king's judgement became portable and transferable. The king could still be called upon to arbitrate, but that would have been for disputes involving the higher ranks of Northumbrian society. For the everyday, run-of-the-mill dispute, the king's man was sufficient to uphold the king's law. He acted in the name of the king, on behalf of the king and anyone who disagreed, was disagreeing with the king. And that was usually fatal.

But if the king was the lawgiver he was also the protector and defender of the realm. In fact, early medieval society was in some ways a pact, a covenant, between those who wielded the sword and those who drove the plough. Peasants worked the land on the understanding that their lord would protect them, and the king's men understood that that protection was the due of their peasants. Of course, that didn't mean a peasant would receive kind or considerate treatment from his lord, but it did mean that if anyone was going to mistreat a peasant it was going to be his liege lord rather than some interloper.

Oath breaking and oath taking was the glue that bound Anglo-Saxon society together. But what happened when the king died? Did the loyalty of his men seep away with the king's blood, or was allegiance transferred to the king's heir? Of course, before a warrior could transfer his loyalty he had to survive his king, and there was a strong sense of shame attached to fighters who escaped a battle in which their lord died. A member of the king's warband was expected to die with the king as well as live with him. Sometimes, when a king was killed in battle, the victors tried to persuade his remaining warriors to transfer their allegiance to the winners. This made obvious sense: not only would the victors gain some battle-hardened warriors, but they'd save themselves the risky task of finishing off men who were determined to fight to the death. Sometimes the appeal worked – for with the death of the man to whom they were oathbound there was no real shame involved in changing sides – yet, as often, men chose to fight and die with their king. However, if a successor was known and respected among the warband – say a son or kinsman of the king – then loyalty might be transferred, and men would live to fight another day and for a new man. It's also true to say that as the years progressed and the armies wielded by kings grew, then loyalty gradually transferred to the office of the king rather than the particular man who held the office at that time. After all, it was much easier to be personally loyal to a king when you were one of maybe 200 men who lived, fought and rode with him virtually full time, than if you were part of an army 3,000 strong and only rarely saw the king. The early warbands were driven by a desire for honour and glory, the later armies were motivated by a desire for land and wealth.

The Royal Stable

Below the king were the princes and princesses. Sons were obviously valuable in that they provided additional martial power to the king's warband. At a time when a warband might number 200–300, a few tough princes made a small but not negligible difference to a king's might and were usually dependable, and, if the king was lucky, loyal. However, daughters – and sisters – were, if anything, even more valuable to a king. As princesses, they could be married off to the sons of other kings or to the kings themselves, thus forging alliances and extending kinship – and all the ties that brought – with men that might just as easily have been raiding and warring with their fathers save for the obligations of marriage.

Of course, princes could be traded to rival kings too, as guests and as hostages. It was normal practice to send sons to neighbouring courts to be raised by the king there. The nearest modern analogy is probably fostering or boarding school. The king would send a son – and the boy might well still have been a boy of maybe 8 or 9 – to live as part of the warband of a neighbouring king. That king would then have the obligation to raise, feed and train his royal guest. This had the effect of building and solidifying relationships between neighbours, since princes were frequently exchanged. From the viewpoint of training future kings, it gave these young boys a chance to understand life in a different court, to forge friendships with men who might be their allies in future, and at worst, to gather intelligence on the strength and abilities of a rival.

As far as hostages were concerned, it was normal practice to require hostages of a defeated enemy. In fact, the kings of Northumbria generally preferred to leave a defeated king on his throne and acquire his allegiance through hostage taking, rather than despoiling his kingdom. Magnanimity brought its rewards, and a vanquished enemy treated generously could become, in time, a trusted ally. Hostage taking was one of the key guarantees of this process. However, to properly comprehend the Anglo-Saxon view of hostage giving and taking we have to reverse our understanding of the word. For us, in our obviously more advanced world of terrorist hostage taking and Mafia kidnappings, we understand some- one being taken as a hostage as meaning that if something goes wrong between the two kingdoms, the hostage will pay for the infraction with his life. But for the Anglo-Saxons, the primary meaning of hostage giving and taking was that nothing could go wrong between the two kingdoms because they had become kin. Hostages were given and taken in order to build trust, rather than as a hedge against suspicion. The key social component of hostage giving was that it produced a kin relationship between kings and kingdoms, and betraying kinship was almost unthinkable in Anglo-Saxon society. While Anglo-Saxons, being human, did sometimes do the unthinkable, the more usual result was stable alliance and a degree of trust. Even if a king broke the terms of an agreement, the ties of kinship and the obligations to hospitality were such that it was rare for a hostage to pay the penalty.

On first defeating another king, the normal process was for the victor to appoint himself the over-king of the vanquished lord, and to show his magnanimity, the victor would take the eldest son of the beaten king into his court to raise as his own – plus a tribute of gold, since he was now the over-king. If everything went to plan, then that eldest son became integrated into the court where he had taken up residence, trust was fostered and a rock- solid alliance was forged where everyone knew who was top king. The eldest son would then return to his own kingdom on the death of his father and take over its rule, bringing with him the culture of his hosts. Of course, if the defeated king did decide to chance his luck, the prospects for hostages could be bleak, but if anything, wrath and retribution was more likely to be directed at the rebellious king and his kingdom. An oath broken invited the most terrible retribution, and any sub-king who failed in his rebellion was not likely to live long enough to try again.

In Northumbrian history, the most notable example of attempting to build relationships occurred between Oswiu and Penda, king of Mercia. Penda had killed Oswald, Oswiu's brother and the previous king of Northumbria, and Oswiu ruled Bernicia at Penda's suffer- ance. But despite Oswiu being subordinate to Penda, one of his sons married one of Penda's daughters, and one of his daughters married Penda's son, Peada, who was baptised and became a Christian. Despite these multiple blood ties, something still went badly wrong with the relationship: Penda invaded, refused 'an incalculable quantity of regalia and presents as the price of peace' (Bede, *Ecclesiastical History of the English People*, p. 183) and forced an outnumbered Oswiu into battle, which was where things went wrong for Penda. He lost the battle and his life, and Oswiu found himself, rather unexpectedly, high king of Britain.

The marrying of a Northumbrian prince and princess to Mercian examples of the same is evidence that people at this level of Anglo-Saxon society were unusually mobile with respect to the rest of the population. A king couldn't travel far from his kingdom for long periods without the risk of losing it. At the other end of the social scale, the peasants prob- ably rarely moved more than a few miles from their birthplace. But princes and princesses could turn up almost anywhere as a result of marriage, fostering, hostage giving, exile or simply visiting. Since most Anglo-Saxon kings claimed descent from Woden, there existed some sort of kin relationship between almost all of the royal houses. Even when there was no kin relationship between kings, a royal family in exile could usually find a welcome in a distant court: among the Northumbrians, Edwin took shelter with Raedwald in East Anglia, while Oswald and Oswiu – fleeing from Edwin a few years later! – found asylum in Dalriada, which wasn't even an Anglo-Saxon kingdom (it encompassed much of what is today Northern Ireland and Argyll in Scotland). The fortunes of kingship being particularly fickle in the early medieval period, an exile might easily become a king, so it paid to put some obligations in the bank for future withdrawal should a group of bedraggled refugees turn up looking for sustenance and shelter.

Be my guest

The continuing importance of hospitality for medieval culture is underlined by the play made of Harold Godwinson's stay at the court of William the Bastard ('the Conqueror' was known as 'the Bastard' by his contemporaries, and by many UK Northerners, to this day. Our memories are long!) by the latter's propagandists. During this time, the two men fought side-by-side, besieged several castles and hunted together. So when Harold met William on the field at Hastings it was seen as shocking that two men who were effectively kin could come to such a pass. The questions this placed against Harold's response to William's hospitality meant that William the Bastard received the allegiance of more of the local English nobility than he would have done otherwise. Although William was undoubtedly one of the most effective propagandists of his time, any spinner or PR worth their salt will tell you that the best and most effective way of influencing public opinion is to simply push it further in a direction it was already inclining towards. Harold Godwinson, like his father, was viewed with suspicion by many of the nobility, as an oath-breaking chancer. In a world where reputation was all, to incur doubt on the reliability of your promise was a serious and possibly country-losing business.

On the road again

The king and his retinue did not have one settled place to live. Instead, they moved around the kingdom in what was probably a regular cycle, staying for a month in one place, a couple of weeks at another. This was, in effect, a form of taxation, as the local inhabitants and nobility were expected to provide food and sustenance for the court on its peregrinations. The constant moving also served to make it harder for enemies to find the king. There were a number of permanent residences, most notably Bamburgh, Ad Gefrin, Carlisle and York, but Northumbria was a large place and there were many other places that the court stayed that have been lost over the years. But wherever these were, it's likely that the king and his retinue spent a significant part of the year living in tents, whether that was while moving between the more far-flung of the permanent residences or simply because tents were the only available dwelling place in an area to which the court had repaired to eat its way through a seasonal bounty.

The Second Tier

Beneath the king and his blood relations was the next-highest tier of Anglo-Saxon society. Prior to the conversion to Christianity, this consisted of the kingdom's elite warriors, who were a mixture of made men (that is, men who had made good from a variety of backgrounds by proving themselves in war), men who were raised (the scions of existing warband warriors) and people who were related to the king more distantly, mixed in with warriors from other courts who had come to serve at a foreign court in the hope of glory, plunder and renown. Joining in with the warriors, and not necessarily distinct from them, were bards.

The king's advisors were largely taken from this strand of society, but the personnel advising the king could and did change according to the particular problem he was seeking counsel on. After all, even today we would likely seek advice from different people as to whom we should marry or what career to pursue. In the early medieval period, the kings of Northumbria turned to different people when deciding whether to go to war, which princess to marry and which king to marry their own daughters to. Although being advisor to the king was an influential position, it was, depending on the king, potentially a risky one as well. It took a self-confident king to accept the fault of a failed raid or broken alliance as his own: how much easier to blame an advisor. Being counsellor to someone like Penda, the warlord king of Mercia, was a dangerous business; the calculation was whether the rewards offered by Penda's rise to power over the other English kingdoms was worth the ever-present risk of falling from his favour and watching your body flop to the ground as your head fell to the floor nearby. Not that the king's advisors always had a choice: if the king called on one of his men, he had to answer, whether he willed or not. From such a situation many an Anglo-Saxon must have eventually escaped back to his holdings glad to be still alive. Kings were a capricious lot.

The Warband

From its semi-legendary beginning with Ida to about the middle of the eighth century, the warband was the central polity of Northumbrian society. What was the warband? It was the group of men, maybe 300[35] warriors under Æthelfrith and the early monarchs, who lived with the king, followed him as he made his peripatetic way around the kingdom, and fought for him with the implicit and explicit understanding that they would die for him. These were the men whom the king rewarded with gold and honour, and for whom he provided food and lodging. Oh, and drink. Lots and lots of drink. It was an intensely communal life, of a sort that perhaps only soldiers on detachment in enemy territory can understand today.

The warband was a masculine culture, but that does not mean its older members were unmarried. Given the premium on physical strength that effective fighting required at this time, it's likely that the bulk of the combat would have been carried out by the younger, hotter-blooded men in the warband, while the older heads provided counsel, leadership and orders – in that regard, much like armies today. On the other hand, it's unusual for a general to die in battle in the modern age, while for Northumbrian kings it was dying from natural causes that was unusual.

Still going where other people won't. British soldiers today. *Wikimedia Commons*

The sons of the king's followers were inducted into the warband from an early age, so there was a strongly familial strand to the relationships there. This placement had the side effect of helping to ensure the loyalty of the senior men in the warband. Since their sons were under the care and in the direct line of sight of the king, any ideas about setting up a little kingdom of one's own, or striking for the crown, must surely have been tempered with the knowledge of what might happen to their boys. It's difficult from our vantage point many centuries later to tell whether it was the unstated threat or the obvious trust involved in giving sons over to the warband that dominated; we suspect that it would have varied depending on the personalities and conduct of the people concerned.

Although warbands were an early incarnation of the Musketeers' motto '*unus pro omnibus, omnes pro uno*' (all for one and one for all), individual warriors did sometimes go off with small bands of retainers to fight discrete actions, but the warband remained crucial to the king's power – and his survival. Even when warriors disappeared on skirmishes, the king must have retained enough men to ensure a fair chance of his own survival should a neighbour pay an unexpected visit. So the sorties likely never amounted to more than a quarter of the available warriors.

Life for a warrior in the warband involved constant travel, as the king moved around his kingdom, and an ability to sleep pretty well anywhere. According to Beowulf, the usual bed for one of the king's warriors was the bench where he'd been eating or the floor to which excessive drink had consigned him. The normal pattern of a warrior's day was to practise his trade, prepare his weapons and look after his animals during the day, and then go to the hall or tent with the rest of the warband in the evening, eat, tell tall tales, boast, riddle and listen to songs, drink too much and fall asleep. It was a life that demanded as much of the liver and the memory as it did of the biceps.

But after a long service, a trusted warrior would be rewarded with land. He would then perpetuate the cycle by providing good, strong council and leadership to a locality, acting in the name of the king. Trusted warriors would be able to train the local militias and raise strong sons and beautiful daughters who could go on to serve the king, or maybe, replace him.

Blood money

Anglo-Saxon Britain was a society where, if you killed a man unlawfully, you paid the price. Literally. This was the system of weregild, the blood money owed by the killer to the relatives and lord of the man he killed in lieu of the blood feud that was the only other means of redress at the time. Admittedly, paying the weregild didn't always prevent a blood feud, but it generally ensured that the killer was not outlawed by the king. To be outlawed was the greatest punishment a king could enact: the Viking word for an outlaw was *nithing*, literally nothing. The Anglo-Saxons had cognate names for an outlaw, all indicating that the man was now prey to all, and anyone could kill him and incur no penalty. He was a wolf's head, a man to be hunted down and killed like an animal.

To avoid such a fate, it behoved most men to pay the weregild if they could. The idea and practice of weregild remained remarkably consistent throughout the early medieval period, with the amounts payable staying pretty much the same as far as the sources allows us to ascertain. In Kent in the eighth century, where a shilling was set at the value of a cow, a nobleman was worth 300 shillings, a freeman 100. The apparent cost of a life might be more in other realms, but that was because the value of a shilling was set at the price of a sheep. There, the respective blood money was 1,200 shillings for a member of the nobility and a bargain 200 shillings for a freeman. Body parts had their value too. Under King Alfred's law code, cutting off a nose cost the cutter 60 shillings, an ear was worth 30 shillings and a finger was worth 9. It's interesting to note that a woman's weregild was the same as that of a man of the same rank. Even killing a slave incurred a cost, although in that case it was thought of more as a punishment for depriving the slave's owner of his property than as payment for murder.

In Viking culture, it was occasionally possible for a man who had been declared an outlaw (a *nithing*) to fetch up at another court, offer his sword for hire and to thus rebuild his life and his honour.

KINGS AND BISHOPS AND ABBOTS

While in pre-Christian Northumbria it was not particularly clear who was ranked second in the kingdom after the king, following the conversion that position was definitely occupied by the bishop. The exact status of the bishop varied somewhat, depending on the closeness or otherwise of the relationship between the monarch and the primate, but there were no secular figures that approached the bishop in importance. As an example of how sticky the relationship between king and bishop could become, we need look no further than the strife between Wilfrid, a Renaissance churchman 700 years before there was a Renaissance, and Ecgfrith, the king of Northumbria, which led to Ecgfrith expelling Wilfrid. The quarrel centred around the division of Wilfrid's huge northern diocese into smaller bishoprics, but one suspects the encouragement Wilfrid offered Ecgfrith's queen to retain her virginity may have contributed towards the souring of relations between king and bishop. Wilfrid travelled to Rome to make his case to the Pope, and was upheld, but he managed to put out Ecgfrith's successor kings too, so that he spent most of his diocesan life in exile, travelling to and from Rome trying to get the Pope to take his side in his endless arguments with kings and brother bishops. These trips were an early example of a problem that would come to come to bedevil relations between the English Crown and the See of Peter, culminating in Henry VIII declaring himself head of the Church in England.

But in most cases the relationship between crown and mitre was considerably more harmonious. Bede makes much of the closeness between Oswald and the first bishop of Northumbria, Aidan, with the king even acting as the bishop's translator. Later kings would likely have found the intelligence that the bishops could bring to their councils in terms of advice and information about other kings invaluable.

As the Church developed, the heads of monasteries grew in importance too. While there was undoubtedly a genuine desire to withdraw from the world and its temptations, the necessity of dealing with kings and kings' men meant that the abbots of places like Monkwearmouth and Jarrow, Hexham, Melrose and Ripon assumed a role comparable to that of the king's councillors in earlier days. The monastic movement also had the initial advantage, in the eyes of the kings, of providing land, lodging and purpose to men that the king would probably have had to stump up for himself: retainers too old for battle, or who had grown weary of blood found homes and vocations in monasteries, relieving the king of the necessity of settling land on them in recompense for their services.

The monasteries were also useful for aggrandising the king. If a king commissioned a manuscript from a monastery, then the scribe would pay tribute to the king's generosity, thus ensuring credit to the monarch and a place for his name in a text that was holy in itself: worthy results for this world and the next!

From a historical point of view, the relationship between king and Church was almost symbiotic: the king protected and endowed the Church, the Church legitimised the king in this life and guaranteed his salvation in the next.

However, Bede tells us about an unintended consequence of kings' support for the Church. Later on in the kingdom, taxation on the nobility was such that up to half their land might be lost to the king on their death. The Church, on the other hand, held its property and land in perpetuity. Some of the nobility decided that the best option, there-fore, was to declare your household a monastery and yourself the abbot – then your land and possessions could legitimately be passed on intact to your successor as abbot (who just so happened to be your son) as well as sparing you the military demands placed on the nobility while you were alive. So you got to avoid uncomfortable and possibly fatal expe-ditionary trips to neighbouring kingdoms and see your children inherit the lot.

Bede worried that the number of people becoming monks would lead to a fatal weakening of the kingdom, and there is a case for saying that the loss of fighting men did weaken Northumbria, but it must also be noted that the nobility became monks for honourable reasons too. Being a warrior was a bloody and brutal business. Without the promise of feasting in Valhalla with the gods that the pagan religion promised, there were fewer positive reasons to keep on fighting, and the new faith provided a different path to eternal fulfilment. That path was so attractive that two kings of Northumbria in the eighth century, Ceolwulf and Eadberht, abdicated and became monks, ending their days at Lindisfarne and York respectively. Something deep had changed in the culture of the Northumbrians.

[manuscript text — Life of St Wilfrid]

...pdicatore ... ... inprospn

& aduersis eqli lance patient portabat; dans sep

tā spirituali q̄ secularib; dona & munera tā large

in nullus ei eqlis inuenie bat; DE EDIFICATIOHE DO DOI

AD HERE BAT iois f secundum IN HAGUSTALDENSAE

psalmista indesinent dño. ponens in eu spē suā; Ca XIX

reddens q; dño suo dulcissima q ei omia concedit;

Hā in hagustaldaesae adepta regione a regina sca

æþldryþe dō dedicata · domū dño in honorē beati

AHDREE apti fabre facta fundauit; cuius p fundicate

inetra cū domib; mirifice politis lapidib; fundata ·

& sup tā multiplice domū columpnis uariis & porticib;

multis suffulta; mirabiliq; longitudine & altitudine

muroy ornata · & uariis liniaru anfractib; uiarū

aliquando sursū · aliquando de orsū p cocleas circū duct

tā; ñ est me p paruitatis hoc sermone ex plicare ·

qd ipse psul animaru · a spū di doctus ope facere

excogitauit; neq; ulla domū alia citra alpes montes

tale edificata audiuimus; p orio beatae memorie

adhuc uiuens grae di acca eps q; magnalia ornamen-

ta huius multiplicis domi · de auro & argento lapidib;

q; priosis · & qmodo altaria purpura & serico induta

decorauit · qs ad explanandum sufficere pot ·ē

redeam ad ppposita; DE SANATO PUERO SEMI Ca XX·

Vo edificantes nāq; ce intarii muroy VIVO ·

huis domi altitudines · q dā iuuenis ex seruis di de

pinna in hor me pcerptatis elapsus ad terā de orsum ·

A page from the *Life of St Wilfrid* by Stephen of Ripon. *Wikimedia Commons*

. Bamburgh Castle today. *Bamburgh Research Project*
(BRP)

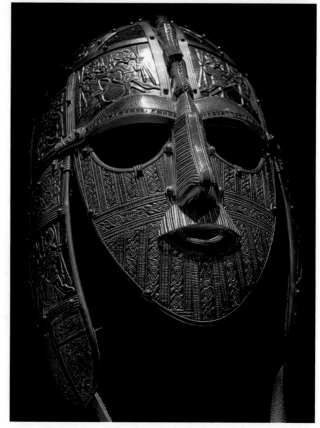

. A reconstruction of the Sutton Hoo helmet.
Wikimedia Commons

3. King Edwin of Northumbria as imagined in Victorian times. *Wikimedia Commons*

4. Items from the Staffordshire hoard. We think this was plunder or payment from Northumbria. *David Rowan/Wikimedia Commons*

. The Cheviot Hills. *Simon Fraser, Northumberland National Park Authority*

6. Great Whin Sill. *Simon Fraser, Northumberland National Park Authority*

8. St Peter's, Wearmouth. © *Andrew Curtis*

7. Hadrian's Wall. *Simon Fraser Northumberland National Park Authority*

9. Benedict by Fra Angelico. *Wikimedia Commons*

10. The ruins of Lindisfarne Priory. These remains are what's left from when the priory was re-established in 1093. *English Heritage*

11. Holy Island causeway. *Gail Johnson*

12. St Aidan. *Gail Johnson*

13. Whitby Abbey. *Chris Kirk/Wikimedia Commons*

14. A reconstructed Anglo-Saxon Shield. *Paul Gething*

15. Medieval peasant hoeing. *Wikimedia Commons* 16. Medieval peasant ploughing. *Wikimedia Commons*

18. A modern copy of an Anglian ring lying on unpolished garnets. *Paul Gething*

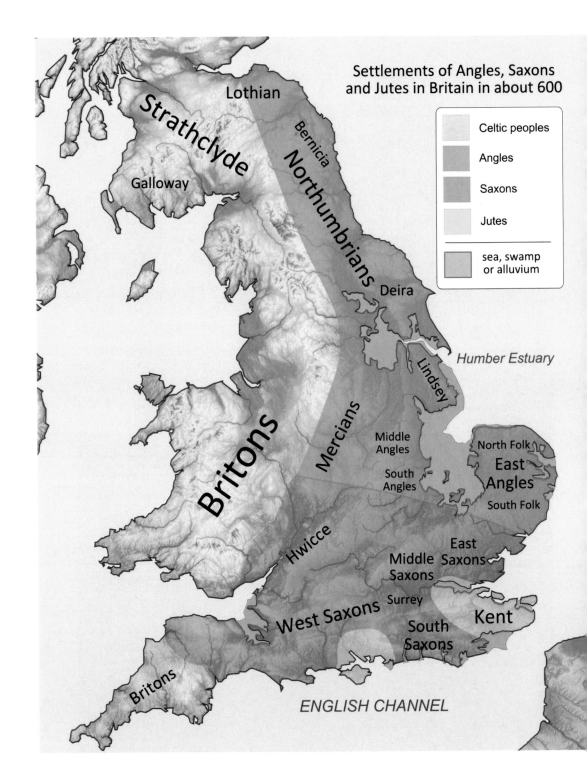

Settlements of Angles, Saxons
and Jutes in Britain in about 600

	Celtic peoples
	Angles
	Saxons
	Jutes
	sea, swamp or alluvium

Strathclyde

Lothian

Galloway

Bernicia

Northumbrians

Deira

Humber Estuary

Lindsey

Britons

Mercians

Middle Angles

North Folk

East Angles

South Angles

South Folk

Hwicce

East Saxons

Middle Saxons

Surrey

West Saxons

South Saxons

Kent

Britons

ENGLISH CHANNEL

17. Map showing the distribution of kingdoms and very different coastline in AD 600. *Wikimedia Commons*

21. Fruit leather. *Wikimedia Commons*

22. Smelting. *Paul Gething*

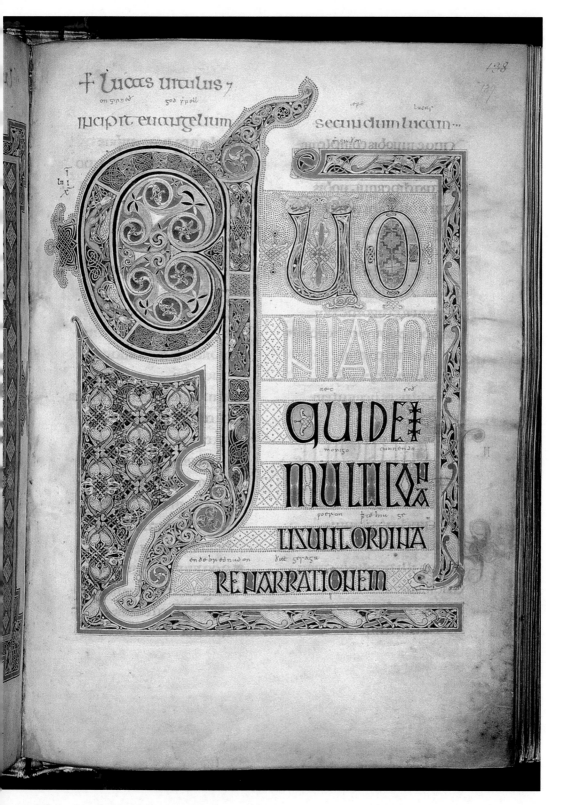

23. Lindisfarne Gospels folio. *Wikimedia Commons*

24. Lindisfarne Gospel. *Edoardo Albert*

25. Styca excavated by Dr Hope-Taylor in the 1960s. *BRP*

26. Lindisfarne Gospel detail. *Edoardo Albert*

27. Viking sword pommel. *Wikimedia Commons*

28. Reconstructed Anglo-Saxon buildings in Bede's World, Jarrow. *Bede's World*

ꟽAKERS ANꝺ ꟽENꝺERS ANꝺ GROⱲERS

Taking another step down in Northumbrian society, we come to the artisans. The crafts-men ranked below the warriors and the religious, but the top flight among the artisans – the weaponsmiths and goldsmiths – were only just below the top tier of society and, being guardians of secrets to which their superiors were not necessarily privy, they could command considerable status, outranking even minor religious and military figures. Of course, the majority of craftsmen, dealing with everyday goods and necessities, had no such presumptions, and generally sought out their fellow craftsmen's company. For instance, in York, all the butchers lived in The Shambles ('shambles' is the old word for butchery). However, beware instant linguistic archaeology. Coney Street was not the place to buy a rabbit: Coney is in fact a corruption of *Konungr*, the old word for king.

For more about the artisans of the time, see the chapter on technology.

Apart from the makers, there were farmers, the top level of whom were retired nobility or the sons of nobles acting as landlords and land managers, overseeing their holdings and controlling their farmers and peasants.

ꝺEASANTS

Resting at the bottom of Anglo-Saxon society, supporting everyone else and almost cer-tainly outnumbering everyone else were the peasants. And we know virtually nothing about them. They are well-nigh invisible. There are almost no graves, there are very few records and there is little reference to their lives in the surviving literature. They are the unseen people, as hard to trace as the wind. They were probably the indigenous population, whose ancestors had first settled to cropping the soil, and who remained as immovable as the Cheviot and as remote.

One of the few sources we have on the life of the peasant is Aelfric's Colloquy, a dia-logue dating from the end of the tenth century. In it, a monkish teacher asks after the labours of the ploughman, the shepherd and the oxherd, as well as more prosperous people such as the hunter, the birdcatcher and the merchant. The ploughman laments:

> Master, I have to work so very hard. I go out at the crack of dawn to drive the oxen to the field and yoke them to the plough. For not even in the bitter winter would I dare to stay at home for fear of my lord; but, when I have yoked up the oxen and fastened the plough and the ploughshare to the plough, then I must plough a whole field or more for the whole day.
> **Teacher**: Have you any mates?
> **Ploughman**: Yes, I have one boy who drives the oxen with a goad. He is hoarse from shout-ing and the cold.
> **Teacher**: Do you do anything more during the day?
> **Ploughman**: Yes, indeed, I do very much more. I have to fill the stable with hay for the oxen, water them and take their dung outside. Alas, I have to endure such hard work since I am not a free man.
>
> (Aelfric's Colloquy, translated by Ann E. Watkins. (http://www.kentarchaeology.ac/
> authors/o16.pdf))

Hard labour: ploughing. *Wikimedia Commons*

Even among the peasantry there were gradations however. It was possible to own a piece of land that belonged to a thegn (one of the gradations of Northumbrian nobility, ranking below an earl) – it was their land as they had tenancy rights – but they had to pay a rent to the thegn. Then there was a group of peasants who also had tenancy rights on their land but owed a duty to their thegn for the land; that is, they had to work for their lord for a day or two a week. The people below this, generally known as churls, owed their entire labour to their lord, so would have to work for him pretty much full time. The churls did have some land to live on, but it was a hard and basic existence.

Added to this, most free men owed at least some military service to the king, so part of their working year would be taken up by performing a service for the king and training for any potential strife.

Home is where the heart is

It's hard for us to realise today how insular most Anglo-Saxon society was. The majority of people were born, lived and died within a few square miles. Bede famously never strayed far from the monasteries of Monkwearmouth and Jarrow, and he was a supremely cultured man. The ordinary man knew his neighbourhood with the intimacy of generations. Travel could bring advantages however. In fact, one of the ways a freeman could become a thegn was by completing three overseas journeys, at his own expense. So it was possible to rise to the nobility simply by making three trips abroad: as if three trips to a Costa could earn you a knighthood today.

Princess far from home

The Bamburgh Research Project (BRP), when excavating the burial ground at Bamburgh Castle, found the remains of a high-ranking Norwegian woman. She was buried around about AD 680 and most probably had come to Bamburgh as a bride. It's impossible to tell from the remains whether she was a princess or simply of very high rank, but the fact that she was buried in Bamburgh 100 years before the trade links between Northumbria and Norway become entrenched is intriguing, and a salutary reminder of how far afield people in the highest echelons of society travelled. We know that she was Norwegian from isotopic analysis of the dentine of her teeth. Sadly, this Norwegian traveller died young; she was in her early twenties at the time.

She had no marks of stress in her bones, indicating a life without hunger. Well fed, tall and strong, she is probably one of the very first Scandinavians to enter Northumbria, heralding a far more aggressive incursion just over a century later.

Bare boned.
Norwegian female
during excavation.
BRP

SLAVES

Slavery among the Anglo-Saxons was not the absolute ownership of the early days of the USA. There were rules to keeping slaves, and some peasants availed themselves of those rules to sell themselves into slavery. For while the Anglo-Saxons may have been mainly a free people, for the poor that freedom sometimes represented little more than the freedom to starve. Accepting slavery meant a reasonable prospect of food and the chance of buying back your freedom when times had improved.

A better way of viewing slavery in the Anglo-Saxon milieu is to think of indentured labour: a slave owed his labour to his master for as long as his master owned him, but that ownership incurred obligations on the master, and the slave could manumit his servitude by saving money and buying his way to freedom.

Slaves were a lucrative business, however. Anglo-Saxons fetched top prices in the slave markets of Europe. Famously, it was the sight of handsome Anglo-Saxons for sale in Rome that inspired Pope Gregory to send a mission to convert these people who were so beautiful that they were '*non Angli, sed angeli*' (not Angles, but angels). Supplying the slave markets of Europe would have required local agents in Britain, but given that there were multiple routes into slavery, it was not too difficult to meet demand. People could be put into slavery as a punishment: for example, if they had defaulted on a loan. Losing a battle was often a route into slavery, particularly for any poor unfortunate who'd been pressed into service to make up the numbers. Without much in the way of battle skill to bargain with, the easiest way for the victors to turn a profit on such an individual was to sell him into slavery. And sometimes people sold themselves into slavery if they couldn't afford to eat. In some ways, this resembled an early form of pawning, with the collateral being your own body. A poor man might sell himself into slavery when his crop failed and he was unable to feed himself, with the intention of redeeming his freedom once he had saved enough money.

Anglian widows

The attrition rate among warriors was high, so second and third marriages for women were not uncommon. (Although, on the other hand, the attrition rates of childbirth were also high, so men also had successive wives.) The question arises of where did the nobility get their spouses from? Was the Northumbrian nobility entirely composed of descendants of Ida's warband, the men who had first wrested control of Bamburgh from the native British? The short answer seems to be no, but with reservations. As far as we can tell, there was quite extensive intermarriage, but that was mainly with courts of a common background and outlook to the Northumbrians: mainly the other Anglo-Saxon kingdoms, and then the coastal Norse peoples across the North Sea. There were probably even marriages with the native British nobility, despite the centuries of strife between Britons and Anglo-Saxons. In fact, it would have been much more likely for a Northumbrian princess to marry a prince of Dalriada than a peasant of her own people. This was a society that was stratified along social rather than racial grounds.

Interview with Alex Woolf

1. Who are and you what is your area of expertise?
My name is Alex Woolf and I teach Mediaeval History at the University of St Andrews.

2. Describe your specialism simply.
I am principally a textual historian but have some training in archaeology and Old English. I have published mostly on Dark Age Britain and Ireland.

3. Can you describe the social system of Northumbria in layman's terms?
So far as we can tell Northumbrian society was organised through both landholding and kinship. As with other parts of early medieval Britain, land was divided equally between male heirs. Settlements were organised into small 'shires' like Islandshire or Hexhamshire, consisting of a single dale or equivalent parcel of lowland. At least as late as the end of the seventh century, and probably later, some of these shires were largely inhabited by British-speaking, as opposed to English-speaking, populations. These areas probably paid higher tribute levels and had less influence on the governance of the kingdom as a whole.

4. How does this work in principle?
This means that most householders were quite closely related to most of their neighbours. They would have farmed their land with their extended family and in most cases with some slaves. Taxation, in agricultural produce, and most dispute settlement and judgement would take place at the level of the shire. The farmers in a shire would probably also share the same unenclosed upland grazing and may well have co-operated in annual round-ups of sheep and cattle. Most shires would have been under the jurisdiction of a royal officer who may or may not have been a local man. A few shires were wholly in the lordship of a major church, which would have exercised the rights usually held by the king.

5. How do we know, and what are the sources?
The sources for Northumbrian social structure are a mixture of circumstantial evidence produced by Bede and the writers of saints' lives as well as the survival of archaic institutions into the later middle ages when administrative documents begin to survive.

6. Are there any specific examples of this, such as documents or excavations?
One of the best textual sources is a work known as Historia de Sancto Cuthberto, a collection of documents relating to the land holding of the Church of St Cuthbert put together in the tenth and eleventh centuries from earlier sources. This includes, for example, the record of a grant of the shire of Cartmel (now in south Cumbria) to the Church, with all the Britons living in it. Archaeologically, sites such as Yeavering and Millfield and Sprouston probably represent the administrative centres of shires.

7. What techniques do you use to interpret the way poor people lived?

Settlement morphology (i.e. shape) and distribution probably tell us more about the lives of ordinary people than anything else but to date, relatively few settlements have been well investigated archaeologically. It is fairly clear that nucleated settlements were not very common, although the excavations at West Heslerton appear to indicate that they were not unknown, and this probably means that the open field system of agriculture practiced in much of England by the twelfth century was not widespread. Most settlements seem to have been made up of between two and four households, probably representing the collaboratively run farms of close kinsmen.

8. Does Northumbria have a discrete social system?

Across the British Isles very similar social systems existed in this period and were modified locally due to the environmental conditions. Parts of Yorkshire may have closely resembled much of southern and eastern England, whereas the organisation in Bernicia would probably have been more like that in Wales and the north where similar constraints on livestock management and crop production prevailed.

9. Did it change after the Roman collapse? If so, how?

During the later Roman period a considerable amount of production in this area was probably geared towards supplying the army. This would have encouraged production for a market and probably a more rigid social hierarchy dominated by those who actually procured the army contracts. After the Roman Army and state disappeared, most production would have been geared towards subsistence, kings and churches taking tribute in much the same kind of foodstuffs as ordinary people consumed.

10. Are the peasantry/poor/slaves visible in the records or archaeology?

Slaves are very hard to identify in the archaeological record as they probably lived alongside their owners. Indeed the social distance was probably more like that between servants and masters in an early modern farming context than the stereotype based on recent American plantations. The free population was probably not as clearly divided between peasantry and nobles as would be the case in the later middle ages, with a more varied distribution of wealth. As late as the Norman Conquest much of Northumbria was owned and farmed by a class who lay somewhere between what we would consider peasants and lesser gentry, known then as thegns and drengs. Most of the archaeology we can identify probably belongs to this group.

11. How did they live? What were their lives like?

Almost everybody lived by farming and most craft production was carried out on individual farms. The better-off householders and their wives would probably be able to avoid the least pleasant tasks most of the time, though at the lower end of the wealth range slaves and masters probably mucked in together most of the time. At harvest and round-up time it is likely that everybody had to pull their weight. Women were probably largely employed in dairying and cloth production whereas most of the ploughing and livestock management would have been a male preserve. At times, there may have been plenty of food and fun to be had but these sorts of societies were very susceptible to bad weather, crop failure or loss of livestock through disease or rustling. When that happened starvation and malnutrition would take their toll.

12. Is there anything you would like to add?
The big distinction amongst the peasantry would have been between those who were wealthy enough to do honourable service, that is to say those who had a good horse and some weapons and could afford to leave the farm to run by itself whilst they attended the king or other lord, and those who performed only base service of labour and food renders, because they could not afford to leave their holding for too long at a time. The biggest division in society was probably between the free, who bore weapons and held land, and the slaves, rather than between peasants and nobles.

7

CULTURE

I'm a strange creature, for I satisfy women,
a service to the neighbours! No one suffers
at my hands except for my slayer.
I grow very tall, erect in a bed,
I'm hairy underneath. From time to time
a good-looking girl, the doughty daughter
of some churl dares to hold me,
grips my russet skin, robs me of my head
and puts me in the pantry. At once that girl
with plaited hair who has confined me
remembers our meeting. Her eye moistens.

(Anglo-Saxon riddle from the *Exeter Book*, translated by Kevin Crossley-Holland. The answer
is at the end of the chapter. [Accessed at http://www.tfl.gov.uk/tfl/corporate/
projectsandschemes/artmusicdesign/poems/poem.asp?ID=99])

ƿꞰⱯꞇ!

If one word can sum up any culture, the clanging syllable that begins *Beowulf* defines the
world of the Anglo-Saxons: *Hwaet* 'listen'. Stop what you're doing, stop your drinking,
your talking, your boasting, for something marvellous and intriguing is about to be spoken
into existence. Nowadays, when we want to find out something, when we want to amuse
or intrigue ourselves, we have a wealth of means by which to do so, and most of them
involve looking. In the early medieval period, people had to listen. Essentially, knowledge
resided with the wise: a priest, be he pagan or Christian, a traveller with first-hand tales
of the strange ways and wonders to be found beyond the horizon, a bard with stories and
songs of the exploits of heroes and the ways of gods and saints.

This was a fundamentally conservative (small *c*) culture that looked backwards in order
to find a way forwards. Knowledge was not freely available but had to be sought, usually
by travelling, be it near or far, to find someone who had that knowledge. However, this

was specialised information. Primary information, be it how to make a fire, what to do to find water or where north lay, was diffused throughout the culture. Everybody knew how to do these things – they had to. This generalised knowledge fits perfectly with the definition of culture employed by archaeologists, which has a culture as being anything that provides a specific identity to a group of people living together in a particular way. Thus the Oldowan culture refers to a Palaeolithic culture that made stone tools, choppers, scrapers and awls, in a specific manner. The Anglo-Saxon culture produced people who could make their way and their living in a hostile world by the mastery of a range of practical skills. But, of course, this technical definition of culture is not the one in everyday use. And, in deference to the vernacular, culture, as the complex of language, stories, songs and fashion, is what we're going to look at in this chapter.

Harp strings

In 2003, the Museum of London began excavating at Prittlewell in south-east Essex. What they found there was a burial of a man who had been laid to rest in what was basically a subterranean bedroom, with rich goods laid out around him and hung upon the walls. Given the value of the items buried with the man, he must have been of high status, and among the objects that he was taking with him into the afterlife was a lyre, which was reconstructed by instrument maker Zachary Taylor. Taylor came to the conclusion that the wood must have been manipulated while it grew in order to provide the special characteristics necessary for the lyre's frame. If this is correct, then Anglo-Saxon instrument makers practised an early form of bonsai.

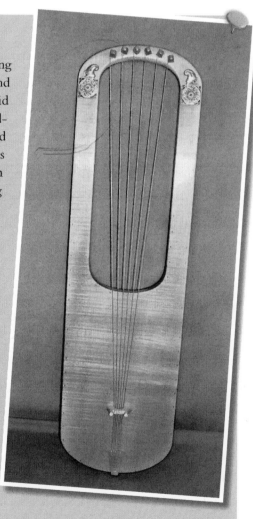

A reconstruction of the Sutton Hoo lyre. *Wikimedia Commons*

The world is a big place

One of the key cultural changes that occurred when the Anglians came to Northumbria was an expansion of horizons. This might seem odd, given that much of Britain – although only the bottom half of Northumbria – had been part of the Roman Empire only a few generations before, but with the withdrawal of the legions there was a contraction, a constriction, in the mental space occupied by many of the British kingdoms. Admittedly there were exceptions to this, notably in Ireland, but on the mainland the native British tended to become more insular. This was not surprising, really, as they were trying to withstand the bands of Anglo-Saxon invaders coming over the waves. But this was simply the end-point of a process: the British had turned inwards over the last century or two of Roman rule. Britannia was a rich province, but no Briton ever became a Roman senator and it stood apart from the rest of the empire: literally, being an island. The withdrawal of the legions exacerbated these cultural tendencies.

So when the Anglo-Saxons came, they brought with them a seafaring culture that had continuing strong links across the North Sea to the homelands of the newcomers, and to their cousins in Norway and Sweden. The eastern flank of Britain is indented by rivers that reach far inland, cutting through the generally flat land that lies on the right-hand side of the country, and the invaders made great use of these watery highways into the interior. Once their kingdoms were established, the Anglo-Saxons continued to use the sea and rivers as their roads. While it would have taken a week or more to travel overland from Bamburgh to York, the two chief settlements of Northumbria, the journey could be accomplished by ship in a day. So, for the class of people that moved – basically the warriors and the scions of kings – there was a broadening of horizons with the replacement of the British rulers with Anglians. (There was no change for the peasants though. They were the opposite of rolling stones, staying put and farming the land through the millennia.) Indeed, travel was regarded among the ruling class as desirable in itself, and profitable too. As mentioned previously, three trips abroad, paid for from one's own purse, allowed a man to become a thegn, a high rank in Anglo-Saxon society.

Although it's impossible to prove at this distance, we suspect that one of the reasons that travellers were welcomed and venerated was the intellectual wealth that they brought with them, particularly in the form of new stories. After all, in a world where there wasn't a great deal to do during long winter nights other than sit around and tell stories, a new tale was a big event. Travellers brought stories and news; no wonder they were regarded with delight. When, at the start of the poem, Beowulf arrives at the court of Hrothgar, the king throws a feast for him. We should expect similar treatment to have greeted real-life aristocratic travellers pitching up at new halls.

We sometimes wonder whether an under-appreciated reason for the eventual success of Christianity in Britain was that the Bible is chock full of really good stories – new stories for the Anglo-Saxons.

Painted people

The Picts were famous for being the painted people, covered in tattoos. We don't know if the Anglo-Saxons followed that custom. There have been no fleshed archaeological remains to indicate that they did, although Anglo-Saxon designs do seem quite suitable for tattooing. Within the broader cultural ambit of the northern European world, there are surviving reports from Ahmad ibn Fadlan, a tenth-century Arab, of people he called 'Rus', who scholars believe to be Vikings. Ibn Fadlan describes them as being tattooed from fingernails to neck with dark blue or dark green tree patterns. It seems very unlikely that the Northumbrians, who decorated everything and anything, would not have decorated their bodies. We think they were tattooed, we just can't prove it!

HARD MEN, SWEET WORDS

Elsewhere we have compared Anglo-Saxon kings and their warbands to Mafia gangs running protection rackets: pay tribute or else. While this is an analogy, and thus necessarily imperfect, there is some truth in the comparison. However, there is one area in which the analogy falls down completely – language. Goodfellas use a language stripped of syntax, grammar and most words of more than one syllable; if you ever want a deeply depressing experience, listen to an FBI wiretap of gangsters plotting to off someone. But the hard men who made up the retainers and warriors of Anglo-Saxon Britain valued verbal skill and linguistic brilliance almost as highly as skill in arms. To be a proper man meant being able to fight a duel, stand in the shield wall, compose a riddle, extemporise a poem and sing songs. Beauty mattered to these men, whether it be beauty in words or appearance (we'll get on to appearances later). Anglo-Saxon warriors were deeply enculturated, and it was not just the warriors. Bede recounts the famous story of the poet Caedmon. Caedmon appears to have been of fairly low rank, as he looked after animals. He must have been a sensitive man, for:

> it sometimes happened at a feast that all the guests in turn would be invited to sing and enter-
> tain the company; then, when he saw the harp coming his way, he would get up from the table
> and go home.
>
> (Bede, *Ecclesiastical History of the English People*, p. 248).

From this we learn that being able to sing and play the harp was a normal and expected social skill among the Northumbrians, which was why Caedmon found his incapacity so excruciatingly embarrassing.

Before the advent of Christianity there was little in the way of pictorial representation and even afterwards, paintings were rare, confined mainly to monasteries and churches. Starved of visual representations, people had to paint pictures with words. If you've ever read a story out loud to an imaginative child, do you remember the rapt expression and the gamut of emotions running across their face as the story took them on wild adventures?

Singing for his supper. A good bard was a valuable commodity. Here the Icelandic *scald*, Bersi Skáldtorfuson, attempts to keep his captors sweet. *Wikimedia Commons*

The words make the world of the story come to life and the child lives it. Sadly, few adults these days retain the ability to be transported by words that they had as a child, but we suspect that in the early medieval period, grown men would weep when they listened to Beowulf's death, or cheer the hero on as he pursued Grendel's mother down into cold waters. One of the great shifts of sensibility over the last century or two has been the transference of the chief arena of the imagination from the aural to the visual.

Another great difference is our addiction to novelty: new films, new songs, new episodes of our favourite television programme. The Anglo-Saxons liked new things as well, but they were comfortable with the old tales. Each telling had contemporary elements woven into it, allusions to the people present calculated to make them guffaw or grimace, but usually the story itself was well known. This didn't make it less enjoyable. There is a comfort in familiar things that is felt all the more keenly in an acutely unstable world.

The Music of Words

That the Anglo-Saxons were keen poets is almost certainly true. That almost all their poems have been lost is definitely true. So we'll never know for certain whether *Beowulf* was a lone peak in the Anglo-Saxon poetic tradition, merely a foothill to scale before greater epics, or a generally representative example of the quality of their verse. There are surviving fragments of other poems, such as *The Battle of Brunanburh*, a 73-line poem incorporated into the *Anglo-Saxon Chronicle*; 325 lines of *The Battle of Maldon*, which tells the story of the Anglo-Saxon defeat at the hands of the Vikings in 991; 50 lines of a poem called the *Finnesburg Fragment*, which recounts Hnæf's fight when besieged in a fort; and a couple of pages that were found stiffening an Elizabethan prayer book that told part of the adventures of Waldhere, a hero of Aquitaine in France, and a popular figure in the Middle Ages. But that's pretty much all that's left of centuries of epic poetry.

The same is true for other forms of verse: we have just enough to give us a taste of what the Anglo-Saxons composed but nowhere near enough to slake our thirst, nor even to know if what we have is representative. Running through most Anglo-Saxon verse is a deeply elegiac mood, perhaps best exemplified in *The Ruin*, a meditation on a Roman town, once great, now fallen to ruin. The poem begins:

> *Wrætlic is þes wealstan,   wyrde gebræcon;*
> *burgstede burston,   brosnað enta geweorc.*

Bearing in mind Bede's point that 'verses, however masterly, cannot be translated literally from one language into another without losing much of their beauty and dignity' (Bede, *Ecclesiastical History*, p. 249), the beginning of *The Ruin* can be rendered:

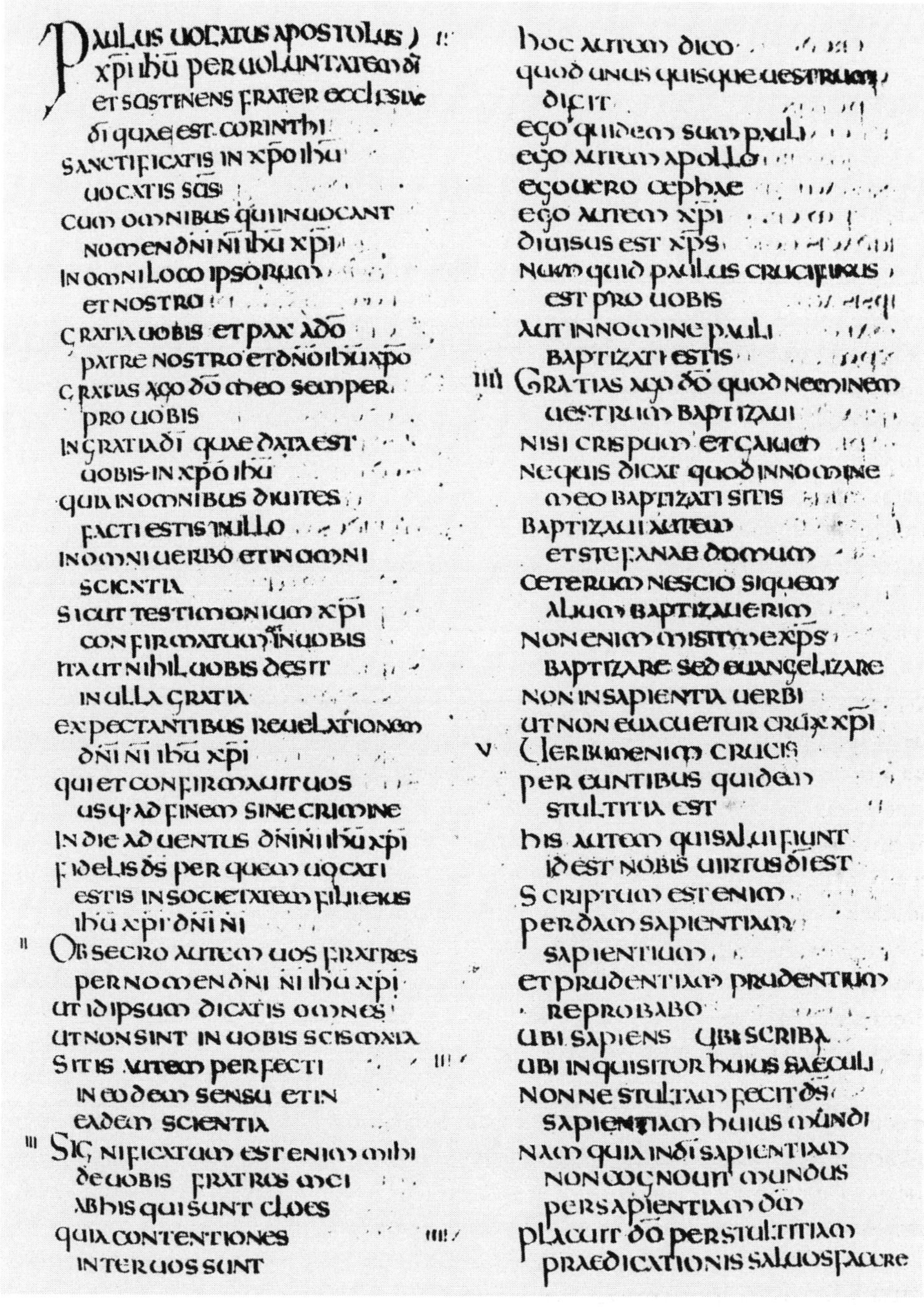

PAULUS UOCATUS APOSTOLUS
XPI IHU PER UOLUNTATEM DI
ET SOSTINENS FRATER ECCLESIAE
DI QUAE EST CORINTHI
SANCTIFICATIS IN XPO IHU
UOCATIS SCS
CUM OMNIBUS QUI INUOCANT
NOMEN DNI NI IHU XPI
IN OMNI LOCO IPSORUM
ET NOSTRO
GRATIA UOBIS ET PAX A DO
PATRE NOSTRO ET DNO IHU XPO
GRATIAS AGO DO MEO SEMPER
PRO UOBIS
IN GRATIA DI QUAE DATA EST
UOBIS IN XPO IHU
QUIA IN OMNIBUS DIUITES
FACTI ESTIS IN ILLO
IN OMNI UERBO ET IN OMNI
SCIENTIA
SICUT TESTIMONIUM XPI
CONFIRMATUM IN UOBIS
ITA UT NIHIL UOBIS DESIT
IN ULLA GRATIA
EXPECTANTIBUS REUELATIONEM
DNI NI IHU XPI
QUI ET CONFIRMAUIT UOS
USQ AD FINEM SINE CRIMINE
IN DIE ADUENTUS DNI NI IHU XPI
FIDELIS DS PER QUEM UOCATI
ESTIS IN SOCIETATEM FILII EIUS
IHU XPI DNI NI
OBSECRO AUTEM UOS FRATRES
PER NOMEN DNI NI IHU XPI
UT IDIPSUM DICATIS OMNES
UT NON SINT IN UOBIS SCISMATA
SITIS AUTEM PERFECTI
IN EODEM SENSU ET IN
EADEM SCIENTIA
SIG NIFICATUM EST ENIM MIHI
DE UOBIS FRATRES MEI
AB HIS QUI SUNT CLOES
QUIA CONTENTIONES
INTER UOS SUNT

HOC AUTEM DICO
QUOD UNUS QUISQUE UESTRUM
DICIT
EGO QUIDEM SUM PAULI
EGO AUTEM APOLLO
EGO UERO CEPHAE
EGO AUTEM XPI
DIUISUS EST XPS
NUM QUID PAULUS CRUCIFIXUS
EST PRO UOBIS
AUT IN NOMINE PAULI
BAPTIZATI ESTIS
GRATIAS AGO DO QUOD NEMINEM
UESTRUM BAPTIZAUI
NISI CRISPUM ET CAIUM
NE QUIS DICAT QUOD IN NOMINE
MEO BAPTIZATI SITIS
BAPTIZAUI AUTEM
ET STEFANAE DOMUM
CETERUM NESCIO SI QUEM
ALIUM BAPTIZAUERIM
NON ENIM MISIT ME XPS
BAPTIZARE SED EUANGELIZARE
NON IN SAPIENTIA UERBI
UT NON EUACUETUR CRUX XPI
UERBUM ENIM CRUCIS
PEREUNTIBUS QUIDEM
STULTITIA EST
HIS AUTEM QUI SALUI FIUNT
ID EST NOBIS UIRTUS DI EST
SCRIPTUM EST ENIM
PERDAM SAPIENTIAM
SAPIENTIUM
ET PRUDENTIAM PRUDENTIUM
REPROBABO
UBI SAPIENS UBI SCRIBA
UBI INQUISITOR HUIUS SAECULI
NONNE STULTAM FECIT DS
SAPIENTIAM HUIUS MUNDI
NAM QUIA IN DI SAPIENTIAM
NON COGNOUIT MUNDUS
PER SAPIENTIAM DM
PLACUIT DO PER STULTITIAM
PRAEDICATIONIS SALUOS FACERE

A page from the *Codex Amiatinus*. *Wikimedia Commons*

Well-wrought this wall: Wierds broke it.
The stronghold burst ...

Snapped rooftrees, towers fallen,
the work of the Giants, the stonesmiths,
mouldereth.

(*The Earliest English Poems*, translated by Michael Alexander, p. 28)

This short extract in the Old English illustrates some of the key metrical and alliterative devices that gives Anglo-Saxon its particular recitative power. Nowadays, poetry is a solitary pursuit, generally pursued by teenagers who need to get out more. Nothing could be further from the Anglo-Saxon scop, who was the voice and memory of his people. Speaking out loud in the hall, the one thing a poet couldn't afford to do was dry up. So Anglo-Saxon poets built up a stock of half lines that could be used to express essential ideas: for instance *gear-dagum*, *aer-dagum* and *eald-dagum* all mean 'a long time ago'. But note that these three ways of saying the same thing all begin with a different sound but continue with *d*, which brings us to the heart of Old English poetry. Poems were constructed of half lines, of varying numbers of syllables, but with four main words stressed. Each line was broken by a caesura in the middle, which may have been further accented on the lyre or drum. In its most basic form, the rhythm is:

Bang ...   Bang   :   Bang ... Crash

Generally, the first three stressed words alliterate, but the pattern was sometimes stripped down to just the first stressed word after the caesura alliterating with one of the stressed words in the preceding half line.

J.R.R. Tolkien, who was professor of Anglo-Saxon at Oxford University, peppers *The Lord of the Rings* with verse written in this Old English style. The Rohirrim, whom he explicitly modelled on the old Anglo-Saxons, in particular make use of the style:

Death in the morning and at day's ending
lords took and lowly. Long now they sleep
under grass in Gondor by the Great River.

(J.R.R. Tolkien, *The Return of the King*, p. 125)

Perhaps the finest surviving Old English poem is *The Dream of The Rood*, a perfect union of Christian message and Anglo-Saxon medium. The poem, in which a dreamer beholds Christ's cross and hears the cross speak to him, combines the riddling form familiar to Anglo-Saxons with a clear exposition of Christian doctrine: this was a poet in perfect command of the differing demands of his poetic form and religious subject. The poem must have been held in high regard in its day, since apart from the complete text in the Vercelli Book,[36] parts of it survive cut as runes into the Ruthwell Cross, an eighth-century freestanding cross, and inscribed into the reliquary called the Brussels Cross, made to hold fragments of the True Cross sent to Alfred the Great by Pope Marinus I in 884.

A page from the Vercelli book.
Wikimedia Commons

Beowulf shears off the head of Grendel

Beowulf. Open Library

This is tragically short commons from the work of a professional class of poets. In a culture where glory and renown were important, even vital, kings employed poets – or 'scops' to use the Anglo-Saxon word – whose job it was to tell tales and sing the praises of the king. The measure, of course, was whether the song lasted any longer than the king who'd commissioned it. And that probably depended as much on the skill of the scop as it did on the deeds of the king. So, even in Anglo-Saxon times, it paid rulers to employ the best eulogists, or spin doctors, as we'd call them today.

As for *Beowulf*, the consensus among scholars today is that it was a praise poem that the kings of East Anglia had written, probably in the eighth century, extolling the predecessors and ancestors of their royal house.

But apart from the music intrinsic to the rhythm of the words, the bards accompanied their recitals with instruments, notably drums and the Anglo-Saxon lyre, a form of the harp with around six strings (the lyre found at the Sutton Hoo burial had six strings). The lyre could either be plucked, like a modern harp, or strummed, like a guitar. We suspect that the audience would have enthusiastically joined in, singing and banging on the table.

Another important role of the storyteller was spreading news. In a society without media of any description and originally no written word, the storyteller would have spread news of births, marriages and deaths. A pivotal battle might happen 50 miles away, but news would only reach a community by word of mouth, perhaps long after the event. When a king died and was succeeded, the first a village knew of its new overlord was from the storytellers, who passed on the information. Thus, news gained a high currency and a person visiting a community would have the attention of all who lived there, eager for information from afar.

Taking it with you

Guli the Russian, a trader of the time, made a fortune from the thirst for foreign trinkets and exotic slaves. He traded around Britain and Ireland, through the Mediterranean and on as far as the Caspian Sea in the ninth century. Although he was called the Russian, Guli was in fact from Ireland, although of Viking stock – he earned his name from the Russian hat he wore – and, in an age when there were no banks, he found somewhere safe, portable and close to hand to store his wealth: his wife's body. She wore their accumulated wealth in jewellery and necklaces. A little later, in the tenth century, the Arab traveller Ahmad ibn Fadlan described the way Viking traders garlanded their women with their wealth.

> Each woman carries on her bosom a container made of iron, silver, copper, or gold, its size and substance depending on her man's wealth. Attached to the container is a ring carrying her knife which is also tied to her bosom. Round her neck she wears gold or silver rings; when a man amasses 10,000 dirhems he makes his wife one gold ring; when he has 20,000 he makes two; and so the woman gets a new ring for every 10,000 dirhems her husband acquires, and often a woman has many of these rings.
>
> (Johannes Brøndsted, *The Vikings* [transl. by Kalle Skov] p. 265)

RIDDLE ME THIS

In a primarily oral culture, and one with a lot of time to fill during the winter months, riddles passed much time and provided rich diversion in the king's hall and the monastic refectory. We have some examples of riddles, with subjects ranging from aspects of nature such as wind and sea and sun, to the close at hand: the bookworm that eats the words of the wise but learns nothing from his meal and the ox that breaks the ground when living (by pulling a plough) and binds the living when dead (oxhide was made into ties). However, the vast majority of Anglo-Saxon riddles, as with Anglo-Saxon poems and songs, has been lost to us over the years; either never recorded and forgotten when the last memory failed, or written down but lost to flame, decay or a scribe needing vellum to start a new book and scraping off an old sheet that no one was interested in anymore.

The riddles were in prose or poetry, and were often humorous. A good riddle could keep discussion and argument going in the hall for an evening or longer, with various proposals for its solution being tried out and rejected or modified through the night. The riddler, and no doubt the audience too, expected the solution to be greeted with an exclamation of delight. It was like the punchline of a joke, with the solution unveiled with all the drama of a stage magician and the audience oohing and aahing as they saw how the pieces snugly fitted together. Riddling was an art and a science, demanding elegance of expression, precision in language and an almost forensic attention to detail. The surviving Anglo-Saxon riddles go some way to revealing one of the key differences between the past culture of Northumbria and the culture today, and that's what we're going on to in the next section.

DEDICATED FOLLOWERS OF FASHION

Anyone watching a film set in medieval times would be forgiven for thinking that people then lived in a monochromatic world in which it was perpetually winter. Everything is grey, gloomy and drained of colour. If there's one thing we'd like anyone reading this chapter to take away with them, it's this: it wasn't like that. Early medieval people (in fact, all medieval people) loved colour, and splashed it around as much as they possibly could: on their clothes, on their houses, in their books and probably on their bodies too. We tend to think of the medieval period as black-beamed houses and whitewashed walls, as if the Tudors lived four centuries before their time and the iconoclasm of the Reformation had not changed tastes utterly. But if we could go back in time and approach a medieval town it would appear more *Balamory*[37] than Stratford-upon-Avon.

People had learned how to extract dyes from nature – the brighter the better – from stones, from plants, from almost anything. Lincoln green came from weld (*Reseda luteola*), a tall-stemmed biennial plant that likes waste ground. Madder (*Rubia tinctoria*) produced red dyes and woad (*Isatis tinctoria*) blue. Lapis lazuli from the Badakhshan region of Afghanistan was imported for the intense blue it imparted to inks and dyes. To help dyes set, early medieval dyers used an easily procurable liquid: urine.

Beauty and beautification was a serious business for Anglo-Saxons, and for the men as much as the women. In fact, nothing was more likely to get these psychopathic peacocks combing their beards and shining their torcs than the prospect of battle. The sight of men going into battle would have been as impressive for the vivid colours on display as for the flashing weapons: gold and silver jewellery glinting in the sun, buckles shining, colourful cloaks, yellow leggings, tunics woven in plaid, gaily painted shields. But aside from the impact of colour, styles and designs told of affiliations to tribes, lineages and localities, rather as modern people wearing a football team's shirt advertise their support for the club, but still maintain individuality.

In fact, it's just as well these men were so strong, otherwise they'd have been weighed down by all the jewellery they wore when going into battle: bracelets, armlets, earrings, pendants, buckles. Pretty much anything that could be tipped or trimmed with gold or silver would have been so furnished.

Great ingenuity was exercised in producing the best effects from the available materials. For instance, garnets were cut thin. Then a thin sheet of gold was stuck onto the back of these jewels, but this gold foil was stamped with a microscopic pyramidal shape, just 0.3mm high, that cast light in all directions. Its effect on the garnet was to set the deep, rather dull red of the jewel on fire, as if it burned from within. The sun, or torchlight, shining on these jewels would have scattered everywhere, casting brilliant highlights into dazzled watching eyes.

While only the nobility could afford fancy jewellery and gold and silver, the peasants were probably just as keen to brighten their lives: naturally derived dyes could brighten clothes and dwellings, flowers and foliage brought colour and perfume within. Although peasants worked hard, there were periods of the year, when the crops were sown and growing, that the daily toil eased and they could enjoy some time spent beautifying home and person. Just because people were poor didn't mean that they couldn't show off to their neighbours. Copper and bronze jewellery, and gilded jewellery, were commonplace and probably affordable for all but the poorest. In fact, the slow decline of the Northumbrian kingdom can be charted through its jewellery: garnets, in particular, get smaller as the kingdom passes its zenith and enters its decline. At its peak, the garnets were large, precious and from far away, having been mined in Sri Lanka and India. But as we come forward in time, the garnets become smaller and are more often imported from Portugal. This is probably one of the reasons for backing garnets with stamped gold, since this treatment could take a fairly mediocre gemstone and make it special.

The Laws of Duelling

It might seem strange that in a society as violent as Northumbria – it took over 100 years and twelve monarchs before a king managed to die of natural causes – something as savage as duelling would have rules and regulations. But duelling was subject to strict customs that were not written down but codified by the stories of how people had duelled in the past. Any duellist who stepped outside the accepted boundaries of duelling etiquette would have been vilified – a dreadful fate in a society in which reputation was all. He ran the risk of not only being hunted as an outlaw, but worse, of being treated with unbridled scorn.

First of all, the combatants had to establish what sort of duel they were fighting. Duels began with small contests that continued until one or other of the contestants grew too tired to continue and gave in: there were three-shield fights, where the duellists each had three shields and when the last of the shields broke, the duel was over; there were duels fought until first blood flowed; and then there were duels to the death. However, duellists were not bound to keep to what had been agreed. It was perfectly possible for a duel to death to continue so long that both participants became so exhausted that they agreed to leave off the fight. It was not seen as dishonourable so long as both duellists agreed.

Before the duel an area the size of a cloak was usually pegged out as the fighting ground. Given that an ordinary duel could destroy three shields, it's clear that Anglo-Saxon swords were good at hacking through leather and wood. The fighting too was stylised, with a blow being given and then one accepted in what became a ritualised trial of strength rather than the no-holds-barred and frankly dirty fighting that took place in war, where any means would be used to get a man down and a sword in his guts. In the shield wall, a head butt or a kick to the groin was as useful and as usual as a sword thrust. Duels were different. They were public spectacles and it did a warrior no good to win at the expense of his reputation. In fact, warriors generally took care to ensure that they did not triumph as the result of their opponents' bad luck. In *Laxdæla Saga*, which was written in Iceland but reflects the similar culture of the Norse world, Kjartan Ólafsson's sword is bent during a duel. The combatants stop fighting, talk about the matter and the man with the straight sword tells Kjartan to straighten the sword before they resume fighting. In *Kormáks Saga*, one of the fighters, wielding a sword that has become blunt, complains to his adversary that his sword is rubbish and always has been rubbish. The other chap says that his father has a good sword, so they stop for a while, he goes to borrow his father's sword, lends it to his foe to replace his blunt weapon, and they start hacking away again!

The weapons employed were normally sword and shield, but some duels were fought with thrown spears, although these presumably took place at a longer range than the breadth of a cloak.

In a world without courts or police, and where every freeman was armed, duels were one way of resolving disputes. No doubt most arguments between the king's warriors were settled much the same way as we solve things today: by talking. But if an argument escalated, duelling provided a carefully calibrated way of resolving matters. And in a society that accepted fate, whether that be through the Norns[38] or by God's will, then the winner of a duel was vindicated. In this view, it wasn't that might made right, rather that right was proved by might. But sometimes if a duel was obviously mismatched then the weaker party could select a proxy to fight on his behalf, so it wasn't always a simple case of the strongest winning.

Duelling was the pastime and province of the nobility, but kings in general didn't engage in the practice. Kings occasionally offered to engage in single combat rather than pitching their armies into battle, but this seemed to be more a matter of form, since there are no records of this actually occurring. Some kings, such as Harold Hardrada, the legendarily tough king of Norway, probably would have been more than happy to engage in single combat, but frankly you'd have been an idiot to take him up on the offer!

Oh, and the answer to the riddle that begins the chapter: an onion. What else could it have been?

Source books

There are four, just four, main sources for surviving Anglo-Saxon poetry. These are the Vercelli Book, which is in the Basilica of St Andrew in northern Italy. It's an unlikely spot for a book of Anglo-Saxon prose and poetry, but the location may be due to Vercelli having housed a hospice for English pilgrims. It contains 23 sermons and six poems, most notably *The Dream of the Rood*. The Junius or Caedmon codex is in the Bodleian Library in Oxford. It contains Anglo-Saxon poetic retellings of the biblical books of Genesis, Exodus and Daniel, and a narrative poem telling of the fall of Satan and Christ's harrowing of hell and temptations in the desert. The Exeter Book, the largest collection of surviving Anglo-Saxon poetry, is in Exeter Cathedral, naturally. It's the source of such poems as *The Ruin, The Wanderer* and *The Seafarer*, particularly vivid examples of the pathos that underlay the Anglo-Saxon worldview. Finally, the Nowell Codex in the British Library has the only version of *Beowulf*, plus some prose works including King Alfred's translation of St Augustine's *Soliloquies* and the rather marvellous *Wonders of the East*, with its tales of the marvels to be found in far-off lands, including dragons, phoenix and strange races of humans, such as cannibals and people with ears so big they used them as blankets at night.

A picture from the Junius (Caedmon) codex. *Wikimedia Commons*

Theophilus Presbyter's guide to garnets, as employed by Paul Gething

Theophilus Presbyter was a:

> German monk and writer of the 12th century. He is known for his De Diversis Artibus (*c.* 1110–
> 40), a thorough account of the techniques of almost all the known crafts of the early 12th century.
> From his writings it can be deduced that he was a practicing craftsman of the Benedictine order.
>
> (*Encyclopaedia Britannica* online)

Theophilus is the closest thing we have to a first-hand source on how goldsmithing was actually done and how precious materials were actually treated in the medieval period. As he wrote centuries after the golden age of Northumbria, it may seem odd to reference him, but techniques and technology changed so little in the intervening years that his testimony is still very pertinent. He wrote on a selection of arts and crafts, from making stained-glass windows, through blacksmithing to how to make a jewelled chalice from gold and silver. His testimony is invaluable when studying ancient crafts.

Using Theophilus as my guide, I decided to polish some garnets. I reasoned that it would be challenging, difficult, time consuming and a process that required specialist skill. The accounts of modern gem polishing indicate that it is mechanised for a reason: it's hugely time consuming. I thought I would have a go anyhow.

Theophilus recommends using 'tenax' to fix gems to a 'dop stick' (a dop stick is a short piece of wood that allows the gemstone to be manipulated more easily and with less chance of dropping it). The stick is used to grind the gem against progressively finer grindstones until the shape is achieved. Then a surface of lead is prepared from crushed tiles mixed with saliva. The gem is polished against the lead slab until it shines. Finally, a goatskin is loaded with the same preparation and a final polishing is carried out until the gem becomes bright. (Theophilus, *On Divers Arts*, p. 386)

So, that's what I did. In the end, I spent days polishing and shaping garnets, using the methods described above by Theophilus.

Herewith some observations on garnet cutting and polishing, medieval style:

– Spending two hours polishing a garnet and then dropping it on the ground can be quite vexing. You won't find it again.
– Use strong glue to prevent point one becoming an irritating reality.
– Remove modern notions of time from your mind. Polishing takes hours and hours of painstaking, repetitive work. It is strangely enjoyable though.
– Polishing stones gives one hours to think. It is meditative and could easily be seen as a way of communing with God: a physical manifestation of the monastic relationship to the Supreme Being. I can understand how it would appeal to monks in the early medieval.
– While medieval jewellery making was skilled work, I have come to realise that the basics can be quickly picked up. It seems likely that apprentices, novices and even children were employed to do the groundwork. The absence of any evidence for mechanised stone cutting implies that it was all done manually, and therefore slowly.

8

FOOD

Why should we be fated to
Do nothing but brood
On food,
Magical food,
Wonderful food,
Marvellous food,
Fabulous food,
Beautiful food,
Glorious food!

(Lionel Bart, *Oliver!*)

In Northumbria, the daily bread was soup: a boiled pottage of barley or wheat, boiled up with pulses or legumes, that was thicker than minestrone but not as thick as porridge. Barley was the main crop grown, along with root vegetables, and wheat became important later in the history of Northumbria.

Barley and wheat are members of the grass family, and to the modern, urban eye they look very similar. The grain harvested from barley and wheat can be used to make bread, of course, but it can also be fermented into beer, which was both a major source of calories for the people of Northumbria and a way of ensuring that their liquid intake didn't kill them.

Boar town

The Viking name for York, 'Jorvik', comes from the English word *Eoforwic*, which means 'boar town'. There is speculation that the old English name for York arose because the city was producing large numbers of pigs. However, etymological speculation is speculative, and an alternative explanation is that boars were symbols of masculinity and power. All known early Anglo-Saxon helmets had boar crests or symbols, so the name could as easily be a reference to Eoforwic being a gathering place for warriors. Another possibility is that York takes its name from the old word for the River Foss, Ure. Hence Jorvik may be Urevic, a town on the Ure.

Working the Land

In the high medieval period, Northumbrian farmers worked the land in a rotation system and we have no reason to suppose that they had changed their cultivation practices since the early medieval period. So every third year, a field was left fallow. Note that this doesn't mean that the field remained untended, but rather that it was set aside to grow hay to provide winter fodder for animals rather than producing a crop for people. This allowed the nutrients in the soil necessary for a good crop of barley or vegetables to be replenished.

Farmers ploughed the land with a heavy plough that was first introduced into the country by the Romans and that remained essentially unchanged for over 1,500 years. The Roman heavy plough had taken over from the ard, which was basically just a spike dragged through the ground, but had been the principal ploughing tool in Britain until the arrival of the Romans. The Roman heavy plough turned over the soil as well as breaking it up, thus aerating it and bringing new nutrients to the surface. Because it was shaped and, well, heavy, the Roman heavy plough allowed heavier, clay soils that had previously been unworkable to be brought into production.

Driving and guiding a team of oxen over the fields was hard, physical work. Oxen were the preferred beasts for pulling ploughs and generally performing hard labour since the collar harness had not reached Europe during the Northumbrian heyday. Before the adoption of the collar harness (which was invented in China during the fifth century AD), horses were hampered by having to wear a harness that effectively choked them the harder they pulled. Oxen, with their different anatomy, were not so hampered, so they could wear a yoke and pull a plough or cart without choking themselves.

To replenish the soil, Northumbrian farmers grew crops like clover and hay in the third year, as well as putting the field out to pasture so that the grazing animals could help to restore nutrient levels with their manure. A field put out to pasture could also provide plenty of forage food suitable for human consumption, particularly in a thin year. Plants like dandelions, clover and buttercups can all be eaten if necessary. In the earlier part of the Northumbrian period there was plenty of wild land that could be foraged for foods well beyond the usual blackberries and crab apples: mushrooms, nettles, haws, sloes and even acorns. With the rise of monasticism and the apportioning of land to abbeys, and the sequestration of more land by the king, access to wild land became harder, although ancient laws of usage served to ensure that customary uses endured. In the high medieval period this became formalised as the right of pannage, which continued the right of villagers to graze their pigs in oak woodland that belonged to the king or Church, but that they had customarily used to help fatten their pigs during autumn's acorn fall.

ANIMALS

Pigs were the most important source of protein for most people in Northumbria. Pigs were raised anywhere and everywhere, and just about every family kept one or more swine. Pigs are versatile beasts that can be kept in a variety of situations and places. It's worth bearing in mind that the pigs of the time were not the pink, rather indolent beasts of today, but big, aggressive animals, well able to fend for themselves in the wild and to forage in villages and hamlets.

Pig rearing is male chauvinism in reverse. Sows are kept, bred and fattened, so that they produce new piglets and more meat. Male pigs, apart from the occasional fortunate boar tasked with servicing the local sows, are slaughtered for meat as soon as they are big enough.

The pigs themselves were kept in backyards, left to root around in harvested fields, and were fed whatever scraps and waste the family had left over. Pigs will eat practically anything, so they make ideal mobile waste-disposal units. It's a practice that continues today in many parts of the world. When the pig was slaughtered, every part of the animal was used, from trotters to blood to head. In fact, the only part of the animal that couldn't be completely used were its bones, so pig bones routinely turn up in large amounts in any archaeological excavations of houses from Northumbria and the wider Anglo-Saxon world.

Apart from pork, Northumbrians could get protein from eggs, be they chicken, duck or goose, and from butter and cheese.[39]

Cattle were widely kept too, with many families having a cow, but cattle were significantly more expensive than pigs so poorer people were not able to afford them. The cattle were a local variant of the European short horn that was on its way to becoming ubiquitous. Cattle were selectively bred, the females for reproduction and milking; the males mostly slaughtered for meat at a young age, but with selected larger males kept, gelded and trained as oxen. After the adoption of Christianity and the proliferation of monasteries, there was further selection, in that cattle were bred for vellum, the material used for books. For the best vellum, the cattle were particularly well cared for, since blemishes and scratches that would normally be invisible on the animal are accentuated when the skin is turned into vellum, rendering it unsuitable for anything but scrap vellum. For instance, a cow rubbing against a thorn bush and breaking the skin would produce a blemish when the skin is processed, even if the scratch had healed before the animal was slaughtered. The Lindisfarne Gospels required over 200 cattle for their production, but maybe 220 or 230 had to be slaughtered to get blemish-free skin.

Oxen, which are gelded cattle selected for their size and strength, were the main labouring animals, pulling ploughs and carts and doing the other physical tasks that were beyond human strength. Of course, at the end of their lives, the oxen were slaughtered for meat and leather and all the other products that Anglo-Saxon ingenuity allowed.

The best sort of farm animal was tough, could look after itself and required little feeding while producing a useful yield of food. The goat excelled in all this. Famously able to eat plants that any other animal would turn their nose up at, goats can largely be left to look after themselves and they still produce milk and meat – an ideal early medieval domestic animal. The horn was also used, although we can't always tell what for. At Saviour Gate in York, Paul excavated a site that yielded thousands of the inner casings of horns. It's clear that horn was being processed here on an almost industrial scale in the ninth century, but the purpose remains speculative. One possibility is that the horn is translucent and becomes soft and pliable when boiled to remove the outer layer, so these could have been used as a window or lantern covering, an early substitute for the ultra-expensive glass.

Archaeology is mute, for remains have no voices, but sometimes their circumstances give them a history. This was the case in the excavations at Saviour Gate. The archaeologists found a tool kit in a box, wrapped in a bag and put in a bucket with a lead container on the outside, that had been dropped into a well with a dead cow pushed into the well to seal it. It's hard not to believe that a craftsman in ninth-century York, on seeing the Viking boats drawing up on the shore, collected his most valuable tools, dropped them out of sight and then contrived to put off any marauders investigating further by poisoning the well. The fact that archaeologists found the tools over 1,000 years later suggests that the plan was successful, though the fact that the tools were never reclaimed makes one fear for the fate of the man who hid them so well.

Sheep were another self-reliant animal that could largely be left to feed and look after itself, with children detailed to keep an eye on them where necessary in order to protect the flock from wolves and other animals. Agropastoralism, taking animals up to the high ground for the summer and then bringing them down to lower ground in the winter, is a way of life that stretches back into prehistory. Along with goats, sheep provided the primary products of meat and skin and horn as well as secondary products such as fleece and milk. Moving into the high medieval period, Britain was renowned for its wool, and this production had already begun in the early medieval.

Horses were almost exclusively used for riding for most of the Northumbrian period. Riding a horse was intimately linked with status: a rider literally looks down on his fellows. The inheritance laws stated that a percentage of a person's estate should pass to the king, and a man or woman's worth was often stated in terms of horses. Beowulf was given eight horses by Hrothgar, which was riches beyond measure. It's a minor mystery of the time quite why horses were so valued. Horses were not used for battle since the stirrup had not yet been popularised. Warriors might ride to battle, but once they got there they dismounted and joined the shield wall, while the horses were tethered behind the lines. In fact, despite the rather frightening image of medieval knights in line charging abreast with lances lowered, a shield wall that stood firm would have been safe enough – a horse will not run directly into an obstacle.

From little acorns

Pigs traditionally ate acorns, but it is possible for people to eat them as well. They're not the most palatable of foods but in times of dearth, acorns represented a viable alternative food source. To make them edible, Northumbrians ground the nuts and made them into flour, then washed the flour and dried it. Once it was dry it could be baked and turned into an acceptable, if not particularly pleasant, loaf.

LAND USE

The landscape that we think of nowadays as typically English – a patchwork of hedge-defined fields and small woods – didn't exist. The land was wilder and more wooded, with much simply left uncultivated, and the field system was different, defined by strips belonging to different families. Each village or hamlet owned and worked a number of large open fields, but these fields were split into strips that were owned by different families, with their holdings fairly evenly distributed through village land. This served to ensure that everybody had access to the best land and had to share the less productive fields, although relative wealth could be assessed by how many strips each family owned. People also owned land of their own, or rented out strips from a landowner. As the land settled upon monasteries increased in area, it became reasonable for an abbey to allow peasants to work some of the land in exchange for a tithe of the food produced; that way, land that was beyond the abbey's capacity to bring into production brought in a return. The great difficulty faced by peasant farmers was inheritance: a small holding that might support one family perfectly became thoroughly inadequate if it had to be split evenly between the father's surviving and inheriting sons and their families.

The fields themselves were generally ploughed by oxen using heavy ploughs or were dug in the ridge and furrow system, which can still be seen in some fields today that have been used for pasture and have not been ploughed since medieval times. A ridge and furrow field looks like corrugated iron, with parallel ridges and troughs stretching along its length; the distance between the ridges is indicative of when the fields were worked: as a rule of thumb, the narrower the gap, the older the field. Roman fields usually have ridges about 3m apart, while in medieval fields the gap is usually 5–8m. Modern-day Northumberland, being the most sparsely populated county in England, has many fields where the medieval ridge and furrow pattern is still clearly visible – the best time to spot these fields is when the sun is low and shadows clearly reveal the alternating pattern of ridge and trough.

The ridge and furrow system was often dug rather than ploughed, with the furrows being dug out and the spoil producing the ridges. The ridge and furrow system can be ploughed in, but is the result of many seasons' ploughing in the idiosyncratic long shallow S shape that means that the oxen do not have to do tight turns. The difference in height produced different drainages, thus allowing the medieval peasant to hedge his bets by planting crops along the ridge and in the furrow. If the season proved dry, then the seeds sown in the wetter furrow would be assured of enough water to grow; if the year was wet, then the freely draining ridges gave their crop an advantage. Essentially, medieval peasants were creating different microclimates by this method of cultivating land.

hUNTING ANÒ FISHING

Fishing was a specialised profession, including sub-divisions of river and sea fishermen, and the even-more specialised eel men. A bream or trout would no doubt have been a welcome addition to the pot whether it was bought or traded from fishermen or caught by a family member. Hunting, on the other hand, was very much a pastime of the nobility. Trapping and snaring of hares, wild birds and other small animals had the double benefit of protecting crops and providing some extra protein, but the hunting of larger animals and birds was something done with hounds, putting it outside the purvue of most people.

The ÒAILy BREAÒ

The typical day's diet consisted of a coarse bread with some kind of pottage made from barley or wheat, with leeks, onions or a similar vegetable thrown into the pot, some dairy produce, either cheese or milk, and to wash it all down, large volumes of weak beer. Meat was generally only eaten on high days and holy days, and of course the Church required people to abstain from meat on Fridays. There was some fruit in season, such as crab apples and plums, but nothing approaching the year-round availability we take for granted today. Apples were the most reliable and widely available source of fruit, with the added benefit that surplus production could be turned into cider. Coprolites excavated in York show that people in the Northumbrian period ate bullaces (wild plums) whole, since the fruit passed through their digestive system and emerged intact at the other end. We've got much sweeter tastes now, and bullace is largely considered inedible although it makes good jam.

Wine was available in small quantities, but since it was imported it was an expensive drink and was thus confined to richer people. Proving that even if you can't take it with you, people will still try to do so, there are allusions to and representations of wine in richer graves: cauldrons from which wine would be shared communally. Mead, the alcohol derived from honey, was what people used to get drunk. Beer was made, to use the modern parlance, in premium and low-alcohol varieties. Strong beer was the stuff of feasts in the lord's hall and holy days for the lesser folk, small beer quenched the thirst of labourers in the field and rich folk on their travels. Having been boiled and fermented, small beer was free of cholera and the other bacteria that lived in polluted drinking water. Beer was carried out to the fields in pottery pitchers.

It was a rather monotonous although quite nutritious diet that perhaps differs most notably from our own in its lack of sugar. The only available sweetener was honey.

High-energy fruit bars, Anglo-Saxon style

In further proof that there's nothing new under the sun, the Anglo-Saxons had their own version of today's high-energy fruit bars. They took crab apples and other unpalatable fruits and heated them in a pot with some honey so that the naturally present pectin made the fruit start to gel. The product was then laid on a level rock to be heated and dried by the sun, creating a flat layer of concentrated, edible fruit that would keep all winter. This fruit leather made an ideal travelling food as it could be rolled up and popped in a pack, and then popped into the mouth to provide an instant energy rush.

SALT

Salt has been one of the constants of human history, being essential for preserving and flavouring food. In Northumbria, salt was traded extensively as well as being manufactured locally. With access to the sea – and Northumbria was not short of coastline – it's a fairly straightforward business to construct a brine pit. At Bamburgh there's a big pit by the tide-line that was lined with clay and had extensive burning around it. It was probably used to extract salt from salt water. The aim of these pits was to collect seawater and then get the sun to do the legwork of evaporation, leaving the salt residue to be harvested, although the burning around the Bamburgh pit indicates that the process could be hurried. Traded rock salt came from as far away as the Middle East and North Africa. Although it could be used to flavour food, its key use was to preserve food for winter or before travelling. In the days before refrigeration, effectively preventing food from rotting was the difference between starving and eating through the winter. Other ways to preserve food included smoking and pickling in brine.

ENOUGH TO EAT

Teeth are important to archaeologists. When excavated and analysed, teeth can tell us all sorts of things about the person who once smiled with them: the wear patterns tell us about the sort of diet he or she consistently ate and the rings of enamel that are laid down annually in teeth indicate whether the person had enough to eat. So layers that are constant and roughly equal indicate that the person had a good diet. One of the key indicators of wealth for bodies excavated in Northumbria is the presence of these equal rings of enamel in the teeth. In poor people, there are intervals where there is no growth in the teeth, so there must have been times when they were either eating a very poor diet or simply starving. Typically this pattern of low or no tooth growth might occur 10 or 12 times in a lifetime, indicating that while hard times were not constant they were not uncommon either. This does not necessarily indicate a completely failed harvest; more likely there was a harvest but its yield was low, so the person had to make up his or her diet with food that could be eaten but was not very nutritious – the pottage became thinner, with fewer vegetables and pulses, low-calorie plants were foraged from the countryside to bulk out the pot, the beer was watered down. Among the plants scavenged were the tubers of bulrushes, which were roasted – they taste a bit like sweet potato. If things got really bad, people ate oysters. It's one of those curious reversals of history, that a food that is now considered a sign of affluence was consumed by the very poorest in Northumbria. Shell middens, in the early medieval and high medieval periods, are almost always associated with poor areas and poor people.

High-status people had consistently good tooth growth, as did monks. So while monastic law laid down fasting and abstinence, the extensive lands attached to most monasteries ensured a good year-round diet for its inhabitants.

At Bamburgh, there is evidence of people eating cranes, which were probably hunted, as well as sea life such as porpoises and sturgeon; in a time when a significant proportion of the population knew what it felt like to go hungry, pretty well anything that could be eaten would be eaten. However, on the table of the king, variety and novelty were markers of prestige.

Work for idle hands

Wool was ideal for tablet weaving, which was a perfect idle-time occupation, like knitting. Tablet weaving uses a number of small cards (made in Anglo-Saxon times from bone, wood or leather) with holes in them, through which the weft is passed and woven. It produces narrow textiles like belts and trim, but allows more variation in pattern than a normal loom. Tablet weaving is a creative but mechanical occupation, well suited to winter evenings and dim light.

Tablet for tablet weaving.
Wikimedia Commons

9

TECHNOLOGY

Any sufficiently advanced technology is indistinguishable from magic.

(Arthur C. Clarke, *Profiles of the Future*)

There are almost as many definitions of technology as there are ways to change a lightbulb, but we're going with the idea that a technology is something, be it a tool or a method, that allows people to do something that they wouldn't otherwise be able to do. It's a pretty wide definition, taking in things as diverse as domesticating animals and finding your way by the stars as well as the more obvious wheel and fire. For this chapter, however, we're mainly going to look at material stuff, such as iron and stone and the ways the Northumbrians used them, rather than more abstract technologies.

what technologies did the Northumbrians have available to them?

When considering the types of technology that the Northumbrians used, it's important to remember that they did not have access to all the technologies of the preceding Roman civilisation in Britain. The Anglo-Saxons were a mainly agrarian and rural people, and while living in small communities does not necessarily imply a lack of technology, it does make the spread and cross-pollination of ideas more difficult. While Northumbria was a large kingdom, intellectually it didn't approach the accumulated mental capital of the Roman Empire. The fundamental difference lies in the respective societies' intellectual cultures. The Roman Empire was acquisitive: it absorbed useful ideas in much the same way as it absorbed wheat from Africa, tin from Britain and slaves from everywhere. So when the Romans came up against someone who defeated them in battle, they would withdraw, regroup, adopt the most useful of the technologies, techniques and tactics of their enemies, and come back and beat them. The Romans were the historical antecedents of the Borg in *Star Trek: The Next Generation* – and rather than SPQR,[40] their standards might as well have been inscribed 'You will be assimilated' and 'Resistance is futile', the Borg's imperial catchphrases. The empire became the flux that melted together the peoples and cultures of the Mediterranean and north-west Europe. Take the garrison of Hadrian's Wall as an example – it was manned by soldiers from places as far-flung as Syria and Romania.

But when the empire collapsed, its successor kingdoms, realms, duchies and poxy little pirate princedoms became, of necessity, much more insular. When the Anglians conquered and settled Northumbria, the reference zone of the inhabitants shrank to the lands and peoples surrounding the North Sea. The nature of travel also altered, changing from the relatively large-scale movements of people necessitated by the redeployment of formations of the Roman Army and trade that was designed to feed, clothe and keep entertained an imperial city of a million inhabitants, to a much more individual affair. That's not to say the Northumbrians weren't travellers – some among them were indefatigable tourists, traders and pilgrims – but to acknowledge that travel was pitched at a different scale and sometimes oriented towards different ends. For instance, the great Northumbrian and Anglo-Saxon missionary outpouring to their separated and pagan brethren in northern Germany that took place in the seventh and eighth centuries was generally a one-way journey: the missionaries set forth but seldom returned to their own land.

Another consequence of the breakdown of the empire was the hoarding of technological secrets: any small kingdom that happened to have acquired a particularly skilled swordsmith was not going to broadcast to potential enemies the secrets of forging a pattern-welded sword. But once knowledge is concentrated and secreted in such a way, it becomes much more vulnerable. If there is only one person left who knows how to make fire arrows, and he dies through illness, accident or an unfortunate run-in with the king, then that knowledge goes with him. Thus, in the aftermath of the Roman Empire, much of its everyday technology was simply lost. What was retained was generally conserved, with few improvements made over a long period of time. So the heavy plough that the Romans introduced to Britain was retained, essentially unchanged, until the sixteenth century.

Therefore most of the technologies employed by the Northumbrians were essentially Roman, with some adaptations for the new conditions of the kingdom. In particular, the materials required for most crafts and technologies had to be acquired locally, rather than being imported from the farther reaches of the Empire. The caveat to this is that Northumbria did indeed have far-flung trade links (see the chapter on trade for more information on this), but this trade was mostly of luxury, prestige items that would not have travelled far outside the immediate environs of the king and his retainers. We surmise that the people involved in this long-distance trade might have developed a very different sense of identity to the intense local feelings displayed by most people at this time: travelling widely, seldom returning to any base, it's possible that their greatest allegiance might well have been to their immediate kith and kin, and the other people involved in their trading networks.

IRON

Iron was a key component of many of the tools, weapons and implements used by the Northumbrians, so the first question to answer is where did they obtain their iron? The answer appears to be, with some difficulty. To make iron you need iron ore, which is then smelted, and (reasonably) pure iron separated from the slag. But there are very few sources of iron ore in Northumbria. The most ubiquitous source of iron ore was bog ore, which is

Charcoal preparation using child labour (just like the Anglo-Saxons!). *Paul Gething*

not found in toilets but in swamps. Where rain leaches through certain types of vegetation and soil, it leaves iron 'pan' in its wake, which forms a deposit that slowly aggregates. For bog ore to form, there needs to be a thin layer of free-draining topsoil and an underlying clay. Rainwater drains through the topsoil then sits in a layer on top of the clay. Organic material drains through the topsoil into the water, but can't decay properly in the anaerobic conditions produced by the layer of water, and so peat starts to form. The peat creates a hard crust on top of the clay and it's here that bog ore starts to develop.

A narrow valley with peat at the bottom of it quite often contains bog ore, so a skilled prospector will have a good idea of where to pan for it. The great thing about this source of iron is that with enough rain (not usually a problem in Northumbria) it will renew itself every 15–20 years. Given the long time span between crops, we surmise that the lore of where to find good bog ore was passed down through families, from grandfather to father to son, with the old man out on a ramble with his grandson passing a waterlogged valley and pointing into its depths with his spear butt, telling the boy 'Your father and I dug up enough bog ore here to buy three pigs when he was a little older than you are today, and I reckon it'll be ripe for you to dig there with your dad in a few years' time.' Bog ore can provide very good-quality iron but it is a diffuse source. A lot of peat has to be dug to get sufficient bog ore for a sword or a plough.

Although bog ore was probably the main source of locally produced iron, the mines in Rosedale and the foreshore at Staithes were probably more concentrated sources of iron ore. Rosedale was certainly being mined in the high medieval period and we believe its iron would have been exploited in the early medieval period as well. At Staithes, the presence of iron is so obvious, with iron stone lying around pretty well everywhere and more of it constantly being exposed by an eroding coast, that it's impossible not to believe that it was mined here in the early medieval period.

Bog ore and these two mines apart, there were few other domestic sources of iron for the Northumbrian kingdom, so it would have had to trade for this key material. However, Roman technologies such as stamping mills and rolling mills that had allowed for large-scale, almost industrial production of iron had disappeared with the legions. We suspect that the lack of good-quality iron ore may have been one of the underlying causes for the decline of the Northumbrian kingdom, particularly as the size of war bands and armies increased in the eighth and ninth centuries, and thus the demand for iron weapons as well.

Making iron is a very different skill from blacksmithing. It's time consuming, and it needs good-quality ore and charcoal, clay, patience and skill. Making steel is even more difficult. Archaeologists employing reconstructed Anglo-Saxon technology have still not been able to consistently make good-quality iron. Yet the Anglo-Saxons did make some of the best iron and steel ever created.

So we believe that different groups of people made the iron and worked it, and that these technologies were jealously guarded and kept separate. Iron foundries were generally located on marginal land, away from other people, for reasons of both practicality – a foundry needed to be near its supply of charcoal and iron ore – and secrecy – myths and legends are replete with stories of divine blacksmiths and there was a natural awe attached to so fundamentally changing the nature of a substance. Looking at ethnographic parallels in societies where small-scale local iron smelting still occurs shows that the process is shrouded in mystery. Smelters and smiths tended to live outside the boundaries of normal society, and were regarded with a mixture of awe and suspicion by normal folk.

We believe that once the ore was smelted into iron, it was traded to blacksmiths, sometimes over long distances. There is very good-quality bog ore in Denmark and Norway, and given the trade links across the North Sea it seems likely that traders or even the smelters themselves would have taken good-quality iron to the Anglo-Saxon kingdoms to sell to blacksmiths, or trade for British specialities such as horses, hunting dogs, honey, high-quality craft items and slaves.

Iron was a precious commodity and not one to be thrown away when it could still be used. Steel was even more precious. Traditionally, steel is iron that has a carbon content greater than 1 per cent. The carbon changes the molecular structure of the iron, making it possible to sharpen it to a much keener edge, but this structural density has a down side – brittleness. Steel is often brittle and can snap in situations where iron would simply bend.

As an example of how precious steel was, excavations of the Viking settlement in Novgorod have revealed knives with cutting edges that are microscopically thin. These were knives that were used and used and used until there was virtually no steel left in them. The knives have a steel cutting edge sandwiched between iron – steel was at a premium in comparison to iron, so was used sparingly – and the knives were stropped and stropped and stropped until there was nothing left, a process that would have lasted years and possibly even decades. A knife might start off as a proper belt knife and then, as it wore away and became harder to sharpen, it could be relegated to hard craft, such as splitting lumps of wood into small kindling, a task that can often be done more easily with a knife than an axe.

The sword in the stone

Wootz is a type of steel that, when forged into swords, makes wonderfully hard and cutting blades. It's associated with India, where the method of casting it was discovered sometime before the birth of Christ, but the technology was lost around 1700. So far as we know, wootz steel was never made in Britain or indeed anywhere in Europe before the present day. So what do we make of the fact that some of the best-quality Anglian and Viking swords contain wootz? Before getting carried away, we have to bear in mind that the number of swords we're talking about is small, and these swords themselves only contain small amounts of wootz. So one possibility is that an intrepid trader brought a consignment of wootz from India in the early medieval period and sold it piecemeal to the blacksmiths who would give him the best prices for his superlative steel. But from this consignment of wootz, swords were made that have been found in Russia, Germany, Romania, Ireland, Britain, Norway and Sweden – basically all over Europe.

What's more, these swords have the name of their maker, Ulfberht, in raised letters on the blade. The name probably indicates a family group rather than an individual, and a trade that likely lasted over three or four generations, with its secrets being passed down from father to son. These swords were the best swords in the world at the time, and they remain supreme examples of the craft of swordmaking. Their quality arises from the combination of wootz steel with the swordmaking techniques developed by the Anglo-Saxons and their Continental brethren.

But of course, when people are willing to pay a huge premium to acquire an Ulfberht sword, it doesn't take long for other people to start forging them (in the sense of making cheap knockoffs). So we find today some swords, apparently marked as being made by the Ulfberht concern, that, shall we say, you wouldn't have wanted to trust your life to in battle. In short, they're rubbish. The name of the maker is often inlaid into the steel, but just as often with these poor-quality swords the name is misspelt. For instance, there should be a cross after the name, but sometimes it appears jumbled up with the letters. This suggests an illiterate swordsmith copying out marks he doesn't understand to trick his hopefully just as illiterate client into buying a 'genuine' Ulfberht sword. Since the only other way to tell that these swords were fake was for them to snap in battle suggests that Viking warriors really should have paid more attention in their reading lessons.

The mark of the maker: Ulfberht.

STONE

The Northumbrians, in common with the rest of the Anglo-Saxons, found Britain to be a land covered in monumental stone-built villas, forts, baths and, as a special bonus for the people up north, a very large wall. There was therefore no need to engage in the laborious, backbreaking work of quarrying when ready-cut blocks were there already. And sure enough, that's what the Northumbrians did. Just as Bob the Builder advocates, they reduced, reused and recycled Roman buildings and structures for their own use. Thankfully, at least so far as archaeologists and historians are concerned, the Anglo-Saxons were generally averse to using stone – wood was their favoured material – so more of Britain's Roman heritage has survived to the present day than might have done had they been more inclined to the hard stuff.

In a rather pleasing symmetry, Roman stone was mainly reused to make churches for the Roman Church: York Minster and the churches in Hexham and Ripon were all initially built with recycled stone.

As proof of the general Northumbrian lack of use for stone, there is little or no evidence of any quarrying in Northumbria in the heyday of the kingdom. Apart from churches and monasteries, stone is simply not used. Even when building fortifications, the Northumbrians rarely used stone. The stone wall at Bamburgh Castle was so unusual that it was mentioned in the historical sources. But even so, the castle – and remember this was the key stronghold for the most powerful realm in the land – was still mainly made of wood. Stone was limited to the castle's surrounding wall (which may have been surmounted with wooden ramparts), a church and possibly a great hall, which would have been made of stone, wood and thatch.

Houses, in what towns there were and in the countryside, were made of wattle and daub, or planks, with thatched roofs. In other words, mud, sticks and grass.

However, the Northumbrians did use stone to make crosses, and some still stand outside the oldest Northumbrian churches. But unfortunately, Henry VIII seemed to take against them, and many were destroyed during the Reformation.

One tantalising glimpse into Anglian stone comes from the sherd of stone found at Bamburgh Castle during Lord Armstrong's refurbishment in the nineteenth century. It has been interpreted as the arm of an eighth- or ninth-century throne that would have been used by the kings who lived at the castle. The fragment is intricately carved, but weathered by the erosion of centuries, as it stood outside in the West Ward for hundreds of years. Using this remnant as a template, members of the Bamburgh Research Project have reconstructed the throne with the help of the castle stonemason. The reconstruction shows the value of archaeologists working in conjunction with good artisans who are interested in history.

WOOD

If the Northumbrians were reluctant stonemasons, they were skilled carpenters. The Anglo-Saxons were a seafaring folk in origin, and making boats that can ride a North Sea gale is a greater test of carpentry skill than even the largest house on land. These skills were widespread throughout the lands bordering the North and Baltic seas, rich as they were in timber and with water travel being the easiest way to get around. So coppicing trees to harvest strong, straight branches was a common practice, one that had been around since Neolithic times and, in fact, continued right up until the modern era.

If a time scope enabled us to look through the (wooden) door of a (wooden) Northumbrian house we would see many things that are familiar to us today. The (wooden) table would have pride of place, used as it was for eating, preparation and general storage. The planked construction of the table would strike a chord with anyone who's bought an Ikea product. The wooden benches on either side of it could similarly come in a box marked 'Ivar'. On the table there might be (wooden) bowls and cups, turned from deep disks of wood on a pole lathe, which was the staple tool of the Anglo-Saxon carpenter.

There would also be a range of knives, ladles and spoons. All these implements were made from wood (except for the metal blades). They would be created by hand in quiet moments, which was a valuable pastime in the long winter evenings.

Peering into the corner of the room, we would see a bed (yes, you guessed it, made of wood). A stuffed mattress would make the frame softer. Beside the bed would be a large (wooden) chest, containing the precious items that the family owned collectively: linen, clothes and heirlooms. On top of the box we might see a set of panpipes, or a drum (wooden) and a lyre (also wooden). These were the main musical instruments played by the Anglo-Saxons. (There were flutes made of bone as well as wood.)

In a corner there might also be a large bucket, made from planked wood and banded with iron. This would provide the drinking, washing and preparation water for the family.

As our time scope slowly withdraws from the house, we see the children playing outside with wooden toys, dolls, boats and swords.

The Anglo-Saxon world was a wooden world.

FIRE

Making fire was a vital and necessary skill for everyone, and no self-respecting Anglo-Saxon would have gone anywhere without the means to light a fire at hand, or rather, dangling from his belt. Every Northumbrian, including children, wore a belt and on that belt were the key implements necessary for life: a knife (which was carried by children as well as adults as it was the main tool for almost everything, including eating) and a flint and steel for making fire. The steel was made of hardened metal and striking it against a flint created sparks. The spark flashes into life because flint is hard enough to chip off a tiny sliver of the metal when it is struck, and the energy released by the blow and concentrated in the sliver of metal is enough to ignite it. To catch the spark and ignite a fire, the Anglo-Saxons carried char cloth. This was cloth that had basically been turned into the linen equivalent of charcoal by heating the cloth in an anaerobic environment, that is, in the absence of oxygen. Char cloth could even be made by tightly wrapping a wad of cloth and throwing it in the fire. The outer layers will burn, but the centre will char rather than combust. The resultant char cloth is super dry and very flammable: the ideal material to catch a spark and turn it into a flame.

Flint, steel and easily combustible material. *Paul Gething*

If an Anglo-Saxon ran out of char cloth, there were many other naturally occurring materials that would have served almost as well, such as old man's beard (*Clematis vitalba*), thistledown (the dandelion-like seeds of thistle plants), razor strop fungus (birch polypore or *Piptoporus betulinus*) and various other types of fungus, one of which is called King Alfred's cakes (*Daldinia concentrica*). The fungi, when dried out, will catch fire and hold a spark for hours. In fact, these fungi have many uses.

Flint, of course, was one of the main materials used in the stone ages, be they Palaeolithic, Mesolithic or Neolithic and, being flint, the worked arrowheads, axes, knives, scrapers and other implements used in previous ages were still lying around in the Anglo-Saxon age (they're still around now, if you have eyes to see). Now, since flint turns up all the time on medieval sites, we surmise that right through the medieval period people were reusing flints that had originally been shaped and worked by the country's original Stone Age inhabitants. So, we know that the Northumbrians recycled Roman stone, and we believe that they did the same for Neolithic flint. After all, most of these flints were originally shaped to be conveniently held in the hand, being flint they endured through the years, and they were conveniently to hand if you just kept an eye open.[41]

Fabulous fungi

The Anglo-Saxons were early exponents of biotechnology. Knowledge of the properties of fungi not only afforded them alternative sources of food, but tools, medicine and portable fire-starting kits. Take King Alfred's cakes (*Daldinia concentrica*) for example. This resembles a lump of coal, or indeed a badly burned cake, and grows mainly on the dead wood of ash trees. It occurs in black and dark-brown forms and the black one can be used to light a fire when dried out, as its inner flesh will catch and hold a spark from a steel. The ember will continue glowing for hours, or days even, depending on the size of the fungus, making King Alfred's cakes a good way of transporting a fire to a new campsite.

Razor strop (birch polypore or *Piptoporus betulinus*) occurs mainly on birch trees and is a bracket-type fungus. It too can be used to set a fire when dried out, but, as its name suggests, it will also strop a knife to the sharpest of points and strips can be cut off and used as plasters, effectively closing wounds and, since the fungus has antibacterial properties, helping to stop infection as well.

Daldinia concentrica, King Alfred's Cakes. *Wikimedia Commons*

CLOTHING

The typical clothing of a Northumbrian was leggings, a fairly long tunic reaching to the thigh, a belt, linen undergarments if he could afford them, a cloak and a hood. This basic outfit was supplemented in winter with shoes that consisted of a leather sole and leather upper, which were sown inside out and then inverted. These are very simple to make – Paul's made quite a few and he's not exactly a skilled leather worker – which suggests that they were suitable for most levels of Northumbrian society. And while they don't sound that comfortable or weatherproof, frequent coatings of beeswax were enough to keep Paul's feet dry in a pair of these leather shoes through the wettest April on record, and stuffing hay into them kept his feet warm as well. In fact, the shoes weren't the only item of medieval clothing Paul has worn – he's been kitted out in authentic medieval gear for long periods and can personally attest to the clothes being warm, comfortable and dry. In fact, the clothing worn in medieval times is quite similar to the gear worn by early mountain climbers, who cheerfully ascended the Matterhorn in tweed jackets and cotton long johns. Although the medievals didn't have cotton, linen served a similar purpose.

The main fabrics were wool and linen; silk was available, but only in small amounts and for a very few people. The ubiquitous belt was made of leather. So what people wore came essentially from sheep (wool), flax (linen) and cows (leather). Preparing these materials was laborious, but in many ways was ideally suited to the long nights of Northumbria's northern latitudes. When it gets dark at 3.30 in the afternoon, and doesn't get light again until 8.30 in the morning, that leaves a lot of hours to fill. So you either had to sleep longer, and people probably did do that, or you had to develop activities that could be done in semi-darkness and firelight. Things like weaving were ideal activities to fill the long, still hours of winter, since with practice they could be done virtually blindfolded. This may be why much Anglo-Saxon weaving is geometrical: the patterns are easier to make out in limited light.

Blacksmiths had it easy of course, as the forge fires kept them warm through the winter, and they actually wanted dim light to practice their craft. The key to the blacksmith's craft is managing molten metal and to do that, a blacksmith has to know the temperature of different

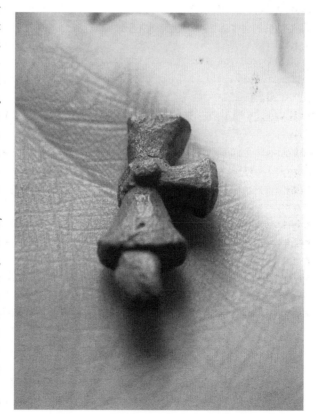

Cross carved from bone. *BRP*

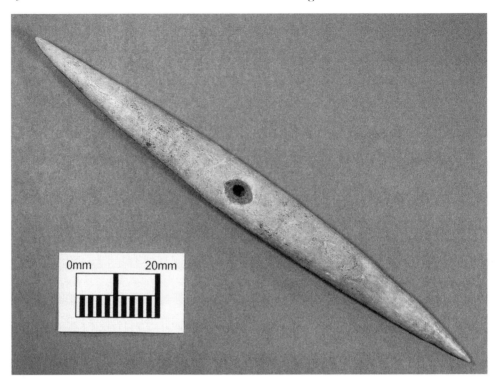

Bone needle, possibly used for net making. *BRP*

parts of his forge. That temperature is revealed by the colour of the fire, but sunlight or harsh artificial light masks the colours.

Constrained by the shifting patterns of light and dark, the Anglo-Saxons had a much more seasonal lifestyle than we do today, making clothes and shoes and mending and matching through the winter, and then moving outdoors as the days lengthened, the fields called and, for the warrior class, the fighting season began.

Being the opposite of a throwaway society, needles played a big part in the lives of many Anglo-Saxons. Very occasionally needles were made of iron, but the vast majority were slivers of bone. In fact, making needles would have been another way of filling winter nights. Typically, needles were made from cattle bones, usually the larger bones, such as from the thigh. The flesh having been eaten and the marrow removed, the last remnants of meat were cleaned off by boiling or the gnawing of a dog. Then the bone was broken with hammer or chisel and suitable pieces were selected and buried or simply left out in the open air to clean and dry. When the piece of bone was ready, it was whittled and shaped into its new life as a needle.

Bone was used for many other purposes apart from needles, including as toggles and buckles (buttonholes only became common in Europe in the thirteenth century. Curiously, the button had been around since the Bronze Age, when it was used as an ornament, but it took centuries for anyone to make a hole to put it through). Small squares of bone with a hole at each corner were used to make complicated patterned braid, which was used for all manner of fastenings and for the hemming of garments. The making of braid was a common pastime for the Anglo-Saxons.

In summary, bone was as useful and ubiquitous a material in that age as plastic is in ours.

Franks Casket. *Michel Wal/Wikimedia Commons*

Water, water everywhere, but not a drop to drink!

In most respects, to successfully hold a fortress like Bamburgh against an attacking force was relatively easy. The defenders had the advantage of elevation and defensive structures. The garrison could rain projectiles and missiles down on the attackers, with little chance of any incoming projectiles striking home due to the height of the castle rock. Starvation, the friend of besieging forces through history, was hard to achieve, since dry goods, such as grain, could be stored in vast amounts on the rock and there was even room for livestock.

The one weakness of the castle was water. It didn't have any. It would be a grim irony indeed to sit on top of an impregnable fortress, staring out across the North Sea and be defeated by thirst.

But the Northumbrian kings weren't going to let a little thing like nature defeat them, and they dug a well in the heart of the castle. The well stands in the keep, but when it was first dug it would probably been in an open area, accessible to anyone who needed it.

The well was dug through 45m of solid rock. The top half was gradually scored through the dense dolerite rock. The rock was picked out with soft iron tools, then weakened by setting fires and then rapidly quenching the hot rock using water painstakingly dragged up from the beach below. Beneath the dolerite sits a plug of sandstone that was softer to dig, but carried a greater risk of cave-ins. It is hard to imagine the amount of work that went into digging a well through 45m of solid rock, but it does show just how grimly determined the Northumbrian kings were to hold what they had taken.

POTTERY

Pottery is not nearly so common in Northumbria as it had been in the preceding Roman period. Many excavations of Anglian sites fail to find a single sherd. Even the richest sites, such as York, have small pottery assemblages from the Anglian era. While absence of evidence is not evidence of absence, it does produce a rather telling pattern. The Northumbrians simply didn't use much pottery.

Most of the pottery we do find was made by specialist potters, but they may have been full-time potters only for part of the year and farmers for the rest of the time. Whether a potter needed to supplement his income outside the pottery depended on where he was. Somewhere like York was big enough to sustain professional potters, but there were few other places with a large-enough population to maintain craftsmen specialising in every-day commodities such as pots.

As to how the pots were made, whether by building up coils of clay or thrown on a wheel, it's probable that both methods were used, although basic farm pottery was largely coil built. The professional potters probably used wheels as well.

But apart from the professionals, nearly everybody at the time would have been able to make a crude pot. Clay was widely available – you only had to dig it up – and every home had a fire in which to bake pots. However, the average Northumbrian just preferred wood.

A modern copy of an Anglian pottery vessel. *Paul Gething*

Bamburgh Castle, the fortress on the rock

There's a reason there's a castle at Bamburgh, and that reason is the great big lump of dolerite rock on which the castle squats. Set in a commanding position on the coast, a fortress on top of the rock allows commanding views over the sea and across the coastal plain to the Cheviot Hills. As such, it's been occupied since Neolithic times and a passing Anglian raider named Ida quickly spotted its defensive and offensive potential. Setting up shop, Ida founded the kingdom of Bernicia around 547 and there are traces of fortifications dating back possibly even to Ida's time.

The first wall followed the lip of the rock upon which the castle came to stand, increasing the difficulty of a fighting ascent even further. It was kidney-shaped because that is the shape of the rock on which it was built. The Bamburgh Research Project has found evidence suggesting that it was stone, consisting either of two parallel stone walls with the gap between filled with clay and rubble, or a single stone wall that had a revetment on its inner face filled with clay. The top of the wall may even have been made of wood, as there was little chance of an enemy setting it alight. In fact, at this early point, the main reason for the stone wall was to prevent a besieging enemy setting flame to the ramparts: the science of siege warfare was not well developed among the early Anglo-Saxons and the small size of war parties made laying a fortress under siege generally impractical. However, as tactics evolved and small bands of marauders evolved into something approaching armies, the fortifications at Bamburgh Castle grew to face the new threats.

The weakest part of a castle is almost invariably its gates and Bamburgh was no exception, so that is where the defences were improved. Today, there are still parts of the eighth- and ninth-century Anglian wall visible in Bamburgh Castle around St Oswald's Gate, which is today a postern gate but in Northumbrian times was the main – and quite possibly the only – entrance to the castle. The relative positions of the Anglo-Saxon and late medieval gates clearly show the change in orientation that occurred over the span of 500 years: the earlier gate looks east and out to sea and is situated over what was probably an anchorage directly below the castle (the wide expanse of beach beneath the castle is relatively modern, for even in the nineteenth century the high tide lapped up against the castle rock); while the later gate looks south and inland. The sea and rivers were the highways of the early medieval period and boats were the preferred mode of travel, whereas half a millennium later people travelled far more by land.

As the eastern side of the castle was protected by the sea and the inland side was protected by the great height of the lump of dolerite on which the castle sat, for attackers, that just left the gate. As military technology and tactics advanced, the castle defences snaked down the rock towards where St Oswald's Gate still stands, making new fortifications and firing zones, and clearing killing grounds behind the gate so that, if any attackers did force their way in past the outer defences, they could be picked off easily once within. Devising a series of defences that allow the castle defenders to fall back, while picking off the attackers, meant that a relatively small garrison could hold the castle and inflict horrendous casualties on a much larger attacking force.

GLASS

Benedict Biscop, the founder of the Monkwearmouth/Jarrow twin monasteries and an inveterate and indefatigable traveller, was determined to have the best for his new monastic foundations. To that end …

> When the building was nearing completion he sent his agents across to France to bring over glaziers – craftsmen as yet unknown in Britain – to glaze the windows in the body of the church and in the chapels and clerestory. The glaziers came over as requested but they did not merely execute their commission: they helped the English to understand and to learn for themselves the art of glass-making.
>
> (Bede, 'Lives of the Abbots of Wearmouth and Jarrow' from *The Age of Bede*, p. 191)

But despite the arrival of Gallic glassmakers and what Bede says above, the craft of glass-making does not seem to have taken wide root in Northumbria. Apart from the grander Church establishments there are virtually no glass remains from the early medieval period.

There is one tantalising glimpse however. A single sherd of glass has been excavated from a secular context. The sherd, which dates from the eighth century, was found at Bamburgh, within the walls of the current castle. It represents the only known evidence of Northumbrian window glass not from a church or monastery (there may of course be other finds in the future). The glass is of fine quality and is incised to make it easier to fit into a pane. The sherd demonstrates just how wealthy and important the inhabitants of the fortress were at this early point.

Glass beads have also been found in the Bowl Hole burial ground at Bamburgh (for more about the Bowl Hole cemetery, see the chapter on burials). These high-prestige items were buried with their owners, a single possession going to the grave with the person who'd born it in life.

Early medieval window glass from Bamburgh. *BRP*

BOOKS

In the space of two generations, the Northumbrians went from being illiterate pagans to Christians who produced books among the most exquisite ever created. The books they made were written on vellum, that is, calfskin. The Lindisfarne Gospels probably contain a small part of the hide of some 200 cattle. To make vellum, the skin was soaked, limed, the hair was removed and then it was stretched on a frame and dried (leather is tanned as well). The sheets were trimmed to size and then individual sheets were sewn together.

As far as writing was concerned, the monk scribes used feather quills and wooden, bone or ivory styli. The scribe dipped his quill or stylus into a pot of ink, wrote a line and then dipped again. It was a laborious business, its discomfort attested to by the scribbled complaints found in the margins of medieval manuscripts as scribes bewailed their lot. Still, it wasn't all sore eyes and cramped shoulders, as one monk wrote in the ninth century: 'Pleasant is the glint of the sun to-day upon these margins, because it flickers so.' (Henry Mayr-Harting, *The Coming of Christianity to Anglo-Saxon England*, p. 88)

Basic black ink was made by taking the branches and twigs of a hawthorn tree, pounding them until they were heavily bruised, and then immersing the wood in water. After the sap had leeched from the wood, it was removed and more bruised wood was added to the same water, usually for eight days. When there was enough sap and resin in the water, the thick liquid was boiled until virtually dry. The final drying was done by the sun, creating a crust that could be powdered. Add water to the powder, and voila – black ink. But if the ink was not immediately needed, the powder could be stored in a bladder, inside a parchment bag, and reconstituted when needed. (Theophilus, *On Divers Arts*, p. 42)

To achieve the astonishingly vibrant colours that we see in the Lindisfarne Gospels and other Anglo-Saxon manuscripts, all sorts of substances were pressed, or rather ground, into use: precious stones such as lapis lazuli, plants including woad and madder, minerals such as iron oxide, in fact, anything they could find that would provide a colour. We suspect that there were monks who spent most of their working lives in what was, effectively, research and development, finding and creating new colours for the scribes.

The St Matthew page from the Lindisfarne Gospels. *Wikimedia Commons*

CHANGING NATURE

We have become used to manipulating matter into different forms, but for the Anglo-Saxons there was still something profound and awe inspiring about the processes of metalworking, glassmaking and other such crafts. Take iron as an example. Ore, a solid, lumpy, rocky substance, is plunged into purifying fire and comes out transformed, its impurities melted and poured away, and its essence exposed and ready to be used to make swords and ploughs and other tools fundamentally necessary to human existence. Or consider the long hours taken polishing garnet to make it into a jewel. And through this process, it becomes red. Blood red. Like the blood of Christ. We suspect that deep religious convictions and beliefs found an outlet in the simple acts of making things, and underpinned them and made them profound for the people undertaking the tasks. This is contemplation in action, an everyday physical meditation.

But before we get carried away into Zen and the art of blacksmithing, it's worth bearing in mind that skill trumped devotion. The skills necessary to make a fine sword or suitably magnificent church ornaments were rare, and monasteries were prepared to accept into their establishments men who were bad monks but good smiths.

> I myself knew a brother (and would that I had not) who was placed in a noble monastery, but himself lived an ignoble life. I could give his name if it were any use. The brethren and elders of the place often rebuked him and admonished him to turn towards a more chaste way of life but although he would not listen to them, nevertheless they suffered him patiently because they needed his outward service; for he was a smith of remarkable skill. He gave himself much to drunkenness and the other pleasures of a loose life. He preferred to remain in his workshop by day and by night rather than take part in singing psalms and praying in the church and listening with the brethren to the word of life.
>
> (Bede, *Ecclesiastical History of the English People*, v.14)

In defence of this unnamed monk, there may have been practical reasons for the monk's failure to turn up for the Divine Office. Once a forge is lit it takes a good half an hour to get up to temperature and the fire has to be constantly tended to maintain the heat. Smiths often work in cycles, having a workpiece gently heating in a warm part of the fire, or 'soaking' in a hotter part of the fire, while they work on the piece in hand. The constant rotation of workpieces means that a smith can work on many items simultaneously, improving his productivity and cutting down on slack time.

The interruption of having to attend services several times a day would have made a smith's working life extremely difficult. When working on a charcoal forge (as Paul often does), taking half an hour to collect the kids from school can result in several hours' work being lost as the forge cools, since everything is taken out of the fire and set to one side so that the building doesn't burn down.

To Bede, employed in the work of praising God, this exemption from services looked like a dereliction of divine duty. But it may have been simple expediency. On the other hand, the smith might simply have been a bad monk!

The colours of fire

Different temperatures in a forge will produce different results in iron and steel. If a black-smith wants to anneal iron to make it more malleable so that he can work it, he needs to take the fire to red and then let the iron cool down slowly. If he wants to temper iron he needs to take the fire to orange, almost yellow, and then quench the iron very quickly. This produces a very hard but brittle iron that, if combined with a small amount of carbon, becomes the even-harder steel. Should the fire get even hotter and go to white, then it might well start sparking as the carbon burns off and, essentially, the blacksmith would lose the steel in his iron. At a fundamental level, these different temperatures produce different qualities of iron because they change the molecular structure of the metal. At a practical level, temperature control is the key skill of the blacksmith.

To complicate matters, different parts of a fire have different oxygen contents too. The top of a fire has a lot less oxygen than the base of the fire. So even though the flames may be the same colour and thus be at the same temperature in different parts of the fire, the metal the blacksmith is working on will receive or lose different properties according to its location in the forge. A blacksmith might want a piece heated in an oxygenating fire or in a reducing fire, depending on what he is doing to that particular piece of metal. Although the blacksmiths in Northumbrian times wouldn't have described a flame as having more or less oxygen, they understood completely the different properties that different parts of the forge imparted to metal. In fact, blacksmiths today are still taught to look for the colours of fire – the 'why' may have changed but the 'how' is the same.

everyday skills

One of the largest differences between Anglo-Saxon society and our own is that then, almost everybody had the range of skills necessary to provide the basic requirements of existence: they could make fire, cobble shoes, weave cloth, farm, hunt, fish, build a house, fletch an arrow and direct a plough. Abandon an early medieval man or woman on a desert island and they would have had no problems surviving. That's not to say that everyone could do everything. While making a nail is not particularly difficult, making a sword is, and the skills required for the former are not sufficient for the latter. So while most people were competent at most things, there were specialist craftsmen in certain areas such as blacksmithing and jewellery making. Technology, technique, information and equipment are the necessary elements in making a good sword or a fine brooch. Most people would have had a basic knowledge of working with metal sufficient to make a knife out of scrap metal (something that could be done over one or two nights by simply using the hearth to heat and soften the metal and hammering it on a stone). But the craftsmanship necessary to make a weapon such as the Bamburgh Sword (see feature on the Bamburgh Sword, p. 75) took a lifetime to acquire.

The position of artisans in society

Most blacksmiths, potters and other artisans occupied a middle rank in Northumbrian society, below the warrior elite. Those who entered religious life could well have achieved senior positions within a monastery, although to be a bishop in this hierarchical society generally required noble birth.

However, many artisans were slaves. War parties were almost as keen to acquire slaves as they were to find treasure, and artisans were valuable. This may not have been quite as terrible as it sounds, as being an artisan slave to a king or one of his major followers at least provided some measure of security: the Anglo-Saxons may have valued their freedom, but too often that freedom translated into the freedom to starve.

Any old iron

In 2010, York Minster Stoneyard – the stonemasons who work permanently maintaining the minster – asked Paul's advice on setting up a new forge. The idea was to create facilities that would allow the stonemasons to sharpen and re-edge their chisels and tools in a more historically accurate manner. But beware asking advice of an archaeologist, for this simple idea grew into a project where two of the stonemasons, an armourer and Paul decided to recreate from scratch tools identical to those that had originally cut and shaped the stone of the earliest phases of the church. This was possible because tools leave characteristic marks in the stone they cut, and from these marks the tools can be recreated retrospectively. But in order to do that, the group would have to smelt iron from scratch. For the tools to be properly authentic, the iron needed to come from sources that had provided the ore for the original tools that had made the minster. So now the Traditional Materials and Technology Group, as the masons, armourer and Paul snappily called themselves, are in the process of smelting ore from a variety of Northumbrian iron sources. The process is being rigorously recorded and samples of ore, charcoal, slag and iron are reserved from each smelt. The iron produced has a unique signature made up of the rare elements contained within the impure iron. Eventually this will be used to map the 'signatures' of the iron and other elements, allowing archaeologists to potentially find just where the iron in their artefacts was mined from originally. It's a big project that all started from innocently asking for a little bit of advice.

Confessions of a twenty-first-century medieval jeweller: an essay by Paul Gething

I've always found it strange that many archaeologists are prepared to pronounce on topics of which they have no practical experience. Obviously, some things from the past are impossible to experience: the Battle of Stamford Bridge or the fear of the evil eye for example. There is not much chance of having first-hand experience of those nowadays. However, there are lots of things that we could try, if we just got off our fat behinds and went and did them. It's as simple as picking up a hammer, banging some flint together or cutting up a bone.

With this in mind, I decided to enrol on a jewellery course before I started to pontificate on how easy or hard it was to make jewellery in early medieval Northumbria.

The tools and techniques of jewellery making have changed remarkably little over the years, at least judging from the illustrations of medieval goldsmiths in a variety of sources. The same hammers, the same hand tools, the same saws. Virtually everything is still done by hand and hardly anything is mechanised. The only obvious difference is that annealing and soldering are now done with gas rather than charcoal, and electricity lights the workshop rather than lamps.

When I began the jewellery-making course, my first impression was of how clean and tidy everything was. It was only after I'd been there a few weeks that I realised that this wasn't fastidiousness but pragmatism. It is a lot easier to find little stones on a clean floor and it is much more straightforward to recover the tiny particles of gold and silver that come off when filing and sawing if everything is swept down regularly. Where there's muck there's brass, but where there isn't any muck, there's gold.

The other thing that struck home was how expensive everything was. A chart on the wall, updated daily, detailed the prices of gold, silver and platinum. Gold and silver are both at a record high at the time of writing. In the early medieval period, gold and silver were very rare. Good sources were either finite, such as Roman leftovers, or very far away. The technology was no longer advanced enough in Northumbria to allow large-scale mining.

So, in an example of how things come around, we're probably better placed today to appreciate the value placed upon gold and silver in the early medieval than at any time since the opening up of the vast gold and silver resources of South America in the sixteenth century. We can appreciate what it is like to recycle gold and to hold it as a truly precious material.

The jewellery class I attended does not deal exclusively with ancient techniques, but it took little effort on my part to avoid modern tools. The first thing I made was a ring based on an Anglo-Saxon design from the eighth century. It was a silver band filed into a loose triangle with a triangular cross section. It had a small garnet set at each of the three angles.

Before I began, I had to decide how big the ring was going to be and do a measurement using the high-tech medium of string. Then I sawed off a measured piece of silver from a strip. This was fairly easy, apart from the fact that it's harder than it looks to saw straight and without wasting metal. The ends were then filed to make them perpendicular. The next step was to loosely bend the strip into shape and hammer it into a rough circle using a mandrel (a steel cone) and a hammer. I closed the circle by soldering the ends together. This involved heating the metal and applying solder, which is soft silver that flows between the two areas to be joined and then sets as solid silver, leaving no obvious gap. I applied a flux, borax in this instance, to keep the join clean and smooth.

Once I'd shaped the basic ring I put it back on the mandrel and hammered it, gently but firmly, into a perfect circle, before remeasuring it to make sure it was the right size.

With the basic ring made, I then filed it for hours. And hours. And hours. I used different grades of file to slowly and carefully remove silver until the shape of the ring emerged from the plain band.

That done, I then spent hours polishing the ring, using progressively finer grades of emery paper. The emery paper of the early medieval was goat skin loaded with powdered pottery in a lipid. I have actually experimented with this and it does work well, although it takes patience to achieve a good shine.

To finish, I had to set the stone. I drilled a hole using a basic handheld drill, measuring the hole constantly and somewhat anxiously to make sure I didn't drill too deep. When the hole was deep enough, I dropped the stone into place and then pressed the silver swarf, which was generated by the drilling, down over the edges of the stone to hold it in place. Then, yes, more polishing. But this was the final polish. The ring was done.

Writing it down, it seems simple enough, but the process was very exacting and took a great deal of skill and even more patience. On the other hand, it was very easy to lose myself in the work, and then the hours drifted away easily. The feeling of having finished the ring and making something unique is very special.

It's strange. When I started the course, I only really hoped to understand the mechanics of how medieval jewellers worked. I didn't expect to understand how they felt. But now I suspect that the pride taken in doing a good job, and the fear of making a costly mistake, transcend time. I know I am not a medieval jeweller, but I have learnt more from making this ring than I could have from any amount of reading.

10

TRADE AND TRAVEL

It is the best of trades, to make songs, and the second best to sing them.

(Hilaire Belloc, *On Everything*)

Trade, the exchange of goods, practices and ideas with other people near and far, is one of the great drivers of human culture and history. When Britain was Britannia and the north-ernmost province of Rome, trade played a huge part in the ordinary and countrywide dealings of the territory with the rest of the empire. But even after the empire's collapse, Northumbria retained surprisingly wide-ranging contacts with other parts of Britain and Europe. In this chapter, we will look at the development of trade in Northumbria, the range of items traded and the key role that the kingdom's currency played in allowing trade to continue and flourish.

SMALL IS BEAUTIFUL: TRADE AFTER EMPIRE

We know a great deal about trade in the Roman Empire, and its value, volume and sheer extent. This is in part because the empire was one of the first great utilisers of the econ-omies of scale: big operations, using scores if not hundreds of workers, produced huge quantities of eminently excavatable items such as amphorae, many of which were conveni-ently stamped with the maker's mark or shaped into distinctive forms that can be identified with a single location. The Anglo-Saxons operated in an almost exactly contrary fashion: on a small scale, independently and using materials such as wood and leather that decay all too easily. As a consequence, we know considerably less about trade in Anglo-Saxon times, and it's likely that many of the holes in our knowledge will never be filled. Still, archaeo-logical and historical discoveries over the last few decades, not least those at Bamburgh, mean that we can now trace some of the developments in trade over the centuries of the Anglo-Saxon and Viking Ages.

Although the legions officially left Britain in AD 410, undoubtedly many legionaries, auxiliaries, and other officers and functionaries of empire stayed. However, as central con-trol collapsed, trade and technology became increasingly tailored to the local environment.

Making things on the grand scale of empire stopped virtually overnight (or over about a century or so – we are talking archaeological timescales here). People began making pots on a local scale for the folk in the immediate area rather than for export. This sort of production continued throughout the Anglo-Saxon era: pottery, ordinary foodstuffs, timber and other staples of life were largely traded in small quantities over short distances.

Although the days of mass-producing olive oil or wine and transporting them across the empire might have been a distant memory, long-distance trade in technology and technological innovations, aspirational goods and, for want of a better term, Anglo-Saxon bling, still continued. Jewellery, swords, horses and even things like stirrups,[42] which in this context lay somewhere between a technological innovation and an exotic collectable, could come from very far away indeed. For instance, garnets have been found in Northumbria and indeed, all over Anglo-Saxon Britain, almost always as jewellery. Examples include the Sutton Hoo epaulettes, the exquisite jewellery from Street House and the many garnets studding the Staffordshire hoard. But these red jewels were not local; tests indicate that the stones originally came from Sri Lanka and the India/Pakistan Kush area, and there is increasing evidence that some of the garnets came from Portugal. Although we'd like to imagine a Sri Lankan peddler turning up, shivering, at Bamburgh, it's rather more likely that garnets were traded down the line, with one set of traders bringing the jewels to the Caliphate and then the hinterland traders, the ones who exploited the uneasy frontier between the Caliphate and Christendom, trading the garnets on until they eventually arrived in Northumbria. In general, the further the goods were traded from their origin, the more valuable they became.

Trade, of course, works both ways, and Northumbria exported exotic valuables of its own to the Carolingian Empire and beyond, notably greyhounds and elkhounds. The British Isles had been known as the best place for breeding hunting dogs for centuries, going back to Roman times, and the new Anglo-Saxon nobility were certainly no less keen on hunting than their imperial and British predecessors, and dogs were pictured in many of the illustrations of the time.

During the time of the Roman Empire, imperial bureaucrats and functionaries had controlled trade, but with the breakdown of central control, the movement of goods became a matter for what were effectively entrepreneurs – freelance traders. There are some interesting ethnographic parallels between the situation in sixth-century Britain and that in nineteenth-century North America. In both cases, incoming peoples were gradually displacing the indigenous inhabitants (Britons and Native Americans being respectively replaced by Anglo-Saxons and new Americans) but, examining what actually happened in America reveals that some of the incomers traded with the natives, some fought them, some married them and some did all three. Thus we would expect there to have been as much trading and mating between Anglo-Saxons and Britons as there was fighting and raping.

The Daily Bread

Exotic foods mostly disappeared from the British diet with the withdrawal of the legions. As an interesting example of Roman fast food, and the breadth of the trade in food across the empire, there's the mysterious case of the rabbit in the jar. Paul excavated a preserved rabbit in a pot in Layerthorpe, York, and since rabbits were only supposed to have been introduced to this country with the Normans, this means that either we have to rewrite our biology textbooks, or that the Romans casseroled rabbits, put them in pots, and shipped them across the empire as an imperial fast food.

In the Anglo-Saxon period, the vast majority of foodstuffs were grown locally. But status played its part in what you ate as much as it did in your clothes, jewellery and weaponry. While the stuff of life probably remained fairly constant up and down the social ladder, those people at the top also ate things that others didn't and couldn't. For instance, at Bamburgh, the excavations have revealed the presence of cranes in the diet in the seventh and eighth centuries. Now cranes are big birds that live in wetlands and mires, so are therefore not easily hunted and brought down. The best guess about how they arrived on the table at Bamburgh Castle is that they were hunted with large hawks, thus bringing together in one neat package some of the principal interests of the English aristocracy over the centuries: hunting, falconry and gamey-tasting birds. Keeping with the big birds, swans were also eaten at Bamburgh, as were other exotic foodstuffs that must have been traded over distances. Most of these are the sorts of foods that can be preserved and transported easily, such as grains and pulses. On the face of it, there seems little of the exotic about beans, but in fact pulses can be food to inspire the archaeological imagination. Take the case of the coprolitic lentil. Coprolites, for those blessed not to know, are fossilised faeces, and excavations at Bamburgh have revealed that lentils were eaten and then excreted on site (the assumption is that consumption and expulsion both occurred here, although in principle it would be possible for a constipated lentil eater to have eaten the lentils en route and only upon arriving at Bamburgh relieve bowels filled many miles away). Since lentils do not grow in Britain, these humble pulses must have been brought to the country from somewhere in the region of southern France or points further flung. So were lentils the ultimate seventh-century gourmet delicacy, traded over hundreds of miles for the king and his household? Could be. But there is an alternative, more humdrum explanation for the lentil poo. Lentils, being easily dried, preserved and transported, could have functioned like the seventh- and eighth-century versions of hard tack aboard ships. Then, when the sailors landed and unburdened themselves of their seaboard fare, the lentil remains joined the general waste from the site. So, either exotic delicacy traded to the high table, or common food of the common, if travelling, man. Both answers are possible. Each offer tantalising glimpses into the society of the time, though neither can be established confidently. However, they both reveal how much more far-flung trade links were in those times than we tend to think today.

Watch out, there are Vikings about

The way we think of the Vikings has swung from one extreme (looters and pillagers)
to another (misunderstood traders and brave explorers) over the last few decades, before
settling on a reasonably sensible median. We could think of them as predatory traders,
or mercantile raiders, the emphasis shifting depending on the men concerned and the
strength or weakness of their targets. Maybe the best way of viewing them is as men with
a keen eye on the main chance: if the odds looked bad, then they would trade and maybe
return next year with more men to pursue sharper methods of exchange; if the opportunity was there and the possible take was high enough, then out would come the swords.
The undefended, richly vested monasteries, conveniently placed on islands, estuaries and
riverbanks, must have seemed like an all-you-can-eat buffet to roving Vikings looking to
score big. No wonder they gorged themselves on plunder.

Still, battle always carried risks. Although some Viking groups were undoubtedly savage
and barbaric, others genuinely preferred to trade. The problem was, if you lived anywhere
near water and saw the square sails and curved prows approaching, how could you tell?

Watch out, Vikings about! *Wikimedia Commons*

The styca in your pocket

How did people pay for the goods that were traded in Northumbria? The old Roman currency had collapsed and, after the withdrawal of the legions, there were very few places where the nominal value of something was different to its worth. The continual debasement of the currency meant a loss of faith in the value of the coinage. This led to people turning to other methods of exchange such as barter. Coinage rapidly slipped from use even towards the end of the Roman era in Britain. But coins that were obviously, demonstrably, made from precious metal retained currency and value. Money effectively became bullion. Viking raiders of course were famous for plundering and robbing, taking gold, silver and jewels where they found them, and it's likely that the early Anglo-Saxon raiders did exactly the same to the Britons. Gold and silver coins were valuable because they contained gold and silver, not because they were faced with the name and likeness of a distant Emperor.

But Northumbria was an exception to this rule. In Northumbria, money was worth something. This tells us something extraordinary about the kingdom. To understand how extraordinary, it is necessary to understand the nature of money in the ancient and early medieval worlds.

Under the Roman Empire, the emperor underwrote the currency. So, even if a denarius was eventually mostly made of copper, it was still worth a denarius because the emperor said it was worth a denarius, and he put his head on the front of it to show that, and the empire effectively underwrote its value. When the western Empire fell, there was no one with the authority to back up a currency. So money returned to bullion and a coin became worth however much gold or silver it contained. If the coin was made of copper, it was worth scrap.[43]

The precious metal view of currency is nicely illustrated in Viking hoards. The Vikings, contrary to more recent views, definitely did believe you could take riches with you, and the richer you were, the more you took. Thus we have found many a buried hoard of coins, mainly silver pennies in urns or pots. But interspersed with these pennies are coins from the further reaches of the Carolingian Empire or even the Caliphate. These exotic coins are included among the silver pennies because they have the same silver content and thus were worth the same as the homegrown (or home raided) pennies. It made no difference to the Vikings whose head was on the coin or how much the Caliph said the coin was worth, or whether the Holy Roman Emperor decreed his coins to be worth 10 silver pennies. This was the age of bite it and see.

But in Northumbria, coins were worth what the king said they were worth. This was one of the things that marked the kingdom out as a discrete political entity. Take stycas (the lowest denomination Anglo-Saxon coin) for example. The very first stycas minted in Northumbria were gold, but the coins were quickly devalued to silver and eventually they were made almost entirely of copper, and thus had no intrinsic worth. Yet they retained a monetary value through the two centuries of Northumbrian ascendancy and control, being worth about £20 in today's money. Stycas held their value because the kings of Northumbria supported the currency, as did the Church. Many coins had the king stamped on one side and the bishop on the other (leaving an open question as to which side would be 'tails' when there were heads on both sides). In uncertain times, the king on his own may not have had the authority to underwrite a currency, but with the Church on board as well, the two pre-eminent institutions of the age had sufficient clout to maintain

the value of the currency. Northumbrian stycas continued in circulation until the fall
of York to the Vikings in AD 867. History textbooks generally claim that they ceased to
be tender after 867, but we would argue that they continued in use for a generation or so,
since stycas are found in hoards buried after 867, and there could have been no reason to
bury them if they had ceased to have any value.

Northumbria is unique among the Anglo-Saxon kingdoms in maintaining a currency
over this period. The other Anglo-Saxon kingdoms only started producing copper coinage
in the centuries after the fall of Northumbria. So, from about 650 to 867, Northumbria
was unique economically as well as culturally and politically. The only other places where
a head on a coin meant something were the Carolingian Empire, under Charlemagne and
his immediate heirs, and the areas controlled by the Papacy.

TRADING FLESH

If other parts of the world had precious metals and jewels as their principal luxury exports,
the English had horses, books and – I'm afraid there's no way to beat around the bush on
this – daughters.

Horses first: if you think that this reflects the contemporary scale of priorities then you
are probably wrong, as women in Anglo-Saxon England had higher status and more prestige than they would achieve for centuries afterwards. Horses from England were traded to
the Carolingian Empire and probably beyond. The best horses were big, had lots of stamina
and didn't fall sick and die easily, although big is a relative term, of course. In general, horses
then were smaller than their modern cousins, since without specific breeding programmes,
horses tend to revert to pony size. Think of the ponies ridden by Native Americans, all
descendants of horses that had escaped, run wild and adopted the smaller, more energy-
and food-efficient stature of the mustang over the generations. English horses were well
known for their relative size, strength and toughness, and at a time when a good horse
commanded more than a Monet, they were a key export. Of course, payment was not necessarily in money. One of the key aspects of this trade in valuable goods was that it created
obligation in the recipient, while demonstrating the open-handed largesse of the giver.
Generosity – with gold and gifts – was a key kingly virtue in Anglo-Saxon society. A king
attracted followers (who would then fight for him) by having a reputation for gold giving.
And attracting the warriors meant, of course, that he was in a better position to get more
gold in order to acquire more followers. It was a self-reinforcing system.

But apart from horses, there was trade in brides and, to a lesser extent, grooms as well.
This is most obvious (and has left the greatest historical traces) among the royal families
of Anglo-Saxon England, but it probably occurred among the lower social orders as well.
But exchanging brides with people in far-flung places not only brought in fresh blood
and welcome dowries, it also brought ideas. The most obvious example of this is the key
role that Christian princesses from Gaul played in the conversion of the Anglo-Saxons
(for more on this, see the chapter on religion). As well as a bishop or priest, a king may
have dispatched an ostler or blacksmith with the party travelling to the new kingdom. And
although the king no doubt kept his best ostler and most skilled blacksmith for his own
court, he might well spare a journeyman for the journey.

SPREADING THE WORD

Northumbria traded in many items highly valued in their day, and these goods would still be regarded as valuable now: jewellery, carefully crafted weapons and highly bred horses. But there was something else, more valuable than gold and rarer than finely wrought swords, that Northumbria was famous throughout Christendom for exporting – books. In a world where every book had to be painstakingly copied by hand, and when the vast majority of people were illiterate, books were surpassingly rare and extraordinarily valuable. To get an idea of just how rare and precious books were, consider Alcuin. Alcuin was the foremost scholar of his day. He had amassed a famously extensive personal library and, not surprisingly, took it with him when he moved from Lindisfarne to York and then on to Aachen. But this huge personal library fitted inside a single large chest.

The monasteries at Lindisfarne, and the twin foundations of Monkwearmouth and Jarrow, with Whitby and, a little later, York, were the key centres of book production in the British Isles and, indeed, northern Europe. Northumbrian manuscripts were traded, given as gifts and exchanged as far as Rome. The trade, exchange and gifting of these books generated goodwill and obligation among the people who received them, be they kings, abbots or even popes. This sort of exchange reproduced, in the ecclesiastical sphere, much of the tissue of mutual obligation and dependence that gift giving engendered between the generous king and his gift-receiving warrior followers. While it would be too much to suggest that Ceolfrith taking an exquisite copy of the Bible[44] to Rome as a gift for the Pope[45] was done to engender a debt obligation on the part of the Bishop of Rome, the gift of similar Gospels and Scriptures to other monasteries, prelates and often newly converted kings, inevitably led within the cultural context of the time to an unwritten acknowledgement of owing.

How could there not be an obligation? Take the Lindisfarne Gospels for example. The resources that went into making this one book almost beggar belief: the hide from 200 cows produced the vellum on which it was written (and not just any cows;

A page from the *Codex Amiatinus*.
Wikimedia Commons

Detail from the Lindisfarne Gospel.
Edoardo Albert

these were the finest beasts the monastery could find, with only a small section of hide from each animal suitable for curing into a form suitable for book production), and the inks were made from precious materials, including lapis lazuli from India and, of course, gold. Although the original leather binding of the book was lost during the Viking invasions, the Gospels would probably have had a golden clasp and bindings. (Given the Vikings' fondness for gold and illiteracy, it's a wonder that any books at all have survived from that time.) To illustrate how much gold was used in the production of books, note that much of the gold excavated at Bamburgh comes from the fittings of books – and this was a centre of royal and military power, not a monastery. In addition to the materials used in its production, it is necessary to factor in the time and labour required to gain an understanding of the undertaking involved. Finally, to really appreciate the value of such a book, the book's actual content comes to the fore – for the richness of ornamentation and material were all merely done to illustrate in physical terms the urgent, transformative call to salvation contained within the covers. For the Northumbrians who produced and read the Lindisfarne Gospels, and who laboured over many other copies of the Scriptures, these words were life. There could be no more valuable export that that.

TRANSPORT

The transport options in Northumbria were limited: walking, beasts of burden (horses, ponies, donkeys and mules, as well as oxen) and ships. (There were occasional examples of other transportation devices, such as ice skates and coracles, but these were so limited as to be curiosities alone.)

Shanks's pony

Walking: almost everyone had access to feet. And they often used them. Great journeys were made in the early medieval period, some covering hundreds, even thousands of miles, and much of that was done on shanks's pony. It was basic, cheap and available. The only real downsides were that it was tiring and potentially dangerous, as it was possible, even probable in some areas, that a traveller would be stopped by ne'er-do-wells and relieved of all his valuables. The kings and their officers tried to maintain the law, but in more remote areas it was very difficult and once a person had been robbed, catching the culprit was well-nigh impossible. To make matters more difficult, the roads were not real roads. Dirt tracks, mostly the relics of a pre-Roman landscape, criss-crossed the land. Think Ordnance Survey footpath rather than cobbled road for a comparison. The only exceptions were the arterial Roman roads that kings often ordered to be maintained.

Two legs good, four legs better

For those with money, a horse or pony was another option. Horses, though, were valuable animals. Hrothgar presented Beowulf with eight white horses with gold tack. The gift, from a king to a hero, was meant to demonstrate just how invaluable Beowulf's services were, but from our point of view it's instructive that 'invaluable' translated into horseflesh.

Moving from poetry into archaeology, the sixth- and seventh-century burials at Sutton Hoo contain the cremated remains of horses that were buried with warriors, demonstrating how important the horse was to a warrior. It's generally believed that the Anglo-Saxons did not fight from horseback however, so it's slightly curious that horses were so valuable to warriors then. The argument is usually given that without stirrups it was impossible to fight successfully from horseback. However, it is worth bearing in mind that the Romans, particularly in the eastern empire, had Cataphracti: heavily armoured, mounted warriors who performed well on horseback despite having no stirrups. With this in mind, the Sutton Hoo helmet panel, showing a mounted warrior riding down a footman, looks less like a fanciful notion, and more like a scene from a battle.

Ships

The terrible roads were a possible reason for the popularity of boats and ships as a mode of transport. However, it could be argued that the Northumbrian love affair with the ship meant that they didn't need roads. Anyhow, the roads were poor and the ships were not.

Take the ship buried at Sutton Hoo as an example. (Admittedly, this is East Anglia, but the Angles of East Anglia were closely related to the Angles who settled in Northumbria and the boats that had brought them across the North Sea would have been very similar.) The main Sutton Hoo burial ship is over 90ft long. That's a third of a football field, or three London buses end to end if you're inside the M25! As the burial place of a king it was one of the biggest and best ships of the time, but it is still an extraordinary vessel.

It was clinker built, with overlapping planks forming a strong, rigid structure with enough flexibility to keep out the seas.

It was a huge open boat rowed by 40 oarsmen and guided through the water by a large steering paddle that was lashed to the starboard side of the hull.

(A.C. Evans, *The Sutton Hoo Ship Burial*, p. 27)

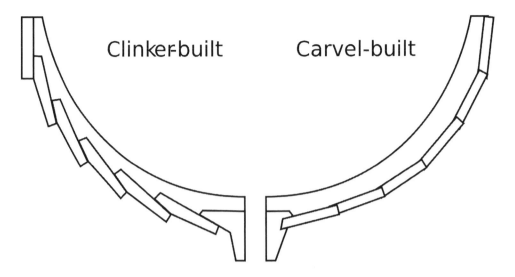

The difference between clinker and carvel boats. *Wikimedia Commons*

The ship was not something knocked together for the royal funeral, for it had enjoyed a good working life, with the remains showing several repairs to the fabric.

The Bayeux tapestry depicts the ships used by William's army to cross the channel. These vessels used sails as well as oars, a method almost certainly employed earlier by the Angles to get from Germany to Northumbria – it's a long way to row.

The Angles, like the later Vikings, were expert seamen. They managed to sail great distances using limited equipment. To do so, they had to navigate great distances and one tantalising possibility for how they did so is suggested by mentions of a sunstone in *Hrafns Saga*. This was probably a type of crystal that polarises light, allowing the sun's position to be seen even on cloudy days. If the Vikings knew this, it is possible that the Angles possessed the same technology. They also seem to have been experts in judging wind speed, sea currents and location by the colour of the seas. These skills are a mystery to most people now, but to early medieval seamen they were second nature.

A much more common sight than the great ship of Sutton Hoo were smaller boats. Rowed by a couple of men, these were used to transport relatively small cargoes. As they were able to navigate shallow rivers, they were the lifeblood of Northumbria.

Slightly larger vessels with optional sails plied the rivers and hugged the coast while still being capable of relatively long journeys. By sea and river, the journey from York to Bamburgh could be done in a day or two, rather than the week to 10 days it would have taken on foot.

One important thing to note about Northumbrian ships and boats is that before the arrival of the Vikings there was no real need for warships to be different from everyday ships. Viking raids, however, meant that the Angles had to rapidly develop aggressive ships to counter the new threat, while also maintaining roads inland to allow a rapid response to Viking incursions. Northumbria never really succeeded in doing this, which was perhaps another reason for the kingdom's decline.

The three types of trade

Anthropologists have established that there are three basic types of exchange:

1. Reciprocity. People of roughly equal status exchange goods of roughly equal value. This is the basic barter system, growing out of the sort of gift giving that occurs in family and related groups.
2. Redistribution. Items are sent to a central location and then redistributed from that centre by an organising authority.
3. Market exchange. The classic trade system. Traders bring goods to a central market and then bargain over the goods. Markets can function both internally, as market towns, and externally, as ports where traders of different nationalities meet and haggle.

11

BURIAL AT BAMBURGH

One place I don't want to go
Down in the ground where the dead men go.
                    (The Pogues, 'Down in the Ground Where the Dead Men Go')

Archaeologists are mosaicists. They take a huge amount of detailed information and attempt to form a coherent picture from the sometimes disparate data. Postholes, pottery and people all go towards forming the picture, and at Bamburgh Castle the people were the ones buried in the Bowl Hole cemetery.

Bamburgh Castle is a big place. It was restored in the nineteenth century by the Victorian industrialist Lord Armstrong and people still live in parts of the castle, while the rest is open to the public from Easter to the autumn. So one question facing archaeologists is where to dig. Legendary archaeologist Brian Hope-Taylor had excavated part of the castle in the 1960s, so when the Bamburgh Research Project began its work, it could refer to the very sketchy references of his excavations. But the location of those excavations and the information from them was not in the public domain. So they did the first thing that all good archaeologists do: they looked at maps. Old maps. On the oldest map of all, the first Ordnance Survey map of the area in 1860, there was a note outside the castle walls, saying 'Old Danish burying ground'. Unfortunately, there was no arrow saying 'dig here' so the archaeologists of the BRP went to look at the rough area indicated on the map. But the reconnaissance simply revealed a huge area of sand dunes. Graeme Young, one of the BRP directors, did some research to find out why the first Ordnance Survey had marked a Danish burial ground on its map – after all, Bamburgh is a long way from Denmark. It turned out that the cemetery had been revealed by a storm in 1817. This was presumably the evidence for the Ordnance Survey designation. An excavation in 1894 had found several cist burials, two crouched burials and an infant.

Having established that there was indeed a reason for the map indicating a burial ground, the next question was where to look for it. Some of the team thought it would be on the ridge leading down to the beach as it is higher land and although wooded now, it was probably clear in the early medieval period, while the foreshore would have been liable to flood. But Paul, following a hunch that would live in local archaeological legend, set off in

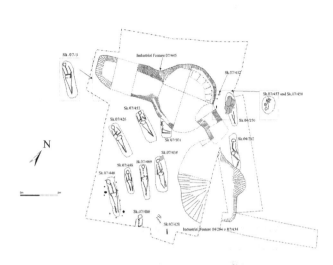

A map of the Bowl Hole cemetery. *BRP*

a slightly different direction, and after wandering for 10 minutes with a party of students he suddenly had an extraordinarily strong gut feeling that he'd found the site.

'Stop. This is it. We need to dig here.'

They dug a 1x2m hole and found a burial almost immediately.

This was one of those moments that make being an archaeologist, despite the wind, rain and back pain, worthwhile. It later transpired that Paul could have stopped anywhere within a 30m radius and they would have found a burial, but for those few moments it was an epiphany. On the other hand, the burial site covers an area about half the size of a football pitch – digging anywhere outside that would have uncovered only sand.

That very first find was later interpreted as a bag containing skeletal remains that had been reinterred when a later grave was sunk on the site of a previous burial. For beneath the first bones, the archaeologists found a fully articulated skeleton. What seems to have happened is that a body was buried in the cemetery's first phase of use in the late sixth and early seventh centuries, but after some years any marks showing the location of the body were lost. Then, about forty years later, when a new grave was required, the gravediggers found skeletal remains as they dug into the ground. They collected the bones and put them in a bag, buried the new body and put the original inhabitant of the grave back in the ground with a companion.

The Bowl Hole cemetery, as it was named, is about a quarter of a mile from the castle. The exact location has been kept secret to ensure that vandals and the overly curious don't trample and destroy the site. Active digging at the Bowl Hole stopped in 2007 (the archaeologists spent almost 10 years working there) and the area has quickly returned to its natural state, so that barely a trace remains of the trenches. The excavated remains are now in laboratories and storage, awaiting investigation. In a curious link with the anti-quarians who had first discovered remains at Bamburgh, a lady of the village walking her dog saw the archaeologists during the excavations and stopped to talk. The lady told the archaeologists that when she was a child she used to come to this area with her grandfather and they would often dig for skeletons while picnicking. Apparently, the bones were taken to a museum in London. Sadly, the BRP has never been able to trace which museum the remains were taken to.

Analysing the inhabitants of a cemetery allows archaeologists to compare ancient DNA with its modern-day counterpart. A comparison of the DNA of living local people with the people buried some 14 centuries ago reveals considerable continuity: many of the residents of Bamburgh today are descended from the people buried in the Bowl Hole.

ÖUN SAILING

The question arises of why the inhabitants of the castle chose the Bowl Hole site to inter their relatives and friends. Before we can answer the question, we have to imagine the coast as it was at the time when the cemetery was in use. The key difference then was that the sand dunes, which now stretch south from Bamburgh and are a Site of Special Scientific Interest for their rare plant and insect life, are new. The dunes only appeared in 1819 when a particularly violent storm moved huge amounts of sand up the coast and deposited it at Bamburgh. Before the storm, the sea washed the base of the rock upon which the castle stands. The cemetery was situated on a flat, long, shallow decline down to the much-narrower beach that existed at the time, so the dead were buried with a perfect view of the sea. The burials were orientated towards the sea so that if the dead should stand

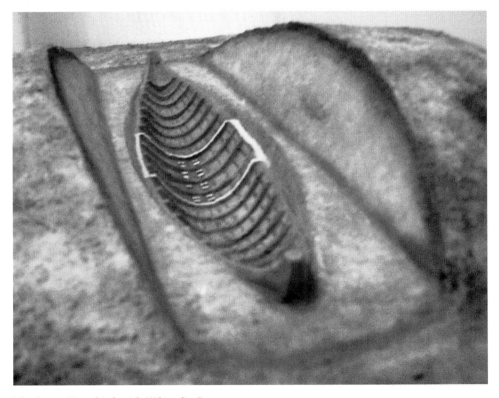

The Sutton Hoo ship burial. *Wikimedia Commons*

up in their graves, they would look out to the North Sea. Christian burial traditions do suggest an east-west orientation for graves, so it may simply be serendipitous that the sea lies to the east at Bamburgh. But the earliest graves date from either pre-Christian or very early Christian times, which would suggest other reasons for their orientation. The most obvious guess is that a seafaring folk might want to bury their dead with a view of the sea, but it could also be that they were laid to rest pointing towards their ancestral homelands, over the sea.

GRAVEYARD HISTORY

Bowl Hole cemetery, Bamburgh:

	Young adult	Middle-aged adult	Older adult	Adult
Female	12 (43%)	9 (32%)	7 (25%)	0 (0%)
Male	9 (29%)	6 (19%)	15 (48%)	1 (3%)
Unknown	3 (50%)	0 (0%)	2 (33%)	1 (17%)

The first inhabitants of the cemetery were interred in the late sixth and early seventh centuries. There was then a hiatus of 30–40 years, followed by two further phases of use. Bodies continued to be buried here until the end of the eighth century. The people digging the graves knew that they were burying bodies in a site that had been used for burials, but the exact locations of individual graves appears to have been lost fairly quickly, as later graves quite often cut through previous burials, necessitating the removal and reinterring of the remains of the previous occupant. There's a ditch on one side of the burial ground that suggests there was once a small building there, which might have been a chapel.

The earliest burials are almost certainly pagan, and the last are certainly Christian, but for the intermediate burials it is harder to judge the adherence of the burial party. It is always worth bearing in mind when working with human remains like these, that we can't attribute any beliefs at all to the dead man or woman based on how they were buried for the simple reason that it's the living that bury the dead. We might hope that they would respect the wishes of the deceased, but all we can say for certain is that burial practices reflect the beliefs of the burial party.

As to whether or not the graves are pagan or Christian, the presence or absence of grave goods is not definite proof one way or another, since the practice of burying Christians without portable wealth for the afterlife developed slowly. Weapons were also sometimes buried with the dead, but curiously, the presence or absence of weapons in graves is related to times of trouble, but in exactly the opposite manner to what one would assume. From our vantage point, we'd expect prestigious warriors killed in battle to be buried with their swords, so there should be more burials with weapons in times of strife. This was the prevalent view among archaeologists for decades, but work done by Dr Heinrich Härke shows just the opposite: swords are buried in peacetime, but when there is war and fighting, the number of weapons buried decreases dramatically. This is a great example of science in action, confounding our expectations. On reflection, it seems absurdly clear that in dangerous times sensible people don't bury perfectly good weapons in the ground. They need them in their hands.

Although few grave goods were found in the Bowl Hole cemetery, there is one mystery: red stones. A number of the graves contain peculiar red stones that are not local arranged around the heads. A number of theories, including one that the stones were used in some sort of game of chance, have been entertained but abandoned and as yet no one knows what the stones were for.

The remains, a thoroughgoing mixture of men and women and adults and children, are homogenous in one respect: they were all high status. There is no evidence on any of the skeletons of lack of nourishment. Nutritional dearth is indicated on skeletons by lack of growth in teeth and stress to the skeletal structure, and the teeth and bones here all show that their owners had access to a good diet throughout their lives.

ÕIE ḢARÕ

One of the bodies excavated was missing a skull. At first glance, it would seem to be the obvious cause of death. It's certainly possible that the young man was decapitated, but since the body was found with a pillow stone in place, it's more likely that the skull eroded out of the ground and has been lost over the years. But if not through decapitation, then how did he die? By being cut nearly in half. The young warrior – he was in his early twenties when he died – was cut with a sharp instrument, presumably a sword or an axe, at an angle from his scapular right across his chest. Looking at the angle of striking, it appears he must have met his end either by someone striking him from horseback, or from above when he was kneeling on the ground. Since it was rare for warriors to fight from horseback in this period, the more likely scenario is that the young warrior was somehow incapacitated during battle, say through being stunned by a blow to his head or from loss of blood, and dropped to his knees. But even then he did not fall. It was only when an enemy saw him thus disadvantaged and struck downwards with full force, through mail, cloth, skin and bone, that the young man died. Although he fell on the battlefield, his own people were at least able to recover his body and give the dead warrior a fitting burial.

The young warrior's remains are a graphic, if slightly appalling, illustration of just how strong and able the fighters of the time were. It's no easy business to cut through meat and bone even on a chopping board; how much more difficult on a battlefield with a man on his knees, swaying maybe, but still defiantly upright.

Analysis of the body showed that the man was from the eastern seaboard of Britain, somewhere between Scotland and Yorkshire. Although it's impossible to be any more precise, it seems likely that he was a local, and was buried near his family. As to when he died, it was around AD 650, which was when Oswiu was king of Northumbria. There were no grave goods to accompany him into eternity, and the body was buried in a Christian attitude, so given that the date was after the conversion of the kings of Northumbria we can reasonably assume that he was laid to rest in a Christian burial rite.

Respecting the past

Most archaeology is unproblematic: you're revealing foundations, pottery and the detritus and monuments of the past. But it's a different matter when excavating cemeteries. Here, we are dealing with people who once lived and had hopes and beliefs and expectations the same way as we do. How would we react to being told that our remains would one day be dug up and analysed and scrutinised? Our answers would no doubt vary: some people would be unconcerned, others appalled. The investigation of human remains is vital from a scientific viewpoint, as skeletons and other human remains reveal details about our past that are inaccessible otherwise. However, it's important to remember that we are dealing with a different order of remains when excavating people. Bodies should be treated with respect at all times, and when our investigations are complete and all the science is done, the bones will be returned to the ground whence they came, to continue their long sleep into eternity.

The king's man

One of the most extraordinary finds in the Bowl Hole cemetery was that of another warrior. The fact that he was a warrior is not surprising – high-status men at this time were almost all either warriors or priests – but what is fascinating is where he came from. Isotopic tests of the dentine in his teeth reveal that he was born somewhere in an arc centring on the Isle of Iona in the west of Scotland. Carbon 14 tests indicate that he died around AD 635. Putting the evidence together with the known historical facts, we reach the conclusion that this man, interred in the ground far from his native earth, came to Northumbria with Oswald when the exiled king returned from Iona. Sadly, from the bare bones alone we have no way of telling what motivated this warrior to leave Iona and throw in his lot with Oswald. Was it friendship or an eye to the main chance, a longing for adventure or a hunger for glory? We'll never know.

The king's man was a grown adult when he died but still quite young, probably in his late twenties. Unlike the warrior mentioned earlier, his remains give no clue as to cause of death, so it could be anything from disease through to disembowelling: soft tissue wounds leave no traces on a skeleton.

Boning up

While there is an undoubted frisson attached to uncovering skeletons in the ground, the business of actually interrogating the remains for what they can tell us about the person and the time when they were a real, live, breathing person only begins in the laboratory. The key responsibility of the excavator is to get the remains from the ground to the lab intact; it's an exercise in preservation rather than analysis at that stage.

The skeleton is the key. Although it represents bare bones to most people, to the osteologist, the skeleton is a rich source of potential information. The general morphology of the skeleton shows age, sex and general well-being. There are specific indicators, such as the notch on the pelvis that shows gender, while the overall size and fusing together of bones indicate age. Well-developed muscles need firmer attachment to the bone, so hard use and strength are shown in the bones and can aid in interpretation.

The bones also contain all sorts of sciencey goodness at a microscopic level. By investigating DNA and RNA residue it is possible to identify a wealth of information about the past life of the previous owner of the skeleton, such as what illnesses he or she had and the relative ease or difficulty of his or her life.

Rings laid down within the structure of the bone indicate periods of plenty and periods of poor nutrition. Like the dendrochronologist, you can tell a lot from rings under a microscope. Trauma is also a good indicator of previous activity. Breaks and cuts to the bone all provide valuable information about the past. However, trauma to the flesh is not marked in the bones, so there are limitations.

Then we get to the teeth. The rate at which teeth erupt from the jaw are excellent indicators of the age of an individual at death. The wear and tear indicates the quality of the diet: the finer milled the flour, the more expensive it was, and the less wear it had on the teeth. But caries, caused by sweeteners such as honey, also indicate that the eater could afford a rich, and expensive, diet. Contained within the teeth is dentine, which is perfect for providing an isotopic signature. This gives excellent evidence of where the individual spent the first few years of his or her life and, as such, provides much information to scientists studying the movement and interaction of different people and peoples.

Taken as a package, the bones can tell us a huge amount. The job of the archaeologist is to flesh this out.

Interview with Graeme Young

1. What is the Bamburgh Research Project?
The Bamburgh Research Project is a not-for-profit
archaeological research project set up in 1996 to
study Bamburgh and its vicinity. There are good reasons to have such a project focussed on Bamburgh,
such as its role as a major royal centre for the kingdom of Northumbria in the early medieval period.
In addition, the natural setting of the site makes
it an ideal candidate to have been occupied as an
important settlement since prehistory.

2. Why did you decide to set it up?
There is a whole gamut of academic reasons that
can be made to justify an archaeological research
project sited on Bamburgh but the reality is that
I have known and loved the castle and the area
since childhood and it would have been impos-
sible for me to have resisted the urge to investigate it for long.

3. What's your role in the project?
I am one of four directors forming the executive committee of the Bamburgh
Research Project. At the moment I am primarily responsible for direct-
ing the archaeological work being undertaken in the West Ward of the castle.

4. What's been your most important find?
In a way the most important find may be the archive and excavation trenches from Dr
Brian Hope-Taylor's excavation work undertaken at the site in the 1960s and 1970s, as
this gives us the chance to ensure that his work is completed and written up along with
our own. The loss of such work would certainly have been very sad for early medieval
archaeology in the north-east. In terms of the archaeology that we have done ourselves,
the evidence for the wider interpretation of the site, which has revealed the location of the
industrial area in the central part of the West Ward together with the evidence for buildings, including quite early stone architecture, stands out. Personally, it's the way archaeology
can paint a picture of the past that endlessly fascinates me: the big picture rather than the
individual find, however exciting or rare that may be.

5. What's your most interesting find?
Thinking about the special finds that we have recovered over the years it's difficult to
pick out individual items. Certainly the ninth-century decorated gold artefacts we have
found in recent years have been spectacular in their beauty and the detail of their decora-
tion, though I still have a fondness for a fragmentary jet crucifix that we recovered from

the late medieval midden layer, as the wear pattern on its surface showed that it must have been a much-loved possession. I think that items like that, which give you a real sense of connection to someone who died hundreds of years ago, do have a tendency to stick in your mind.

6. How long have people lived at Bamburgh?
We have clear evidence of the site being occupied since the prehistoric period. Our earliest finds so far come from the base of a re-excavated Hope-Taylor trench and are a few fragments of Neolithic flint, which pushes the occupation of the castle site back to around 5,000 years ago. In the wider Bamburgh area, Mesolithic flints have been found at a number of sites. These date from the time of the hunter-gatherers many thousands of years ago. A time before farming was adopted.

7. How much longer will you be excavating for?
It's difficult to say with certainty. We would certainly, at the very least, wish to publish an investigation that reached the levels that Dr Hope-Taylor reached. That will probably take another five years or so. Personally, I would love to excavate a full sequence to the bedrock over a limited part of the West Ward, and for that we are probably looking at another decade or more of work.

8. What's the project's role in training the next generation of archaeologists?
We run a training excavation each summer, and have done this at some level since the late 1990s. In most cases, we provide the necessary training in field techniques that universities require from their archaeological students, but we have always aimed to be an inclusive project. We welcome members of the public and very much hope that we have done our bit in popularising archaeology as well as making our contribution to training a new generation of professional archaeologists.

9. How many archaeologists have you trained so far?
I did a calculation quite recently and estimated that around 1,000 students have passed through the dig up to the end of last season. Hopefully they all learned at least a little from their time at Bamburgh. Even if we have inspired only the tiniest fraction of them to stay involved in the discipline then it will have been time well spent.

10. Do you have to be at university to sign up for the project or can anyone interested in archaeology apply?
We very much aim to be welcoming to anyone who is curious about how archaeology works or who has always hankered after a chance to try it out. Most seasons we get a good cross section of people through the dig, and we are proud of that.

11. Where do applicants come from?
We advertise in various popular archaeological journals as well as via the Internet, through our own and other sites. We also run a blog that seems to be increasingly popular, and have

done public lectures since we first started. Popular television programmes such as *Meet the Ancestors* and *Time Team* as well as our own videos have also helped to get the message out. As a consequence we have a varied base of applicants from around the world, not just the UK. We have a solid application base from the USA and Canada, but can add to that many European countries and Australia too.

12. What's the age range?
We are happy to accept all ages from teens to retired pensioners and most seasons will cover that full range, though there tends to be a bias towards late teens to early twenties due to a core group of high school and university students who are planning a career in archaeology.

13. Do you all have beards?
No. I can confirm that there is a low beard ratio among the directors and senior staff. However, Gerry carries the flag for the bearded community but I am sure Clare will be happy for me to confirm her beardlessness.

14. What question do you wish I'd asked?
If you had asked what the best thing about digging at Bamburgh has been then I would have been able to tell you that my abiding memories from the project are of the fun we have had and the people we have met. We have without a doubt produced a hugely important data set but most of all I think we have made a small mark on many people's lives for the better. And you can't say fairer than that.

Interview with Sarah Groves

1. Who are you and what is your area of expertise?
I'm Dr Sarah Groves, a physical anthropologist.

2. Describe your specialism simply.
Physical anthropology is the study of human remains to understand how people lived and died in the past.

3. Can you describe the burials/skeletons in Northumbria/ Bamburgh in layman's terms?
The Bowl Hole cemetery is an early medieval burial ground used over a period of several hundred years. The burial ground is one of the largest and best-preserved early medieval cemeteries in the north-east of England. We have excavated ninety-one graves, around a third of the cemetery.

The burial practices at Bamburgh were quite simple. Most were cut into the sand or clay soil, but some have stone linings called 'cists'. About 37 per cent of the burials were associated with simple grave goods including knives and belt buckles, beads and pins, and one burial had a large bone comb and a set of latch-lifters or simple keys. Animal bones were also present in some of the burials, mostly those of men, suggesting that they were linked to the social identity of the people.

Most of the adults buried at Bamburgh were tall and robust. This relatively tall adult height suggests that these people were well nourished during childhood.

Analysing the skeletons has enabled us to identify a wide range of illnesses and injuries in the population. Most of the adults and some of the children suffered from dental decay, dental abscesses and tooth loss, with some older adults having lost all their teeth during life. While dental disease is primarily caused by poor dental hygiene, it may also have been exacerbated by a diet rich in meat, sugars (from fruit and honey) and refined starches (from good-quality bread). The prevalence of dental disease at Bamburgh is much higher than that seen in other early medieval populations from the north-east, suggesting that the people buried at Bamburgh may have eaten a better, higher-status diet. Interestingly there is also a difference between men and women at Bamburgh: men had far more dental disease than women, perhaps indicating that they ate a different diet. It seems likely that the lifestyle of men in early medieval Bamburgh involved feasting and drinking, but it seems that women partook less than their menfolk, or took better care of their teeth.

Another indicator of dietary excess from Bamburgh is the presence of gout in several individuals. Gout can be caused by excessive consumption of red meat and alcohol, and together with the evidence for dental disease, helps to build a picture of the diet and lifestyle of these people.

Rather surprisingly, a large proportion of the Bowl Hole population didn't have a local isotopic signature. Only eight were born in the local Bamburgh area, 13 had signatures from the kingdom of Northumbria, 23 were from western Scotland or western Ireland, and 26 came from other areas of the British Isles. Six of the samples had signatures that were similar to those seen in Scandinavian countries and seven suggested origins in southern Europe, possibly the Mediterranean area.

4. What are the dates at Bamburgh?
The radiocarbon dates from nine skeletons range from the seventh to ninth centuries AD, and the types of artefact found with some of the burials also support this date range. The earliest burials may be from the late-sixth to mid-seventh century and the latest may be from the late-seventh to late-ninth century.

5. How do the burials/skeletons inform us about wider Northumbria?
Studying this cemetery has made me realise that people living in early medieval Bamburgh really weren't that much different to us today. The information from isotopic analysis shows us that they were a community of people who had travelled from across the British Isles and even further afield in some cases. They were cosmopolitan people with contacts across the North Sea and possibly down into the Mediterranean.

They suffered from many of the same health conditions as we do and clearly cared about their elderly and infirm. Very young children were often buried very close to or even inserted into the grave of an older adult, perhaps as part of a family plot, or in the hope that the adult would look after the child in the afterlife.

The presence of some of the 'non-local' people at Bamburgh may be explained by what we know about the kingdom of Northumbria in the early medieval period. Northumbria had strong links with the early Christian communities in western Scotland and western Ireland and had trading links across the known world.

6. Are there any specific examples of this?

One individual from Bamburgh (sk 101) probably needed special care from the community throughout his or her life. This person is very unusual; the teeth suggest an age of between 19 and 24 years, but the state of development of the skeleton indicates an age of between 10 and 16 years. It seems that this person suffered from a condition that affected and stunted their growth and made it impossible for us to be sure about his or her sex.

7. How is the burial practice/skeletal analysis of Northumbria/Bamburgh different from other places, if at all? Does it fit into a wider picture?

The types of artefacts found in the Bowl Hole burials are typical of a 'Final Phase' cemetery, when graves were very sparsely furnished, possibly due to the influence of Christianity. However, some of the practices stand out as unusual. The proportion of prone (face down) burials is high in comparison with other sites in the north of England. The precise meaning of prone burial is unknown but it has been thought that people who died while doing religious penance were buried prone. The high proportion of prone burials at Bamburgh may be due to the strong links between Bamburgh and the religious communities at Lindisfarne.

Bamburgh is unique in its dual role as a royal settlement with very strong links to early Christianity. It may be that the variety of burial practices at Bamburgh reflects the range of people from across Britain and Europe who lived there.

12

DECLINE AND FALL

But then the Great Darkness came, and they passed away over the Sea, or fled into far valleys, and hid themselves, and made songs about days that would never come again. Never again.

(J.R.R. Tolkien, *The Two Towers*)

In the seventh century, Northumbria was the pre-eminent kingdom in Britain. Its kings were high kings, its territory stretched from Edinburgh to well south of the Humber and the prestige of its monks and holy men was unrivalled among the Anglo-Saxons.

So what went wrong? How did all that power slip away? There were many factors that contributed to Northumbria's decline and in this final chapter we investigate them and suggest that maybe, as with Mark Twain, the reports of Northumbria's death are somewhat exaggerated.

OUT ON THE EDGE

Northumbria was not exactly central. Its position on the periphery of Europe and the edge of Christian civilisation was well known and deeply felt by its people. Bede begins his *Ecclesiastical History of the English People* by situating the country with respect to the rest of the continent.

Britain, formerly known as Albion, is an island in the ocean, lying towards the north west at a considerable distance from the coasts of Germany, Gaul, and Spain, which together form the greater part of Europe.

(Bede, *Ecclesiastical History of the English People*, p. 44)

While its location may have been advantageous in Northumbria's early history, when its sea-orientated people served as the mediators and channels for Irish scholarship and Christianity to spread through Britain, as the rest of the continent slowly re-established political and cultural structures the kingdom became more distant from the new currents of power and thought. In the second half of the eighth century, Charlemagne established his empire and refounded the idea of Europe. As a result, trade increased with the Mediterranean countries, North Africa and the Caliphate. But even using the sea and rivers as roads, Northumbria was a long, long way from the action. In particular, silver, the metal from which money was made through most of Europe – gold having become too rare for such use – came almost exclusively from the Caliphate. The silver mined from Cumbria had long been exhausted.

show me the money

As far as Christianity was concerned, Northumbria was an early adopter. But although the religion was directly responsible for the cultural flowering of Northumbria's golden age, it may also have been indirectly responsible for the kingdom's decline. To put it simply, the religion became too successful. The vast majority of gold in Northumbria became locked in Christian objects – gold crosses, gold chalices, gold book clasps. There were obvious and valid religious reasons for this, since holy things deserved the honour and sacrifice of the most valued and treasured materials. But for an economy to function, money has to circulate. It's like blood: leave it too long in one place and a clot will form. Christianity had the unintended effect of draining liquidity from Northumbria's economy[46] and the replacement for gold adopted by the rest of the continent – silver – was, because of distance, difficult for the Northumbrians to obtain. Gold, of course, had always been valuable. The Staffordshire hoard is mostly gold, and much of the endemic raiding between kingdoms in Anglo-Saxon Britain was, simply, to grab gold. For a king to prosper and attract warriors it was imperative for him to have a reputation for generosity – a great king spread his wealth to his followers. The easiest and quickest way to gain the gold was to take it. Thus a crude sort of liquidity ensued, with gold circulating around the kingdoms of Anglo-Saxon Britain in the wake of successful wars and raids. But with the rise of Christianity, the generosity and gift giving that was characteristic of Anglo-Saxon society was directed to the Church, most notably in gifts of land and gifts of gold. But this immediately put a dam in the money flow. It was all very well stealing the golden torc from a defeated enemy and either wearing it yourself or melting it down for bullion, but it was quite another thing to raid a church, steal a crucifix and melt that down. The first act was the socially sanctioned act of a warrior that would bring renown as well as wealth, while the second was a sacrilege that would not only bring vilification but eternal damnation.

So with the gold locked away and silver hard to come by, the primary sources of wealth in the early medieval period slowly dried up in Northumbria. The only alternative was trade. And, yes, Northumbria was well known in Europe for dogs and horses, but valuable though these were in the early medieval period, they were never going to bring in as much money as the silver mines of the Hindu Kush. The decline in Northumbrian wealth is quite clearly marked by the slow decline in the quality of stones used in its jewellery: from the finest, large garnets, imported all the way from India and Sri Lanka at the height of the kingdom's power and wealth, the gems gradually became smaller and more local, with most mined in Portugal.

Now money isn't everything, but it is the foundation of most worldly enterprises. With less wealth, Northumbrian kings found it harder to recruit warriors, which made it harder for them to win battles, which made it harder to plunder more gold, which made it harder to attract warriors. It was a slow, but inexorable, tightening, and it slowly choked the kingdom.

AND THEN THE VIKINGS CAME

In AD 793, Vikings attacked Lindisfarne. The Viking Age had begun.

The Norsemen were cunning, or clever if you prefer a less pejorative term. They had very clear ideas of what they were setting out to do, they gathered information and intelligence, and they acted on it. They were probably aware that Northumbrian strength had become depleted, partly as a result of its generations-long struggle with the rising kingdom of Mercia. But much of the wealth that Northumbria had acquired during its political heyday was still present, transformed into sacred vessels and instruments in churches and monasteries that were conveniently placed near the sea and rivers, and even more conveniently were unprotected by fortifications. It was a veritable smorgasbord and the Vikings helped themselves. But the pattern of the raids reveals that the Vikings saw what they were doing in a very different light to the locals. For the Northumbrians, the raids were unparalleled acts of devastation and destruction. For the Vikings, the raids were like harvests, reaping crops of gold, silver and slaves. So the usual pattern was to steal portable wealth from a monastery and to take the young and healthy to sell as slaves, but to largely leave the buildings intact. Then, when the monks a few years down the line had begun the laborious work of rebuilding, the Vikings could return and harvest the next crop of human beings and divine offerings.

Although the age started with raids, it developed into a full-scale invasion, with standing armies taking the field and the Vikings conquering the Midlands, East Anglia and the southern part of Northumbria, famously making York their capital. However, Bernicia, the northern part of Northumbria, held out, and Bamburgh was never conquered. But with the central belt of the country under the control of the Norsemen, what remained of Northumbria inevitably became isolated from the rest of Anglo-Saxon Britain.

Apart from cutting Northumbria off from the rest of the country, the arrival of the Vikings didn't help the kingdom's economic situation either. While the Christian Anglo-Saxons couldn't melt down golden crosses and other religious items, the pagan Vikings certainly had no such compunctions. The Vikings liquidated the money that had become locked in Northumbria and elsewhere in Anglo-Saxon Britain as religious art by literally melting it down. Then that gold financed and lured further raids: in effect, the Anglo-Saxons financed their attackers.

The traditional view of Vikings. *Wikimedia Commons*

Although part of Northumbria survived, it had to acknowledge the Danish kings of York as its overlords, and pay them too. Thus further wealth was drained from the system.

who shall rule?

The laws of succession in Northumbria were unclear. The lack of clarity has its roots in Anglo-Saxon custom, where hereditary privilege played a part but the ability to wield a sword and lead a warband generally trumped birth. The matter was complicated by Northumbria being the amalgamation of two kingdoms, Bernicia and Deira, each with royal lineages that could legitimately claim the throne. Thus, the death of a king was a fraught time, as there were many potential claimants to the throne, and even once a king was installed it was quite possible for rivals to claim that the rule should be theirs. For a while, under kings as dominant as Edwin, Oswald and Oswiu, Northumbria enjoyed relative internal peace, but the eighth century, although a time of cultural flowering, was a period of chronic political instability, with one king following in the murdered or deposed footsteps of another with depressing regularity. No kingdom could hope to survive such turmoil unscathed, and Northumbria didn't.

Other Anglo-Saxon kingdoms, notably Wessex, solved the problem of succession much more successfully. The key change was writing. Once things started to be recorded, then the succession became immutable; there was still the old tradition, that basically equated to 'might makes king', but a codified law and the law of the jungle can't co-exist for long – one of them has to take precedence. To cleave to the old ways meant that a king was regarded as a barbarian by his peers – written laws and clear rules of succession were integral to the adoption of Christianity and the reintegration of the country into the wider civilised world. The question as far as Northumbria is concerned is why a kingdom that became thoroughly Christian and literate so quickly failed to adopt adequate laws regarding the royal succession. We suspect, although there is no proof for this, that one reason may have been the ongoing tension between the heirs of the royal houses of Bernicia and Deira, each of which could lay claim to the throne. In such circumstances, it behoved both families in the short term to maintain a certain ambiguity about the rules. In the long term, of course, it led to their destruction.

poured out as a libation

Northumbria's prodigality with its most gifted sons and daughters may also have contributed to its decline. As the pre-eminent centre of Christian scholarship and missionary activity in north-west Europe, it dispatched the best and brightest monks and religious of two or three generations to Europe to attempt the conversion of the ancestral homelands of the Anglo-Saxon peoples. The volcanic Wilfrid set the whole enterprise off as a by-product of one of his many disputes with King Aldfrith. The king had dismissed Wilfrid from his post and exiled him from the land (this was not a one-off occurrence in what must have been the most turbulent example of Church and state relations until Thomas Becket and Henry II). In response, Wilfrid set off for Rome to have his case heard by the

Pope, and on the way stopped in Frisia (the coastal areas from the Netherlands through Germany to the border of Denmark) and set about converting the locals. A generation later, Alcuin was headhunted by Charlemagne to be the emperor's intellectual right-hand man and the schoolmaster of Europe. Willibrord went with a symbolic twelve companions to complete the conversion of the Frisians. Black Hewald and White Hewald set off to evangelise the Saxons, but were martyred. And these are just the names that were recorded. There were many more who set off, in search of learning, for the love of travel or simply to spread the Gospel, who never returned to their homeland.

To support the evangelisation of its own people, and then the peoples of Britain and Europe, Northumbria became a veritable publishing factory. Monkish scribes laboured through the long hours of a northern summer's day, producing manuscripts from the most exquisite to the more functional. While some were retained for domestic use, many were dispatched abroad. Indeed, Northumbrian manuscripts crop up all over the place, from the version of Bede's *Ecclesiastical History of the English People* in St Petersburg (it was rescued from the book burners of the French Revolution by a Russian diplomat), to the *Codex Amiatinus* in Florence. In a society bound together by the mutual obligations of gift giving, sending manuscripts abroad was both an act of pastoral generosity and a binding together of the widely scattered missionary networks in north-west Europe. As Northumbria grew poorer, sending manuscripts abroad might also have served to ensure reciprocal gifts of the precious materials required for producing and adorning books, such as gold and lapis lazuli. So while Northumbria sent forth its children, those emigrants, mindful of their home, did help to keep the monastic scribes working.

SWORDS AND PLOUGHSHARES

Good-quality iron is hard to come by. Northumbria has little in the way of natural resources for iron production beyond bog ore, which while of reasonable quality does not produce much by way of quantity. This was not a problem in the early days of the kingdom, when war bands numbered in the tens rather than the hundreds, but as armies grew larger, more weapons were needed to equip them. Much of the best iron in the eighth and ninth centuries came from Central Europe and Denmark. But once that iron was required to outfit the Viking armies that invaded Britain and other parts of Europe, the trade understandably died off. After all, if you were a foundryman in Denmark, why bother sending your iron off to faraway places when the local kings, enriched by plunder, wanted to buy your wares?

Faced with the arms race of the Viking Age (it was, quite literally, an arms race, as Viking raiders returned as Viking armies, thousands strong), Northumbria found it very hard to compete. Today, Northumberland is the most sparsely populated county in England and, while Deira was probably more densely populated than Bernicia, it's unlikely to have ever supported a large number of people. The kingdom had relied on a small, professional army. This had served the kings well when dealing with the other Anglo-Saxon kingdoms, which fielded similar forces, but, to adapt the boxing phrase, a good large army will always beat a good small army. Once the Vikings started deploying large armies of experienced warriors, Northumbria couldn't compete. Three hundred men can't stand against 3,000 similarly armed men (even the Spartans lost eventually). Heroic failures are all very well for inspiring songs but if there aren't some stories of stirring triumphs for a couple of generations then the war is lost.

That's not to say the Northumbrians didn't fight well. Although Deira fell and York became the Viking capital, Bamburgh remained untaken until that French offshoot of the Norsemen, William, despoiled the north in 1068.

The Achievement of Northumbria

For the brief period of its heyday, Northumbria was the most important kingdom in Christendom. Indeed, one of the reasons for its importance was the role that it played in expanding Christendom, first over the rest of Britain and then into north-western Europe. But then it was largely forgotten. Its work was done. Northumbria set the tone for the rest of Britain, and in that process King Oswald played a key role. Without his encouragement and support it's unlikely that the Anglo-Saxon kingdoms would have been evangelised nearly so quickly, and a pagan Britain would inevitably have been marginalised. Without Christianity, there would have been no codified law, no continuity, no history.[47] In his death and sanctification, King Oswald provided a template into which the brawling, warring kings of Anglo-Saxon Britain could plausibly fit themselves without irretrievably distorting either their cultural identity or their newly adopted faith.

When Oswald died at the Battle of Maserfield, the victorious Penda chopped his body up. Big mistake. The royal relics, credited with miraculous powers, in no small measure fuelled the cult of Oswald that spread through Britain and Europe. In some ways, Oswald was almost an Anglo-Saxon Arthur. He was a thinking-man's king for a ruling class trained in violence from birth, and his story resonated with Biblical and symbolic themes. As a child, he went into exile, as did the young Jesus. He returned with a small group of trusted warriors and won the battle against great odds to reclaim his kingdom (there are echoes here of Moses leading the Jews through the wilderness and Joshua's campaigns to conquer the promised land). He was literate and spoke a number of languages. Then, in his last act, he died a martyr fighting a pagan, and his mortal remains immediately started producing miracles. With his example exported across Europe by expatriate monks, Oswald became a prototype of Christian kingship for the medieval period. So while Northumbria declined in terms of its direct manifestation of power, its influence grew immensely through the examples of leadership, sanctity, scholarship and devotion that it provided.

The kingdom was dead, but Northumbria lived on.

The Song Remains the Same

More than 1,000 years after the heyday of Northumbria, what remains of this kingdom by the grey sea? In material terms, not much. There are the luminous manuscripts, some stone crosses and jewellery, and various pieces of ironwork, but that's about it. Northumbria was no Rome. But even though the political entity that was Northumbria died 1,000 years ago, the identity of modern-day Yorkshire and Northumberland is still deeply Anglo-Saxon.

Although the Vikings were invaders, they shared deep roots with the Anglians and, to be honest, once they set up shop (and houses) in York and elsewhere they proved reasonably decent overlords. But that French Norseman William the Bastard was a different matter altogether. The year 1066 is the schoolboy date, but for northerners, 1068, the year William came north and laid the land to waste, marks the date when the north became the north, in fire and suffering and blood. Frenchmen – French speakers – ruled England and in some ways we can date the cleavage in the national psyche between northerners and southerners to William's depredations in the north. Yorkshire, Northumberland and (although Mexborough-born Paul is loath to admit it) even Lancashire are different to the south. But since the eleventh century, power has been concentrated in the south, in the Great Wen.

Although the cities of Yorkshire and Northumberland (not that there are many cities in Northumberland!) have mixed populations, the people in rural areas can often trace their ancestry back many generations. Indeed, the Bamburgh Research Project found that many of the inhabitants of present-day Bamburgh are descendants of people buried 1200 years ago in the cemetery that the project excavated outside the castle. So there has been a longevity and rootedness in the population that fly-by-night dwellers in the metropolis might find hard to understand. If people can go to the village churchyard and see there the graves of their grandparents and great-grandparents and great-great-grandparents, it inevitably produces a deep, unstated but unmistakeable connection to the land and locale.

To this day, on the long journey back up the A1 from visiting his co-author in London, Paul knows when he's entered the environs of the old north kingdom. The Angles put out from their old homes in Angeln on the eastern side of the Danish peninsula, sailed around Jutland, across the North Sea and arrived in Britain some 1500 years ago – and stayed. The very name of England has its root in the name the Angles gave themselves, and Northumbria, the kingdom they founded, played an extraordinary part in the formation of the country. Northumbria may have been lost in time, but England endures. Not a bad legacy for a bunch of piratical freebooters.

Of pots and postholes

While we maintain that archaeology is a science, there is a dark art to the discipline. The best field archaeologists have an almost intuitive feel for the subject. It's like with the top sportsmen. Lionel Messi, in the split second he has between controlling a ball and a defender closing in on him, doesn't rationally analyse the vectors of his teammates and opposition, thus working out that if he places the ball past the last defender with a certain amount of spin, then Iniesta, whom he can't even see but who he knows will be running into space, will be clear through on goal. The mental processes that take place in such a sportsman are not rational but super-rational: endless hours of practice allied with a natural talent and an ability to see space all come together in a controlled, supremely directed kick. So it is with the truly great archaeologist. He or she can see something in the ground and fathom what it is. Everybody, all the time, is simultaneously processing a vast amount of information. When an archaeologist looks at a particular piece of ground, he or she does so with eyes that are alive to all sorts of contexts, from the immediate environment to the depths of the geological past. Knowledge like this is the ever-present background in front of which a good archaeologist works.

But when it comes to practical field archaeology, there are all sorts of other cues to help situate the archaeologist in place and time. Even the sound of the trowel turning earth will be different according to the material that it's turning over. Gritty soil makes a harsh, clacking sound, sand produces a scraping, abrasive noise and clay sounds smoother. So the noise of the trowel will tell the good archaeologist what he or she is digging through. Smell, too, provides clues, with a richer, more loamy soil producing the characteristic scent of organic material returned to the earth. Important though the other senses are, sight remains key. Even subtle changes of colour can tell a tale. If something gets redder as it is excavated, then that means there's iron in it, because it's the exposure to atmospheric oxygen that is oxidising the iron and turning it red. The best archaeologists use all of their senses. It is the ability to coordinate all of these sensory inputs with the accumulated knowledge and experience of years, all leavened with the intuitive spark that enables the extraordinary to be discerned against the background of the ordinary, that marks out the great archaeologist from the ordinary one. Archaeologists sometimes call this a gut feeling, but perhaps it could be just as accurately described as a sudden and complete sense of things coming together.[48] Archaeologists who have known this happen often describe the experience as euphoric.

But just as important as these moments of insight is the realisation that you've got something wrong: the gradual accumulation of evidence from a dig suddenly tips the scales against a cherished idea. What do you do then? Do you look for more evidence to back up your theory or do you embrace the fresh outlook and construct a new hypothesis based on the new evidence? Proper science demands the latter of course, but human nature often requires the former. The truly bad archaeologists are the ones who develop a hypothesis and then go out to prove it. The best archaeologists don't see being wrong as a negative. In fact, being wrong isn't wrong. The recognition of error allows for a slightly closer approach to what is true, always bearing in mind the provisional nature of archaeological truth. In fact, without a deep acceptance of the fact that you could be, and probably are, wrong, then as an archaeologist you are just digging holes. You might as well be an antiquarian, simply collecting curious artefacts for pleasure.

To genuinely think about archaeology requires the capacity to excavate, to visualise what was there once from what's in the ground now, and to put what you find into context. That context does not just refer to the site.

After bits of pottery, the classic archaeological find is the posthole: the hole where a post used to be! To effectively do archaeology you need to be able to look down at that posthole and then reconstruct a building in your mind's eye based on the pattern made by the surrounding postholes. But that's not the end of the reconstruction. From there, the building needs to be situated in the village to which it belonged, and in the landscape that held and provided for the village. Even then, that's not the end, for the village and the land are nestled, embedded, within a kingdom and a world, which all feed back to the understanding of the posthole lying dark in the earth before you. This is the joy of being an archaeologist: for a while you can inhabit the past on an intellectual and imaginative level. The past ceases to be a different country: for a moment, in the exaltation and exhaustion of excavation, you live there!

The raw material of archaeology: a posthole. *BRP*

NOTES

Introduction

1. Paul Gething (born Mexborough) insists that we add 'and Yorkshiremen' to the phrase.

Chapter 1

2. Yes, we know 'Dark Ages' is no longer the preferred epithet, and it's true, it is the wrong label in almost all ways, carrying unjustified implications of congenital stupidity and evil. But in one respect at least it really was dark – we still can't see it clearly. Early medieval is the new name for the period sandwiched between the end of the Western Roman Empire and the Norman Conquest.

3. Bede, in his history, refers to the 'capture' of Bamburgh, so it seems likely that there was a stronghold there already. Archaeologically, there is a suggestion of a wooden palisade set into a wide clay bank from the right period, which was quickly replaced with a stone wall. Carbon 14 dates have not yet been done on the remains, so the link between the identification of the remains found and Bede's account remains tentative, but it does tie in perfectly with his description.

4. The poem *Y Gododdin* suggests that the British made at least one concerted effort to reconquer their territory from the Angles. The dating of *Y Gododdin* is difficult but it seems likely to be from close to the time of Ida. Gildas also mentions the British waging war on the Saxons (Angles) and Nennius (in the ninth century) describes Urien of Rheged and the Kings of Strathclyde waging war on the 'sons of Ida'. (Source: Rollason, D., *Northumbria 500–1100*, p. 103)

5. Naturally, this authorship is contested, with David Dumville arguing that the *History* is the work of an anonymous writer based at the court of Gwynedd in 820–830.

6. Although Æthelfrith might have been more John Gotti than John of Gaunt, it's pretty certain that his use of language would have been better, if not necessarily cleaner, than modern gangsters. Listening to transcripts of wiretaps on Mafia bosses is to make one despair of the future of language beyond a limit of four letters to a word.

7. Ziegler, M., 'The Politics of Exile in Early Northumbria' in *The Heroic Age*, 2, autumn/winter 1999; Kirby, D.P., *The Earliest English Kings*.

8. Blair, P.H., *Northumbria in the Days of Bede*, p. 42.
9. Ibid., p. 43
10. It's not clear whether Penda was yet king of Mercia at the time of this alliance, but the victory over Edwin would certainly have helped to increase and consolidate his power.
11. Aidan was actually the second representative sent from Iona; the first missionary failed in his mission to convert the Northumbrians, claiming they were too stubborn.

Chapter 2

12. The subtitle of Charles Lyell's *Principles of Geology*.

Chapter 3

13. Apparently, the typical patterns produced when taking natural hallucinogens like mushrooms are spirals.
14. The various stone ages – Palaeolithic, Mesolithic and Neolithic – lasted for varying periods of time in different parts of the world.
15. Yorkish partisans tend to gloss over the fact that once Constantine became sole emperor he established his new capital at Constantinople, about as far away from York as it was possible to get and remain within the empire.
16. Ötzi the Iceman, the human corpse found in the Alps whose body has been dated back to 3255 BC, was carrying a copper-headed axe and analysis of his hair indicates that it was heavily contaminated with arsenic, suggesting that he was involved with smelting copper.
17. A coffin box made of stone that held the dead.

Chapter 4

18. Of course whether this is actually true is another matter. In fact, there is some evidence that it is secular Europe that is the historical aberration, and that the twenty-first may prove to be a century of religious enthusiasm and revival, with all the possibilities and dangers that these most volcanic of human fervours produce. As an introduction see *God is Back* by John Micklethwait and Adrian Wooldridge.
19. The move from grottos to churches was not instantaneous however. The conversion of the Northumbrians at Yeavering in 627 lasted 37 days and was largely conducted out-doors: beside, and in, the River Glen. An amphitheatre excavated on the Yeavering site is thought to be part of the apparatus for preaching to the newly converted in the open air.
20. Clive Barker borrowed the name for his flesh-sculpting artisans of pain in the *Hellraiser* series of stories and films.
21. Scholarly opinion seems to be swinging back towards accepting that there were some mass movements of people as well as small war bands taking over the leadership of petty princedoms in decapitatory style.
22. This is totally speculative, but one can easily imagine a priest of the Britons consider-ing preaching the gospel of everlasting life to the pagans, then deciding that these despoilers of his land and culture deserved only everlasting damnation. 'Let them die in ignorance and be condemned!'

23. Admittedly, Italy wouldn't exist for more than 1,000 years, but calling them Roman invites misunderstanding.
24. This mission was extraordinary in all manners of ways, not least of which was its logistics. Pope Gregory dispatched nearly 40 men to far-off England; imagine the sheer force of personality required to persuade so many to abandon their lives and homes and trek into the unknown. Compare that to how many Italian priests made the journey to England in the centuries between Gregory's death and the Conquest: five. This serves to give some idea of the scale of Gregory's enterprise and the breadth of his vision.
25. Blair, P.H., *Northumbria in the Days of Bede*, p. 107.
26. Bede notes that Iona first sent a bishop of 'austere disposition' who had no success preaching and returned home complaining that the Northumbrians were an obstinate and barbarous people. Given that Bede himself was no slacker when it came to monastic discipline, one is tempted to shudder at the thought of a man whom he labelled 'austere'.
27. His son, Peada, in fact married one of Oswiu's daughters, but the marriage was only contracted on the basis that Peada would be baptised and accept Christianity, which he did. Another example of the importance of Christian princesses in the promulgation of the religion.
28. The standard Roman way of cropping the hair was to shave the crown and leave a circular fringe around it. The monks in Ireland appear to have shaved the front of their heads, from ear to ear and over the crown, while leaving the hair at the back of their heads to grow.
29. The Irish custom actually spread and became the norm throughout Europe.
30. Given that Eanflæd became abbess of Whitby after Oswiu's death, one can speculate that there may have been other frustrations for the king caused by their different periods of abstinence.
31. Iona finally fell into line in 716.

Chapter 5

32. This was the largest hoard of Anglo-Saxon gold yet discovered. On 5 July 2009, metal detector Terry Herbert discovered the first of an eventual 3,500 gold and silver artefacts that had been buried in a field near Lichfield in Staffordshire. The recovered items were almost all martial, with virtually no everyday things. Some 5kg of gold and 1.5kg of silver were discovered, most of the highest quality.
33. A law code issued by King Ine of Wessex in AD 694, which was the first written body of law outside Kent to survive.

Chapter 6

34. 'The state is me' was supposedly the reply given by the 17-year-old king to the president of the Parlement when he questioned Louis' financial demands 'in the interests of the state'. We wouldn't be responsible historians if we didn't note that there are some doubts as to whether Louis actually said this, while admitting that it's such a good line that a chorus of historians dancing from here until Doomsday won't stop people from quoting it.

35. 300 is one of those round numbers always trotted out by the annalists and minstrels. It's unlikely anyone did an accurate head count on the Spartans at Thermopylae.

Chapter 7

36. The Vercelli Book is one of the four surviving codices containing Old English poetry. It was discovered in 1822 in the Basilica of St Andrew in Vercelli, north Italy.
37. Anyone guessing from the *Balamory* reference that the authors have young children scores top marks.
38. The Norns were the fates of Norse mythology, apportioning good and evil fortune according to their whim.

Chapter 8

39. Northumberland is still famous for its cheeses. If you ever visit, ask for a platter of local cheeses.

Chapter 9

40. *Senatus Populusque Romanus* (the Senate and People of Rome).
41. If any reader wants suggestions for a good piece of archaeological research, we suggest examining medieval flint: the patterns created when flint is hit with metal are different to those formed when it is struck by a softer hammer such as an antler, so there should be clear evidence to indicate that Stone-Age flints were reused in medieval times. Reference us in your PhD though!

Chapter 10

42. Contrary to what we would expect, stirrups took a long time to catch on. This seems to be because what seem to us the obvious advantages of riding with stirrups were not so obvious at the time – indeed, most of the plus points of using stirrups (stability, ability to endure impacts) had already been achieved by the high-backed saddles of the Roman and Byzantine heavy cavalry, the cataphracts.
43. Currency had been declining in value for most of the Roman period as a result of the continuing debasement of the coinage. Towards the end of the Western Empire, faith in the currency had largely collapsed, while the slow contraction of the empire meant a lack of new booty and a shortage of new silver for coins.
44. The *Codex Amiatinus* is the oldest surviving copy of the Bible in Latin.
45. Perhaps we can discern, through the gulf of centuries, that Ceolfrith's gift of the Bible to the Pope was an acknowledgement of the debt owed by the Church in England to the successors of Peter and their interest in evangelising the English peoples.

Chapter 12

46. Who'd have thought it? Early medieval Europe and post-modern Europe are linked across the centuries by similar economic crises.
47. Apart from oral history, but that is even more prey to the vicissitudes of fortune than written history.
48. Seeing that this is a book about Anglo-Saxon Britain, another, particularly appropriate, analogy is the moment of insight when suddenly the solution to a riddle presents itself.

BIBLIOGRAPHY

Alexander, M. (trans.), *The Earliest English Poems* (Harmondsworth, Middlesex: Penguin, 1977)

Anonymous, *The Anonymous History of Abbot Ceolfrith* in Webb, J.F. and Farmer, D.H., *The Age of Bede* (London: Penguin Books, 1998)

Anonymous, *The Voyage of St Brendan* in Webb, J.F. and Farmer, D.H., *The Age of Bede* (London: Penguin Books, 1998)

Arwidsson, G. and Berg, G., *The Mastermyr Find: A Viking Age Tool Chest from Gotland* (California: Larson Publishing Co., 1983)

Backhouse, J., *The Lindisfarne Gospels* (Oxford: Phaidon, 2010)

Bede, *Ecclesiastical History of the English People* (London: Penguin Books, 1990)

Bede, *Life of Cuthbert* in Webb, J.F. and Farmer, D.H., *The Age of Bede* (London: Penguin Books, 1998)

Bede, *Lives of the Abbots of Wearmouth and Jarrow* in Webb, J.F. and Farmer, D.H., *The Age of Bede* (London: Penguin Books, 1998)

Blair, J., *The Anglo-Saxon Age: A Very Short Introduction* (Oxford: Oxford University Press, 1984)

Blair, P.H., *Northumbria in the Days of Bede* (London: Victor Gollancz, 1976)

Blair, P.H., *An Introduction to Anglo-Saxon England* (Cambridge: Cambridge University Press, 1977)

Blair, P.H., *The World of Bede* (Cambridge: Cambridge University Press, 1990)

Brøndsted, J., *The Vikings* (Harmondsworth: Penguin Books, 1965)

Campbell, J., *The Anglo-Saxons* (Oxford: Phaidon, 1982)

Campbell, J., *The Anglo-Saxon State* (London: Hambledon and London, 2000)

Carman, J. and Harding, A., *Ancient Warfare* (Stroud: Sutton Publishing, 1999)

Carver, M., *Sutton Hoo. Burial Ground of Kings?* (London: British Museum Press, 1998)

Crocker, R. and Hiley, D. (eds), *The New Oxford History of Music: The Early Middle Ages to 1300* (Oxford: Oxford University Press, 1990)

Crumplin, S., 'Rewriting History in the Cult of St Cuthbert from the ninth to the twelfth centuries' (St Andrew's University Thesis, 2004)

Davidson, H.E., *The Sword in Anglo-Saxon England* (Boydell, 1998)

Dickinson, T. and Harke, H., *Early Anglo-Saxon Shields* (The Society of Antiquities of London, 1992)

Eddius Stephanus, *Life of Wilfrid* in Webb, J.F. and Farmer, D.H., *The Age of Bede*. (London: Penguin Books, 1998)

Evans, A.C., *Sutton Hoo Ship Burial* (London: British Museum Press, 2008)

Hawthorne, J.G. and Smith, C.S., *Theophilus On Divers Arts* (New York: Dover Publications, 1979)

Higham, N.J., *The Kingdom of Northumbria AD 350–1100* (Stroud: Alan Sutton Publishing, 1993)

Hindley, G., *A Brief History of the Anglo-Saxons* (London: Robinson, 2006)

Hope-Taylor, B., *Yeavering: an Anglo-British Centre of early Northumbria* (London: English Heritage, 1977)

Kirby, D.P., *The Earliest English Kings* (London: Routledge, 2000)

Lang, J., 'The Rise and Fall of Pattern Welding: an investigation into the construction of pre-medieval sword blades' (University of Reading thesis, 2007)

Leahy, K., *Anglo-Saxon Crafts* (Stroud: The History Press, 2010)

Leahy, K. and Bland, R., *The Staffordshire Hoard* (London: British Museum Press, 2009)

Lucy, S., *The Anglo-Saxon Way of Death* (Stroud: Sutton Publishing, 2000)

Marren, P., *Battles of the Dark Ages* (Barnsley: Pen and Sword, 2009)

Marsden, J., *Northanhymbre Saga* (Kyle Cathie, 1992)

Mayr-Harting, H., *The Coming of Christianity to Ango-Saxon England* (London: B.T. Batsford, 1991)

Mickelthwait, J. and Wooldridge, A., *God Is Back: How the Global Rise of Faith is Changing the World* (London: Allen Lane, 2009)

MOLAS, *The Prittlewell Prince* (London: Museum of London, 2004)

Pierce, I., *Swords of the Viking Age* (Suffolk: Boydell & Brewer, 2005)

Pirie, E.J.E., *Thrymsas, Sceattas and Stycas of Northumbria* (Powys: Galata Print, 2000)

Renfrew, C. and Bahn, P., *Archaeology: Theories, Methods and Practice* (London: Thames and Hudson, 1996)

Rollason, D., *Northumbria, 500–1100: Creation and Destruction of a Kingdom* (Cambridge: Cambridge University Press, 2003)

Rowland, T.H., *Medieval Castles, Towers, Peles and Bastles of Northumberland* (Warkworth: Sandhill Press, 1987)

Rushton, S., et al. (eds), *Bamburgh: Archaeology in Northumberland: Discovery Series 1* (Northumberland: Northumberland County Council, n.d.)

Siddorn, K.J., *Viking Weapons and Warfare* (Stroud: Tempus Publishing, 2000)

Smith, S.T., 'Writing Land in Anglo-Saxon England' (University of Notre Dame, Indiana, thesis, 2007)

Stancliffe, C. and Cambridge, E. (eds), *Oswald: Northumbrian King to European Saint* (Stamford: Paul Watkins, 1995)

Stephenson, I.P., *The Anglo-Saxon Shield* (Stroud: Tempus Publishing, 2002)

Theophilus, *On Divers Arts* (New York: Dover Publications, 1980)

Tweddle, D., *The Anglian Helmet from Coppergate* (York: York Archaeological Trust, 1992)

Underwood, R., *Anglo-Saxon Weapons and Warfare* (Stroud: Tempus Publishing, 1999)

Waddington, C., *Land of Legend: Discovering Ancient Northumberland* (Milfield, Wooler: Country Store Publishing, 1999)

Waddington, C., *Maelmin: An Archaeological Guide* (Milfield, Wooler: CS Publishing, 2001)

Watkins, A.E., (trans.), *Aelfric's Colloquy* (n.d.) (http://www.kentarchaeology.ac/authors/016.pdf. Last accessed 21 February 2012)

Webb, J.F. and Farmer, D.H., *The Age of Bede* (London: Penguin Books, 1998)

Welch, M., *English Heritage Book of Anglo-Saxon England* (London: BCA, 1992)

Williams, Allan, *Estudio Metalurgic De Algunas Espadas Vikingas*, Gladius PDF (2011)

Young, G., *Bamburgh Castle: The Archaeology of the Fortress of Bamburgh AD 500 to AD 1500* (Bamburgh: Bamburgh Research Project, 2003)

Ziegler, M., 'The Politics of Exile in Early Northumbria' in *The Heroic Age*, (2, autumn/winter 1999)

KINGS OF NORTHUMBRIA

KINGS OF BERNICIA		KINGS OF DEIRA	
Esa	500		
Eoppa (son of Esa)	c.520		
Ida (son of Eoppa)	547–559		
Glappa (son of Ida)	559–560	Aelle (son of Yffi)	559–589
Adda (son of Ida)	560–568		
Aethelric (son of Ida)	568–572		
Theodric (son of Ida)	572–579		
Frithuwald (son of Ida)	579–585		
Hussa (grandson of Ida)	585–593	Aethelric (brother of Aelle)	589–604
Aethelfrith (son of Aethelric)	593–616	Aethelfrith (of Bernicia, son of Aethelric)	604–616
St Edwin of Deira (son of Aelle)	616–633	St Edwin of Deira (son of Aelle)	616–633
Eanfrith (son of Aethelfrith)	633–634	Osric (son of Aelfric)	633–634
Oswald (St) (son of Aethelfrith)	634–642	Oswald of Bernicia (St) (son of Aethelfrith)	634–642
Oswiu (son of Aethelfrith)	642–670	Oswiu (of Bernicia)	642–644
		Oswine (St) (son of Osric)	644–651
		Aethelwald (son of Oswald)	651–656
		Alchfrith (son of Oswiu)	656–664

KINGS OF NORTHUMBRIA	
Oswiu	664–670
Ecgfrith (son of Oswiu)	670–685
Aeldfrith (son of Oswiu)	685–704
Eadwulf	704–705
Osred I (son of Aeldfrith)	705–716
Coenred	716–718
Osric (son of Ealdfrith)	718–729
Ceolwulf (St) (brother of Coenred)	729–737
Eadberht (cousin of Ceolwulf)	737–758
Oswulf (son of Eadberht)	758–759
Aethelwald Moll	759–765
Ealchred (son-in-law of Oswulf)	765–774
Aethelred I (son of Aethelwald Moll)	774–779
Aelfwald I (son of Oswulf)	779–789
Osred II (son of Ealhred)	789–790
Aethelred I	790–796
Osbald	796
Eardwulf	796–806
Aelfwald II	806–808
Eardwulf	808–810
Eanred (son of Eardwulf)	810–841
Aethelred II (son of Eanred)	841–844
Raedwulf	844
Aethelred II	844–848
Osbeorht	848–863
Aelle II	863–867

ACKNOWLEDGEMENTS

We have many people to thank, living and dead, starting with the estate of J.R.R. Tolkien for permission to quote from the Good Professor's works in this book. Without his work, we would never have embarked on our respective careers. Everyone at the Bamburgh Research Project has been unfailingly helpful to us; we would like to thank, in particular, Graeme Young, Sarah Groves and Gerry Twomey. Ian Boomer, Clive Waddington and Alex Woolf gave us their time and thoughts in interviews (as did Graeme and Sarah). Jude Leitch of Northumberland Tourism and Sheelagh Caygill of *This Is Northumberland* have helped us over the years, and with pictures and promotion for this project. David and Margaret Whitbread have supported the Bamburgh Research Project and us, their sons-in-law, through a decade and more. Tom Vivian and Lindsey Smith were all we could have hoped for from our editors at The History Press. We are very grateful and not a little chuffed that Tom Holland read the book.

Moving to the personal, I (Edoardo Albert) want to thank my parents, Victor and Paola, for everything and my brother, Steven, for getting me through some bad times. Proving that I should never be let anywhere near an Oscars' acceptance speech, my thanks are also due to my sons, Theodore and Matthew (and for the loan of Theo's laptop to finish the book when my computer was stolen). Last, but never least, Harriet, indexer extraordinaire and extraordinary wife.

I (Paul Gething) would like to thank my grandfather, Ernest Frank Huggett, who taught me to question. I miss you, Old Timer! Thanks also to Jacob Gething, my constant companion throughout my journeys in Northumbria. It has been a blast, Jake! Finally, thanks to Rosie Whitbread, for everything else. I don't deserve you!

INDEX

Numbers in *italics* indicate a picture.

acorns, 119, 120, 122
Æthelbert, 57
Æthelburga, 54–5, 57
Æthelfrith, 11–14, 16, 71, 87, 92, 179
Ælfwine, 13
Æthelwod, 13
Aelfric, 97, 186
Aeschere, 80
Aidan, 17–18, 58–9, 68, 95, 180
Alcuin, 7, 18, 59, 66, 153
Aldfrith, 19, 173
Alexander, Michael, 110
Alfred, King, 7–8, 94, 110, 116, 133–4
Alvarez, Luis and Walter, 25
Angles, 11, 14, 54–5, 100, 155–6, 176, 179
alder, 29, 36, 80
archaeologists, 85–6, 177–8
archaeology, 177–8; definition of, 22; ethics of,
    163; of Northumbria, 20; techniques, 49; *see
    also* landscape archaeology
armour, *see* mail
Armstrong, Lord, 131, 158
art, Mesolithic 34
Arthur, 12, 175
artisans, 97
Augustine of Canterbury, 12, 55, 57, 59, 116

Balamory, 43, 113, 182
Bamburgh, *8*, 10–11, 17, 20–1, 23, 25, 27–9, 58,
    65, 75, *81*, 85, 91, 99–100, 106, 124–5, 131, 137,
    139–140, *140*, 147–9, 154, 156, 158–61, 165–9,
    172, 175–6, 179, 185
Bamburgh Castle, *8*, 25, 58, 131, 137, 139, 158, 186
Bamburgh Research Project, 8, 20, 75, 99, 131,
    139, 158, 160, 165, 176, 186
Bamburgh Sword, 75, *75*–6, 143

battle, of Hatfield Chase, 15; of Heavenfield, 16; of
    Maserfield, 17, 175
Beaker folk, 43–4
beauty, value of, 9
Beckett, Thomas, 64
Bede, 7, 12–20, 51–3, 55, 57–62, 64–6, *66*, 68, 90,
    95, 98, 101, 107–8, 140, 142, 170, 174, 179–81,
    184
beer, 43–4, 118, 123, 125
Benedict Biscop, 59, 61–2, 65–6, 140
Benedict of Nursia, Saint, 52
Beowulf, 74, 80, 83, 93, 104, 106, 108, 121, 155
Beowulf, 63, 69, 70, 74, 80, 93, 104, 106, 108, *111*,
    112, 116, 121, 155
Bernicia, 10–11, 13, 15, 17, 28, 50, 70, 87, 90, 102,
    139, 172–4
Bertha of the Merovingians, Æthelbert's bride, 57
birch, 29, 36, 133–4
birch polypore (*Piptorus betulinus*), 133–4
bishops, 94–5
blacksmiths, 117, 129–30, 135, 143–4, 152
Bob the Builder, 131
bog ore, 76, 79, 127–9, 174
Boniface, 67
Boomer, Ian, 31–2
books, 66, 69, 113, 116, 153–4; production of, 120,
    141, 153–4
Bowl Hole cemetery, 140, *158*, 158–63
Bretwalda, 10, 14
Britain, divided, 15; Romans leave, 47
bronze, 15, 30, 43, *43*, 44, 84, 114
Bronze Age, 30, 42–4, 49, 136
burial practices, 50, 57, 158–69

Cadwallon, 14–17, 57–8
Caedmon, 59, 68, *68*, 69, 107, 116

Caedmon codex, 116, *116*

cairns, *41*, 42

carvel-built ship, 156

Celtic Christianity, *see* Christianity flowing from
    Ireland

Ceolfrith, 65–6, 153, 182

Ceolwulf, 19.

Chad, Saint, 59.

Charlemagne, 9, 18, 64, 67, 152, 170, 174

Charles I, 88

Cheviot Hills, 23, 28, 30–2, 45, 97, 139

Christianity, acceptance of, 16, 18, 54–9, 67–9; and
    warfare, 73; conflict between Roman and Irish
    traditions, 63–5; defeat of Christian king, 17;
    effect on economy, 171–2; first Christian king
    of Northumbria, 15, 54; history in Britain,
    54–65; golden age, 59–70; loss of following
    Roman withdrawal, 54; missions to Europe,
    66–7, 173–4; organization of, 94–5; relation-
    ship with kings, 95

Christianity flowing from Ireland, 21, 52, 54, 58–9,
    63–4, 170, 181

cist graves, 50, 158, 168

clinker-built ship, 155–6, *156*

clothing, 38, 113–14 and 135–6

Codex Amiatinus, *109*, 153, 174, 182

Coifi, 55, 56

Colman, 64

Constantine, Emperor, 46, 56, 64, 180

copper, 42–3, 112, 114, 151–2, 180

Coppergate helmet, 84, *84*, 185

coprolites, 123, 149

coring, *26*

Cresswell Crags, 33

Crossley-Holland, Kevin, 104

culture, 104–117; of the warband, 73–4

cup and ring marks 34, 41, 50

currency, 151–2; depreciation of, 171–2, 182

Cuthbert, 27, 59, 64, 65, 101, 184

Cwenburg, 14

Dalriada, 58, 91, 100

decline of Northumbria, 170–6

deforestation, 30

Deira, 10–15, 28, 70, 87, 173–5

diet, *see* food

Divine Office, 52, 66, *67*, 142

Dod Law, 34

Doggerland, 26, 34, 48

Domesday Book, 11

Dream of the Rood, The, 69, 110, 116

duelling, 114–15

Eadberht, 19, 65, 95

Eanflæd, 64, 181

Ecgfrith, 18, 94–5

Ecclesiastical History of the English People, 12, 14, 20,
    58, 59, 90, 107–8, 142, 170, 174, 184

Eddius, 96, 185

Edwin, 7, 14–17, 55, 57–8, 67, 71, 87–8, 90, 173

Edward the Confessor, 11

elm, 29

Egil, 72

Elmet, 9, 15

Eric Bloodaxe, 21

Exeter Book, 104, 116

farming, 119–20

farmers, 97

Farne Islands, 23, 27, 29, 65

fashion, *see* clothing

fire, 132–3

flint and steel, 132–3, *133*

floods, 23, 26, 34

food, 118–25, 168

forests, *see* woods

forest succession, 29, *29*

forgetting of Northumbria, 7

Franks Casket, 72, *137*

fruit leather, 124

geoarchaeology, 31–2

geography of Northumbria, 23–32

geology of Northumbria, 23–32

geomorphology of Northumbria, 31–2

Gething, Paul, 8, 41, 75, 85, 121, 135, 142, 144–5,
    149, 158–9, 176, 179

gift giving, 13, 15, 70, 152–3, 157, 171, 174–82

Gildas, 12, 179

glass, 62, 117, 121, 140, *140*

golden age of Northumbria, 18–19, 59–70

Great Whin Sill, *see* Whin Sill

green martyrdom, 52

Gregory the Great, Pope, 12, 19, 55, 100, 181

Groves, Sarah, 167

Guli the Russian, 112

Guthlaf, 72

Hadrian, the Emperor, 27, 46

Hadrian's Wall, 13, 16, 23, 27, 46, *47*, 49, 127

Härke, Heinrich, 161

Harold, Godwinson, 11, 91

Harold Hardrada, 115

harp, Anglo-Saxon, 68, 105, *105*, 107, 112

hazel, 29, 83

helmets, 74, 83–5, *84*, 119, 155, 185

henges, 37, 40–1, 49

Henry II, 173

Henry IV, 11

Henry VIII, 95, 131

Herbert, Terry, 181
Hereric, 14
Hewald, Black, 174
Hewald, White, 174
Hilda, 18, 59, 69
Hnæf, 108
Holy Island, *see* Lindisfarne
Honorius, Emperor, 47
Hope-Taylor, Dr. Brian, 75, 158, 165–6, 185
horses, 58, 70, 73, 103, 119, 121, 129, 148, 152, 154–5, 171
hospitality, 90–1
hostage giving and taking, 87, 89–90
Hotspur, 11
house, oldest in Britain, 36
houses, Iron Age, 45, 49; Northumbria, 131
Howick, 36–7, 40, 48
Hrothgar, 80, 106, 121, 155
husbandry, 120–1
Hutton, James, 23

Ibn Fadlan, 107, 112
ice ages, 28, 31–3, 45
Ida, 11, 13, 92, 100, 139, 179
Ine, King of Wessex, 80, 181
Iona, 16, *16*, 17, 54, 58, 61, 64, 163, 180–1
iron, smelting and forging, 75–7, 79, 127–30, 142–4, 174
Iron Age, 44–5, 49, 50

Jarrow, Bede's monastery, 20, 51–2, *60–1*, 61–2, 65, 95, 98, 140, 153, 184
Jesus, 52, 56, 175
jewellery, 112, 114, 117, 145, 148, 153, 171
John the Baptist, 52
Joshua, 175
Judas Iscariot, 56
Junius codex, *see* Caedmon codex

King Alfred's cakes (*Daldinia concentrica*), 133–4, *134*
kingship, 87–9; *see also* law of succession
knights, *see* warriors

landscape and land use, 122–3
landscape archaeology, 48–50
law, 82, 88, 94, 114, 120–1, 125, 155, 173, 175, 181
law of succession, 87, 173
Laws of Ine, 80, 181
Lerins, 61–2
Lindisfarne, 17, 19, 52, 58, 64, 95, 153, 169, 172
Lindisfarne Gospels, 9, 120, 141, *141*, 153, 154, *154*, 184
Lindsey, 9, 72

location of Northumbria, 7
Lordenshaw, 34
Louis XIV, 88
Lyell, Charles, 23, 180
lyre, *see* harp

mail (chain), *81*, 84–5, 162
maps, 10, 24
maritime culture, 106, 131, 155–7, 161
Maelmin, *40*, 41, 185
Mercia, 10, 14–15, 17–18, 57, 59, 90, 92, 172, 180
Merovingian dynasty, 55, 57
Mesolithic, 20, 34, 36–9, 45, 48–9, 133, 166, 180; tools, 46
microliths, 46, 48–9
monasticism, 51–4
Monkwearmouth/Jarrow, *see* Jarrow
Moses, 175

needles, *136*, 136
Nennius, 12, 179
Neolithic, 36, 39–42, 48–50, 132–3, 139, 166, 180
Northumbria, achievement of, 175–6; Bronze Age in, 42–4; changing view of, 20; culture, 18–19, 104–17; decline, 11, 18–19, 170–6; earliest inhabitants, 35–7; history of kingdom, 9–24, 51–70, 170–8; importance of, 21; Iron Age in, 44–5; Mesolithic in, 36–8; Neolithic in, 36–8; origin of 11–12; Paleolithic in 35–6; rise, 13–18; Romans in, 46–7; society 87–103; topography 28–30
Newton, Isaac, 86
Nidud, King of Sweden, 72
Norwegian 'princess', 99, *99*
Nowell codex, 116

oak, 29, 83, 120
Olafsson, Kjartan, 115
Oswald, 7, 8, 12, 16–18, *17*, 20, 57–9, 68, 71, 87, 90, 95, 139, 163, 173, 175
Oswine, 12
Oswulf, 21
Oswiu (Oswy), 12, 17–18, 57–8, 61, 64, 71, 87, 90, 162, 173, 181
Otzi, the Iceman, 180

paganism, Anglo-Saxon, 54–7, 63; reasons for converting to Christianity, 56
pattern welding, 75–7, *77*, 78, *78*, 127, 185
Palaeolithic, 29, 35–6, 48, 105, 133, 180; clothing in, 38; tools, 46
Paulinus, 55, 57
peasants, 97–8, *98*, 102–3
Peada, 90, 181
Penda of Mercia, 15, 17–18, 57, 59, 90, 92, 175

Peter, St, 56, 62, 64, 95, 182
Picts, 18, 107
pilgrimage, 61, 66, 116, 127
poetry, Anglo-Saxon, 68–9, 108–12, 116, 182
pottery, 123, 136, *136*, 148, 158
Presbyter, Theophilus, 117, 141, 185

Raedwald, 14, 90
red martyrdom, 52
religion, 51–70
Rescript of Honorius, 47
Rheged, 9, 179
riddles, 104, 113
ridge and furrow, 122–3
Roman Empire, 7, 9, 13, 23, 45–7, 49, 53–4, 56,
    58–9, 87, 102, 106, 119, 122, 126–7, 129, 147–9,
    151, 155, 179, 182; abandons Britain, 47
Roughting Linn, 34
royal household, 89–93; movements of, 91
royalty, *see* kingship
Ruthwell Cross, 53, 110

salt, 124
Saul, the King of Israel, 13
scop, 70, 110, 112
seafaring, *see* maritime culture
Seamer Carr, 35–6
seax, 78, 83, *83*
Septimius Severus, 47
shields, 79, 80–2, *81*, 83, 114, 115, 184
shield wall, 80, 82, 107, 115, 121
ships, *see* maritime culture
shoes, 135–6, 143
slavery, 100
slaves, 82, 87, 94, 100–3, 112, 129, 144, 172
Smith, David, 34
society, 87–103
spear, 55, 76, 82–4, 115
Starr Carr, 36–7
steel, 76, 77, 78, 79, 129, 130
Storegga slide, 34
stone, as building material, 20, 51, 62, 131, 133, 139,
    144, 165, 179
Stonehenge, 37, 40
stirrups, 121, 148, 155, 182
Strathclyde, 11, 179
styca, *see* currency
Sutton Hoo, 14, 112, 148, 155–6, *160*, 184–5
sword making, 76–9
swords, 42, 44, 71, *71*, 72, 75–6, *77*, 78–9, 83, 115,
    127, 130, 161–2, 174, 184–5
Synod of Whitby, 64

tablet weaving, 125
tattoos, 107
Taylor, Zachary, 105

technology, 126–46
Theophilus, *see* Presbyter, Theophilus
Thor, 56, 63
tonsure, 52, 63
Tolkien, J. R. R., 110
trade, 147–157; in food, 149; three types of, 157
transport, 154–6
travel, 147–57
trees, 28–30, 32, 34, 45 and 132
tsunami *26*, 34

Ulfberht swords, 130, *130*
Ussher, James, 25.

Vercelli Book, 110, *111*, 116, 182
Vikings, 7, 10, 19, 43, 107, 108, 112, 150, 151, 152,
    154, 156, 172–4, 176
Votadini, 46, 50

Waddington, Clive, 48–50
Waldhere, 108
warband, 67, 74, 89, 92–3, 107, 173
warfare, 71–86
warriors, 13, 42, 44, 56, 71–4, 78–80, 82–4, 87,
    88–9, 92–3, 95, 100, 106–7, 115, 119, 121, 136,
    152, 155, 161–3, 171–2, 174–5
Wayland the Smith, 72
Weetwood Manor, 34
weregild, 87, 94
Whin Sill, 27, 32
white martyrdom, 52
Wildwood, 28–9, 36
Wilfrid, 7, 18, 59, 64–6, 68, 94, 96, 173
William the Conqueror, 11, 91, 156, 175–6
Willibrord, 55, 66, 174
willow, 29, 36
wine, 123
Woden, 12, 56, 70, 88, 90
wood, as material, 36, 41, 48, 51, 76, 80, 82–3, 85,
    105, 115, 117, 125, 129, 131–2, 134, 138–9, 141,
    147, 179
woods, 30, 36, 76, 122
Woolf, Alex, 101
Wootz steel, 130

Yeavering Bell, 44–5, 101, 180, 185
Y Gododdin, 179
York, 10–11, 21, 28, 46–7, 52, 64, 85, 91, 95, 97,
    106, 119, 121, 123, 138, 149, 152–3, 156, 172–3,
    175–6, 180, 185
York Minster, 131, 144
Yorkshire, 7, 10, 15, 30, 35, 102, 162, 175, 176,
    179–80
Young, Graeme, 20, 158, 165

Zeus, 70